Martin Renz/Julius Schwarzwälder (eds.)

Spaces of Appearance
Aesthetics and Politics After Analogy

AF286438

Martin Renz is a PhD candidate in American Studies at Goethe University Frankfurt, where he is finalizing his dissertation, entitled *The Prejudice Against Politics: Arendtian Explorations of the Populist Situation*. He has published on the (ir-)reality of free speech in Hannah Arendt's oeuvre (*Philosophy & Rhetoric*, 2025) and works as a freelance journalist for the German news publication *Research.Table*, where he covers science advice, research policy, and university reforms in Germany and beyond. Together with friends and colleagues, he organizes the research initiative 'Ästhetik demokratischer Lebensformen' in Frankfurt. Before embarking on his PhD, Martin studied Philosophy, Political Science, and the Humanities in Berlin, Paris, Frankfurt, and Chicago.

Julius Schwarzwälder studied philosophy and aesthetics in London, Frankfurt, Paris, and Darmstadt. He is a PhD candidate at TU Darmstadt, where he considers some aesthetic effects of the surging use of algorithmics. He has published in *Deutsche Zeitschrift für Philosophie* (on the advent of 'artistic research'), *kritische berichte* (on TikTok and 'micro-genres'), and *form* (on the calculability of 'beauty'). In and beyond Frankfurt, he co-organized the graduate research initiative 'Ästhetik demokratischer Lebensformen.'

Sponsored by Goethe University's Open Access Publication Fund,
Graduate Academy GRADE, GRADE Center Normative Orders,
and Bodo-Sponholz-Stiftung.

Bibliographic information published by the Deutsche Nationalbibliothek

The Deutsche Nationalbibliothek lists this publication in the Deutsche Nationalbibliografie;
detailed bibliographic data are available in the Internet at https://dnb.dnb.de.

First published in 2025 by transcript Verlag, Bielefeld
© Martin Renz, Julius Schwarzwälder (eds.), chapters by respective authors

Book design and typesetting: Paula Heinrich
Cover artwork: © Paula Heinrich
Copyediting: Joe Paul Kroll
Printed by: Elanders Waiblingen GmbH, Waiblingen, Germany
Main typefaces: *Rauschen B* and *Meno Text*

Print-ISBN: 978-3-8376-7761-4
PDF-ISBN: 978-3-8394-0684-7
https://doi.org/10.14361/9783839406847

Printed on permanent acid-free text paper.

Table of Contents

This volume is a collaborative effort.

All contributors took part in an intensive year of workshops and discussions. They read and criticized each other's texts, which led to substantial revisions of almost all contributions in this volume. The concept 'space of appearance' serves as a shared analytical tool, enabling the authors to address their distinct object of concern in a connected and analytically productive way. We encourage readers to consider the texts alongside one another—not despite, but because of these differences.

What Are and To What End
Do We Study Spaces of Appearance?
Martin Renz/Julius Schwarzwälder

How do things and people come to matter to people and things? What makes a thing or an action seem obvious, salient or evident? What, on the other hand, makes them seem obsolete, obscure or out of the question altogether? How are such relations of importance and insignificance produced and institutionalized, how do they get overturned and occluded? Or, in short: in what ways has the semblance of relevance and effectiveness been organized and disorganized?

To address these far-reaching and general questions, we have assembled a variety of essays that, for the most part, take a concrete object as exemplary for the manner in which the perceptive standards of a given political situation may subtly change or consolidate. All essays share an approach in the spirit of a key concept in the work of Hannah Arendt: 'space of appearance.' We believe that this concept, along with the vocabulary that surrounds it and the kinds of arguments it implies, can make a diverse range of objects speak to these questions. Inspecting them in terms of the spaces in and through which they appear allows the framing of the political situations in which they occur to be perceived.

'Space of appearance' figures as the common point of reference that allows for a theorization of the subtle changes in how a given object of interest may differently appear in diverse situations. The differences we are interested in are aesthetic, but their relevance and appeal, we suspect, concerns the specific political stakes to which they are attached. We reject a conception of aesthetics as an 'autonomous sphere' that stands apart from or is even hostile towards politics.[01] As has often been remarked in recent discussions, an 'aestheticization'

---

01   For an outline of recent approaches, see
      Nikolas Kompridis, ed., *The Aesthetic Turn in Political Thought*
      (Bloomsbury Academic, 2014).

of politics need not always be inherently a- or anti-political.[02] With this in mind, we attempt to resist the conception of aesthetics as a mere structurally analogous model or mirror image of politics.[03] Instead, we look for "concrete transactions" between aesthetics and politics: how aesthetics constitutes the effectiveness of politics, how politics influences the way in which the world appears.[04]

Taken by themselves, there is a tendency for each of the two terms that Arendt combined—'space' and 'appearance'—to foster and even provoke misunderstandings

02 In this fundamental assumption, we follow Susan Buck-Morss, "Aesthetics and Anaesthetics," *October* 62 (1992).

03 Curiously enough, in spite of their newfound co-presence, aesthetics and politics can seem as disconnected as ever. Think of some of the words most frequently used to mark the relation between aesthetic categories and political reality. They will most likely include verbs like 'indexes,' 'reminds us of,' 'exemplifies,' 'speaks to,' 'shows,' 'seems to be about,' 'is a model of/for'—notions that indicate relations of representation and analogy between two autonomous or autotelic 'spheres,' 'realms,' 'regimes,' 'domains,' or 'territories' that might be treated as similar, but ultimately separate. For the Kantian origins of this conception, see Theodor W. Adorno, *Kant's Critique of Pure Reason* (Stanford University Press, 2001), 182: "As I have indicated, the essential component of this corrupting tendency that is implicit in the meaning of Kantian philosophy from the outset appears to me to arise from the circumstance that the disaggregated elements constitute separate realms, like countries on a map, lying contiguously, but independently of one another—an image that Kant constantly uses by way of illustration. These separate realms have no authority over one another." For some remarks on how this separation between theory, practice and aesthetics has been constructed and upheld in recent Germanophone philosophy, see Julius Schwarzwälder, "Über einige Bedingungen gegenwärtiger ART (Artistic Research Theory)," *Deutsche Zeitschrift für Philosophie* 72, vol. 1 (2024).

04 To our knowledge, this challenge was first posed in T. J. Clark, *Image of the People: Gustave Courbet and the 1848 Revolution* (Thames and Hudson, 1973), 12: "Even if one distrusts the notions of reflection, of historical background, of analogy between artistic form and social ideology, one cannot avoid the problems they suggest … I want to discover what concrete transactions are hidden behind the mechanical image of 'reflection,' to know how 'background' becomes 'foreground'; instead of analogy between form and content, to discover the network of real, complex relations between the two."

in this regard. If aesthetics is understood to concern 'mere' appearances, a space of appearance would precisely be the superficial kind of illusion that must be disregarded to get to what is of the 'essence' in matters political: rational debate, making and implementing decisions, writing constitutions, the conduct of war. In such a view, appearances would be arbitrary and suspicious, an 'objective' focus on instrumental analyses of the required means to an end would suffice completely; enquiries into how something 'appears' to someone or a group could and indeed should then be supplanted by examining how things 'really are.' But this begs the question of how a relationship between means and ends is constituted and generally accepted in the first place. What counts as instrumentally effective itself changes over time. Any account of instrumental effectiveness must account for the spaces in which this impression comes about. The appearances we are interested in are therefore always 'spatial' in that they pertain to common impressions from which those who share a given space cannot withdraw by their own volition.[05]

  If the meaning of 'space' were reduced to material or physical surroundings, then it could more easily be discussed in terms of architecture and public design. Unlike 'mere' material space, spaces of appearance are constituted by human interaction, they are always performed, at times even staged, and depend upon their continued and iterative enactment to persist. Material objects, by contrast, once produced, are independent of the process by which they were produced. This difference is captured by Arendt in her distinction between 'work,' which produces tangible, enduring objects, and 'action,' which concerns performed interaction whose duration ends with its performance.[06] Spaces of appearance, it could be said, are effects, not 'products,' of action. They are usually connected with, but not reducible to, the built environment in which they occur. In each case, their appearance is of the essence, they dissipate when the action stops.

05 See Hannah Arendt, *The Human Condition* (University of Chicago Press, 1998), 199: "To men the reality of the world is guaranteed by the presence of others, by its appearing to all; 'for what appears to all, this we call Being,' and whatever lacks this appearance comes and passes away like a dream, intimately and exclusively our own but without reality."

06 Arendt, *Human Condition*, 7–8.

The concept 'spaces of appearance' designates a virtual aspect of the in-between, the interstices of the human world, which is different from, though always interwoven with, the physical or tangible aspects of the world. One needs to be sensitive towards the difference between changes in perception and changes in material in order to identify the structures of relevance through which certain historical modes of articulation, conduct, and interpretation establish themselves as appealing or appalling within a specific political situation. As an analytical concept, 'space of appearance' is fine-tuned for such an endeavor. It refers to real and concretely instantiated configurations of action and behavior that concern the way in which people explicitly and implicitly organize their interaction in and perception of the world. Analyzing spaces of appearance allows concretely modulated forms of agency to be explained as always-already embedded. They are irreducible to the intentions of actors but nonetheless provide space for a revelation of "who" someone is.[07]

Arendt's use of the term 'space of appearance' is less than systematic. The same goes for adjacent terms she employs, such as "space of display"[08] or "spaces of freedom,"[09]

07   See Arendt, *Human Condition,* 178. Here, we follow Patchen Markell, "The Moment has Passed: Power after Arendt," in *Radical Futures Past: Untimely Political Theory,* ed. Romand Coles (University Press of Kentucky, 2014), 128: "One way to mark this feature of Arendt's use of 'power' might be to ascribe power in this sense to situations rather than to agents… But that way of talking about the power of a situation … is still quite forward looking and anticipatory, whereas Arendt helps us see that such situations are also powerful in a different sense: their very existence *as* situations is an expression of the power of the past—or, more exactly, of a past that is not quite finished, that has a kind of momentum through the people who find themselves engaged with it. We might underscore this point by ascribing power in this sense not just to a situation as a 'context within which something *consequential* seems bound to happen,' but also to whatever it is that is the focus of people's attention in that situation—to an event, for instance, that we might describe as 'powerful' in something like the same way that we talk about a work of art as being 'powerful': we mean that it holds us in its presence [emphasis added]."

08   Hannah Arendt, "The Crisis in Culture," in Hannah Arendt, *Between Past and Future* (Viking Press, [1961] 1969), 218.

09   Hannah Arendt, *On Revolution* (Penguin Books, [1963] 1990), 264, 275, 277.

which are also used in diverse and sometimes conflicting ways. In a much-quoted passage towards the end of § 27, Arendt writes that

> [i]t is the space of appearance in the widest sense of the word, namely, the space where I appear to others as others appear to me, where men exist not merely like other living or inanimate things but make their appearance explicitly.[10]

At least since Jürgen Habermas's influential essay on Arendt's notion of power, passages such as this have been taken to imply that the space of appearance is an ideal of "undistorted communication," which, if at all, could only be reached under extraordinary conditions.[11] 'Space of appearance' here describes the conditions under which human beings experience their equality and common humanity while also coming to an enhanced self-awareness of their own life and personality. This passage lends itself especially to readings that contrast unpolitical, private spaces—the *oikos,* the private place of reproduction—from the public 'space of appearance' proper.[12]

10   Arendt, *Human Condition*, 198–99.

11   See Jürgen Habermas, *Philosophical-Political Profiles: Studies in Contemporary German Social Thought* (MIT Press, 1995), 177: "She wants to read off the general structures of an unimpaired intersubjectivity in the formal properties of communicative action or praxis." It should be noted that the translations of Haberma's text that we consulted are imprecise in this section. In the original, the quoted passage refers not to Arendt but to what Habermas describes as the phenomenological method underlying her 'philosophy of praxis' in general. A valuable criticism of Habermas's essay can be found in Margaret Canovan, "A Case of Distorted Communication: A Note on Habermas and Arendt," *Political Theory* 11, no. 1 (1983).

12   In *Human Condition,* Arendt introduces the notion of thepublic in two senses. The first proclaims that public is whatever is not hidden, a matter of degree, and thus everything is potentially public and political, see Arendt, *Human Condition,* 50: "[Public] means, first, that everything that appears in public can be seen and heard by everybody and has the widest possible publicity... Compared with the reality which comes from being seen and heard, even the greatest forces of intimate life ... lead an uncertain, shadowy kind of existence *unless and until they are transformed, deprivatized and deindividualized, as it were, into a shape to fit them for public appearance* [emphasis added]."

But not only does Arendt have more to say about the space of appearance, the passage quoted above is in tension with others, such as the following:

> The space of appearance comes into being wherever men are together in the manner of speech and action, and therefore pre-dates and precedes all formal constitution of the public realm and the various forms of government, that is, the various forms in which the public realm can be organized. Its peculiarity is that, unlike the spaces which are the work of our hands, it does not survive the actuality of the movement which brought it into being, but disappears not only with the dispersal of men—as in the case of great catastrophes when the body politic of a people is destroyed—but with the disappearance or arrest of the activities themselves.

The second sense relates to the ordinary usage of the term in distinction from the private, see Arendt, *Human Condition*, 52: "Second, the term 'public' signifies the world itself, in so far as it is common to all of us and distinguished from our privately owned place in it." Just like in the case of her use of 'space of appearance,' where the use of the term differs depending on whether it is contrasted from the private space or from the non-physical, intangible aspects of the 'world,' Arendt's use of 'public' differs depending on whether she speaks, as in the second sense above, of 'the public' in opposition to 'the private' or, as in the first, of 'public' as a matter of degree on a spectrum between 'fully public and seen by everyone' and 'almost completely hidden and not in sight.' Many interpretations "think with Arendt against Arendt" (see Seyla Benhabib, *The Reluctant Modernism of Hannah Arendt* (Rowman & Littlefield, 2003), xi, xx, 198; see also Juliane Rebentisch, *Der Streit um Pluralität: Auseinandersetzungen mit Hannah Arendt* (Suhrkamp, 2022), 11) to favor the second sense that pitches 'the public' against 'the private' as two irreconcilable spheres, but nonetheless argue that her conceptual vocabulary is open to interpretations in the first sense, too. For instance, multiple contributions in Bonnie Honig, ed., *Feminist Interpretations of Hannah Arendt* (Penn State University Press, 1995), such as those by Bonnie Honig and Morris Kaplan, have opened up the notion to also include spaces that are not obviously part of 'the public,' see 126, 130, and 146. Not only do we follow these interpretations; we in fact believe that the formalized public/private-distinction is secondary to the informal processes which situationally produce and reproduce the public/private-distinction in the first place and that Arendt does account for this. This becomes especially clear when connecting Arendt's ideas about the public to a mundane notion of 'spaces of appearance.'

Wherever people gather together, it is potentially there, but only potentially, not necessarily and not forever.[13]

Clearly, Arendt here argues that the space of appearance really does exist on specific occasions—namely, whenever people act. What is more, it is prior to and pre-dates "all formal constitutions of the public realm." It is thus not subsumable under any specific public realm. And even though it does "not [exist] necessarily and not forever," it seems like the simplest, most mundane thing in the "world"—a stark contrast to Habermas's idealizing theoretical abstraction.[14]

This passage speaks to a more worldly aspect of the notion, which connects well with the phenomenological underpinnings of Arendt's theory and more specifically her notion of the 'world.' Accordingly, Sophie Loidolt argues that the reception of "Arendt's notion of 'world' [has] often [been] reduced to the public world and then directly identified with the political space of appearance." Loidolt distinguishes the actually existing political space of appearance from 'space of appearance' in a more "fundamental," phenomenological, and technical sense, in which it is synonymous with the "appearing world."[15] In this latter sense, it captures not an idealized mode of interaction and speech but a general condition of human existence: humans always-already appear in front of others, usually in a world of objects and practices that were there before them and may very well outlast them.

We agree with Loidolt's use of the 'space of appearance' to also describe the appearing world as actors always-already encounter it. Yet the philosophical dimension of this notion as it relates to Arendt's debts to the phenomenological tradition is not the foremost concern of most contributions to this volume. What interests us are the concept's historically realized forms, which ought not be hastily identified with 'the public.'

---

13   Arendt, *Human Condition*, 199.

14   Arendt, *Human Condition*, 182–83.

15   Sophie Loidolt, *Phenomenology of Plurality: Hannah Arendt on Political Intersubjectivity* (Routledge, 2018), 98 and 103.

The Concept in Use:
Mundane Spaces of Appearance

The task at hand is to resist the automatic identification of the technical notion of 'the space of appearance' with 'the public' as it occurs in many interpretations of Arendt and, it is worth noting, also in some passages of Arendt's work itself. This is because 'the public sphere' is never wholly or clearly demarcated. It is but a frayed assemblage of overlapping and contradictory, more or less relevant and more or less hidden zones—there is no *single* public sphere.[16] In its more tangible dimensions, the concept 'space of appearance' might be used to designate the concrete zones in which these publics are actualized. And this is precisely how we propose to use the term, which is why we pluralize it as *spaces* of appearance.

Pluralizing the concept calls for an interplay between the general and the particular, allowing the concept to be critiqued and enriched through its engagement with concrete case studies.[17] The pluralized perspective on spaces of appearance is more open to case studies that reveal the

16   On this point, we broadly agree with Oskar Negt and Alexander Kluge, *Public Sphere and Experience: Toward an Analysis of the Bourgeois and Proletarian Public Sphere* (University of Minnesota Press, 1993), xlviii: "The bourgeois public sphere is anchored in the formal characteristics of communication: it can be represented in terms of a schema of continuous historical progression, insofar as one focuses on the ideas that are realized within it. But if, by contrast, one takes its real substance as one's point of departure, it is not unified at all, but rather the aggregate of individual spheres that are only abstractly related." See also Nancy Fraser, "Rethinking the Public Sphere: A Contribution to the Critique of Actually Existing Democracy," *Social Text* 25–26 (1990), and Michael Warner, *Publics and Counterpublics* (Zone Books, 2002).

17   Our approach is partially inspired by Johannes Völz, who employs the notion of 'space of appearance' similarly to many of the contributions to this volume, even though his essay accepts standard normativist readings of the space of appearance. See Johannes Völz, "Toward an Aesthetics of Populism, Part I: The Populist Space of Appearance," *Yearbook of Research in English and American Literature* 34 (2018), 224. Another approach that employs Arendt to ends similar to our own in this volume is found in an ethnographic study of street parliaments in Kenya, see Stephanie Diepeveen, "Politics in Everyday Kenyan Street-Life: The People's Parliament in Mombasa, Kenya," *Journal of Eastern African Studies* 10, no. 2 (2016), 266–83.

specifics and the particular inherent logics of spaces of appearance in their concretely actualized form. The contributions to this volume critically reassess, specify, and re-evaluate the sometimes rather unclear usage of 'space of appearance' in Arendt's writings, providing a new and useful way of understanding the notion which critically complements the readings mentioned above. This volume should thus be seen as an extensive proof of concept, an invitation to further enquiry along similar lines.

Thus, we suggest foregrounding a more particularist reading of Arendt's usage of 'space of appearance' to designate really existent spaces in the world. This allows the concept to be approached, examined, and applied more rigorously. For instance, one is less prone to fall into the trap of considering only those spaces widely perceived to be the most general and most hegemonic. Mundane, trivial, and vernacular spaces may also come into view, especially in their competition with different spaces of various degrees of size and formalization.[18]

Since spaces of appearance "preced[e] all formal constitution of the public realm," they may also include informal practices that prevalent preconceptions of a situation would deem to be private:

> [W]herever human beings come together—be it in private or socially, be it in public or politically— a space is generated that simultaneously gathers them into it and separates them from one another.[19]

Privacy not only denotes a state of seclusion from an assumed and unified public realm; it can also refer to a relative hiddenness from view, a general space of public irrelevance in which individuality and intimacy may be safely fostered according to the implicit customs of a community.

18   While the notion of the 'vernacular' has recently received renewed attention thanks to Sianne Ngai, *Our Aesthetic Categories: Zany, Cute, Interesting* (Harvard University Press, 2013), 16–18, it should be noted that it was more formally introduced in Miriam Hansen, "The Mass Production of the Senses: Classical Cinema as Vernacular Modernism," *Modernism/modernity* 6, no. 2 (1999).

19   Hannah Arendt, "Introduction Into Politics," in *The Promise of Politics,* ed. Jerome Kohn (Schocken, 2005), 106.

Yet what is generally assumed or supposed to be private may turn into a public and political issue. This can happen to entire spaces. Think, for instance, of the 1960s "kitchen culture" in the Soviet Union, when the "communal apartment" was reappropriated for "citizen resistance" and as a space of display for dissident art.[20] It can also happen to activities that migrate into political spaces of appearance. Activities such as cleaning and cooking, which are all too often considered inherently a-political and an entirely private matter, may take on an explicitly political character when, say, you are cooking or cleaning at a protest camp. In such cases, the public quality of an activity changes depending on the space of appearance in which it is performed.[21] Assigning different degrees of publicity to a given space is nothing that can be done at whim. 'Private' and 'public' are contestable and contested categories, and these struggles are reflected in perceptions of what 'private/public' means and where it occurs. The unofficial slogan of second-wave feminism, 'the private/personal is political,' comes to mind.[22]

But the extent to which such efforts may take root is always conditioned by the political situations that these efforts prefigure and attempt to reconfigure.[23] 'Situation' refers to the implicit background conditions that always-already

20 Susan Buck-Morss, *Dreamworld and Catastrophe: The Passing of Mass Utopia in East and West* (MIT Press, 2000), 199.

21 For discussions of activities like cooking or cleaning being practiced in protest camps, see: Markell, "The Moment has Passed," 130–31, and Nazlı Konya, "Making a People: Turkey's 'Democracy Watches' and Gezi-Envy," *Political Theory* 49, no. 5 (2021): 841. In any case, here we are talking about the very exercise of these activities, and not their social organization, which Honig, *Toward an Agonistic Feminism*, 146 calls "the (sedimented) products of ... actions, behaviors, and institutional structures." While seemingly private matters such as the question of who is typically tasked with wageless reproductive work need to be problematized, practicing these activities itself is usually not political.

22 See Joan W. Scott, "The Evidence of Experience," *Critical Inquiry* 17, no. 4 (1991), and Joan W. Scott, "Multiculturalism and the Politics of Identity," *October* 61 (1992).

23 For the notion of 'prefiguration,' see Hans Blumenberg, *Präfiguration: Arbeit am politischen Mythos* (Suhrkamp, 2014), 11: "the significant antecedent, the prototype [Prägnat], is not born for prefiguration but is made in order that that which is

pervade our perception, which Arendt captures more technically in terms such as "second ... in-between" or the "'web' of human relationships."[24] While these kinds of implicit background conditions frame the way in which action unfolds and appears, they do not predetermine it. Quite to the contrary, the actualization of a situation in iterating spaces of appearance influences how these general, non-universal rules are typically lived and enacted.

Such situational change becomes apparent when looking at history, in which one is often confronted with spaces of appearance and practices whose criteria change drastically while nominally staying the same. Consider, for instance, the peculiar relation between chanting and street protests in the German-speaking world that emerged in the late 19th century. Within only a couple of decades, street protests changed from an activity that was done in stern silence to one characterized primarily by a spectrum of more or less articulate noises and movements, from cheers and jeers to chants and dance.[25] Crucially, what a street protest 'really is' can never be determined by private opinions alone, it depends upon the situationally specific assumptions about what is considered normal and abnormal behavior. Again, we are talking about appearances that are 'spatial' in scope. You might not particularly enjoy, in the early 21st century, the clamor that comes with a protest. But chants and singing are obviously a normal part of protests today. What may indeed change are the criteria "by means of which we regulate our application of concepts, means by which [...] we set up the shifting conditions for conversations."[26] Yet this common ground of our language and perception is never at any one person's disposal alone. It is the situation that supplies the backdrop against which the concrete modulations and

written might be accomplished—as soon as the accomplishment allows that which was to be accomplished to be recognized in it [translation by Joe Paul Kroll]."

24   Arendt, *Human Condition*, 183.

25   Sabine Müller, "Political and Aesthetic Representation: A Problem Solved, or Still a Challenge?," (paper presented at *The Aesthetics of Democratic Life-Forms*, Goethe University Frankfurt, September 23, 2023).

26   Stanley Cavell, *In Quest of the Ordinary: Lines of Skepticism and Romanticism* (University of Chicago Press, 1988), 5.

configurations of these spaces appear, such as whether street protests are generally accepted to be silent or loud events, which in turn is conditioned by what street protests have been taken and are remembered to be.

At the heart of these criteria is the degree of reality implicitly assigned to a specific space of appearance. Think for instance of a play in a theater. Its narrative exists in its own 'universe'—what narration theorists would call its intra-diegetic dimension—and, typically, cannot be influenced by the audience.[27] However, a stage performance also has extra-diegetic consequences in that it affects the audience directly, thereby producing effects in the 'real' world. Thus, even when a completely fictional play is performed, it is necessarily performed in a space of appearance since it will have extra-diegetic effects. While this does not make all theater political, it marks the point where, according to Arendt, the performing arts and politics overlap:

> The performing arts … have indeed a strong affinity with politics. Performing artists—dancers, play-actors, musicians, and the like—need an audience to show their virtuosity, just as acting men need the presence of others before whom they can appear; both need a publicly organized space for their 'work,' and both depend upon others for the performance itself. Such a space of appearance is not to be taken for granted wherever men live together in a community. The Greek polis once was precisely that 'form of government' which provided men with *a space of appearances where they could act, with a kind of theater where freedom could appear* [emphasis added].[28]

Both the performing arts and politics are similar in that they need an audience that they can affect extra-diegetically. They depend upon concretely enacted spaces of appearance, which is a technical way to say that an actor—theatrical or political— needs an audience to act. Without an audience, all acting is mere rehearsal.

27   See Anton Fuxjäger, "Diegese, Diegesis, diegetisch: Versuch einer Begriffsentwirrung," *montage AV: Zeitschrift für Theorie und Geschichte audiovisueller Kommunikation* 16, no. 2 (2007).

28   Hannah Arendt, "What is Freedom?," in Arendt, *Between Past and Future,* 154.

Political spaces of appearance, however, are those spaces that, at least to politicized people, proclaim to immediately concern the non-fictional reality shared with all others. They do this both in terms similar to the extra-diegetic effects of performance art, which attempts to make onlookers perceive the world differently, but also—importantly and curiously—in terms of proclaiming its own reality to be the world immediately shared with all others. Actions considered political are those that affect the real, tangible world—the "reality-diegesis," so to speak—by being perceptibly and causally effective within it.[29] Accordingly, only those spaces of appearance that are generally deemed to be immediately relevant and effective are political.[30]

29   Fuxjäger, "Diegese," 24 [our translation].

30   The question of whether Arendt's account of politics excluded instrumental concerns has haunted Arendt scholarship at least since a question posed in Hanna Pitkin, "Justice: On Relating Private and Public," *Political Theory* 9, no. 3 (1981), 336–37: "What keeps these citizens together as a body? And what is it that they talk about together, in that endless palaver in the agora?" This has been quoted widely and usually affirmatively, for instance by Dana Villa, *Arendt and Heidegger: The Fate of the Political* (Princeton University Press, 1996), 36; George Kateb, "Aestheticism and Morality: Their Cooperation and Hostility," *Political Theory* 28, no. 1 (2000): 133; Peter Euben, *Platonic Noise* (Princeton University Press, 2003), 41; Shmuel Lederman, "Agonism and Deliberation in Arendt," *Constellations* 21, no. 3 (September 2014): 327; Maria Robaszkiewicz and Michael D. Weinman, *Hannah Arendt and Politics* (Edinburgh University Press, 2023), 144.
It concerns the issue whether Arendt's account of political action allows for any kind of instrumental 'content' or whether she wanted, as indicated in Sheldon Wolin, "Hannah Arendt, Democracy and The Political," *Salmagundi* 60 (1983): 15, "[a] pure form of politics" for its own sake. Villa, *Arendt and Heidegger,* 12–25 argues that Arendtian action is "self-contained" and motivated by an "inexplicable need to *aestheticize* action." Villa later revised his view, see Dana Villa, *Hannah Arendt: A Very Short Introduction* (Oxford University Press, 2023), 70. In our reading, Arendt (or anyone else, for that matter) cannot determine the concrete 'content' of politics irrespective of a given political situation, because what counts as the immediately effective, real, and relevant content of politics is always also dependent upon the situationally predominant ways of perception that designate it as such in the first place. Take two exemplary quotes that favor this reading. (1) Arendt, *Human Condition,* 182: "Most action and speech is concerned with this in-between, which varies with each group of people, so that

By contrast, a political space of appearance may lose its political quality when it is widely questioned whether it exerts an immediate effect upon the shared world. People are then prone to denounce such spaces as 'mere theater.' This is typically the case when established politics is unable to produce significant immediate results and thus its influence upon reality is questioned. Arendt describes as much in her account of the Dreyfus affair, when "the whole of France's political life … was carried on outside Parliament,"[31] in the streets and in the press. In spite of parliaments typically being a particularly political space, the French parliament was severely depoliticized in this situation, as it was widely perceived to be ineffective in tackling the most pressing and relevant political issue of the day. This demonstrates that whether a specific space is considered political or not is itself primarily a question of the general plausibility of its claim to relevance and immediate effectiveness.

most words and deeds are about some worldly objective reality in addition to being a disclosure of the acting and speaking agent [original emphasis]." So action is primarily about the in-between or world, which consists of the material environment as well as the "intangible" persistent background conditions of practices that are always-already there before you enter the world, see Arendt, *Human Condition,* 183. The point is repeated in relation to power and the perceptual organization of what actions count as means to an end and which ones do not, see (2) Hannah Arendt, *On Violence* (Harcourt, Brace & World, 1970), 51: "But the power structure itself precedes and outlasts all aims, so that power, far from being the means to an end, *is actually the very condition enabling a group of people to think and act in terms of the means-end category* [emphasis added]." This is to say that power determines what is recognized as instrumentally effective in a given situation and what is not. Or, to be more precise, power is what allows people to organize for joint political action, which ultimately implies the ability to identify aims and act in their pursuit, see Arendt, *Human Condition,* 199–202. Arendt does not exclude instrumental concerns from political action, she only downplays their relevance in light of the performative elements that always also play a role in political action. For a longer account of this argument, see Martin Renz, "The Prejudice Against Politics: Arendtian Explorations of the Populist Situation," (PhD diss., Goethe University Frankfurt).

31   Hannah Arendt, *The Origins of Totalitarianism* (Penguin Classics, 2017), 150.

Our case for 'spaces of appearance' as a useful concept in aesthetico-political research rests on one main advantage: it makes it possible to disclose and analyze not only *whether or not* persons and things appear at all, in a binary sense, but *how* concretely they come to appear in a specific instance. The question of 'how' something appears implies a threefold motion of inquiry. Intertwined with the descriptive gesture that provides details about the tone and shape of something, it may also supply, in the same stroke, an explanation as to why something comes about the way it does, and an assessment of how 'real,' politically speaking, it is taken to be.

The Uses of the Concept

The opening contribution by **Sophie Loidolt** critically expands upon our conceptual differentiation between 'space' and 'spaces of appearance.' Reading the very first pages of Robert Musil's *Man Without Qualities* with support from Alfred Schütz and Hannah Arendt, she tries to clarify the characteristics and pathologies of spaces of appearance. What Musil introduces with offhand irony is a modern world in which neither relevance (Schütz) nor power (Arendt) are self-evident features of spaces of appearance. While the novelist stages this by using a technique of 'zooming in and out' of different zones of relevance, Loidolt's philosophical concern revolves around a particular set of questions: What holds the world together and makes it something in which orientation is possible for people who appear in it and act before one another? What is it in the development of modernity that so unsettlingly questions this orientedness? The paper first develops a notion of spaces of appearance in the plural with the help of Schütz's notion of relevance, before turning to Arendt and the 'space of appearance' (in the singular) as a space where freedom can appear and which needs power to remain in existence.

Problems of political disorientation are also a central theme in the contribution by **Martha Crowe**. She employs the 'space of appearance' to critically examine a cultural intervention aimed at de-escalating political tensions and addressing far-right radicalization in contemporary Germany. Between 2017 and 2019, the Albertinum museum in Dresden hosted a series of public events entitled "We Need to Talk: *'Bilderstreit'* Face-to-Face" (*Wir müssen reden. 'Bilderstreit' mit*

Blickkontakt). These events were organized in response to claims that the museum had been disproportionately sequestering GDR-era art away in storage, an outcry fueled by enduring East-West divisions in Germany. Based in part on an interview with museum director Hilke Wagner—who initiated the event series—the contribution investigates the motivations behind the museum's approach and its resonance with a broader public. Through a close reading of the first event in the series, Crowe proposes that contemporary political threats are not to be addressed through retreat or moral distancing, but through public conversation and discussion. By drawing on the concept of the space of appearance, Crowe's analysis shows that such interventions can enable subtle shifts in how political identities and divisions are perceived and negotiated, offering an alternative to both silence and polarization.

One very specific form of a subtle shift in perception is at the heart of the contribution by **Martin Renz** and **Julius Schwarzwälder.** Through a close reading of John Berger's *Ways of Seeing* and Hannah Arendt's *On Revolution,* they argue that what they call 'un-unseeability' can explain how, from images to political situations, the same things may subtly change and no longer look the same. The relevance of un-unseeability surged once it invaded and changed the meaning of politics in the course of the revolutions of the 18th century. Significantly, these revolutions changed what could potentially be perceived as political. This had consequences for both the spatial and temporal aspects of politics. Politics ceased to be a sphere, instead becoming a potential medium of reality that designates a particular space and the actions that constitute it as immediately effective and generally relevant. At the same time, experiences of irrevocability signaled the advent of a distinctively modern kind of novelty to the political stage. In light of this un-unseeable novelty, issues such as the much-cited 'social question' appear less like a 'cause' than an effect of the type of freedom found in the un-unseeable experiences of the French Revolution.

Spurious claims pertaining to a revolution's 'cause' are also investigated in the contribution by **Raha Golestani.** She examines the unsettled discursive space of the Shiraz Festival of Arts, an annual performing arts event unfolding

23

at a decisive moment in Iranian history: the decade leading up to the Iranian Revolution (1967–1977). Interrupted and overshadowed by the revolution, the festival has become an equally understudied and burdened site, clouded by an aura of nostalgia, grievance, and speculation. Speaking to other voices in the contemporary discussion of the festival, Golestani contextualizes these debates within gendered assumptions about the public roles assigned to aesthetics and politics in pre-revolutionary Iran, and how their 'irreconcilable differences' manifest in the singular circumstances of the festival. The essay's themes, in equal proportions, are paradise (the festival's subversive portrayal as an Arendtian oasis in a desert), art (its artistic strategies for navigating cultural hierarchies), and caviar (accusations of decadence and aestheticization of politics). Almost fifty years after its final act, the essay looks into the festival's prismatic nature and the diverse responses it generates and sustains to this day.

Merve Yıldırım's contribution deals with another attempt to come to terms with cultural differences by considering a building that was never built and a friendship whose historical roots are all too often overlooked. She examines the House of Friendship (*Haus der Freundschaft/Dostluk Yurdu*), commissioned in Constantinople in 1916, as a lens through which to explore the long and layered history of German-Turkish relations. Tracing this diplomatic history from early modern treaties to its wartime culmination, she focuses on the moment when an abstract ideal of 'friendship' was to be spatialized through architecture. Organized by the *Deutscher Werkbund* and framed as a cultural initiative, the project shows how architecture could operate as soft power—designed not only to symbolize but to generate perceptions of proximity, familiarity, and shared purpose. The House of Friendship, according to Yıldırım, must be understood both as a material intersection of the two empires' trajectories and as an effort to shift friendship from the sphere of statecraft into public experience. Conceived during the Great War, it embodied the paradox of seeking to provide stability to something often lacking permanence, physicality to something inherently relational, and appearance to something not necessarily visible. That the building never advanced beyond its foundation stone does not diminish its significance; rather, it reflects the complexities of rendering political friendship into architectural form, thereby offering a reminder defined less by completion than by its unresolved style.

Further discussion of architectural attempts to give concrete shape to a space of appearance is found in **Dorothea Douglas**'s examination of the unusual central distribution node of Germany's largest courthouse at the turn of the century, the main stairway pavilion of the *Landes- und Amtsgericht Mitte, Berlin*. As part of the wave of courthouse construction following the opening of civil proceedings to the public in the wake of Imperial legal codification, a novel topos of interaction between the citizen—understood as liberal and economically rational in the context of the reforms—and the machinery of the administrative state emerged from centralized planning within the Prussian Ministry of Public Works. Unlike conventional readings of main stairways as merely oppressive ante-juridical spaces, Douglas explores how law's novel order was communicated through the tactile experience of movement. Drawing on discourses surrounding the epistemic potential of psychophysical perception in turn-of-the-century Germany, she engages with August Schmarsow's work, which re-centered architectural form around the sensing body. In this framework, the experience of architectural form is linked to the newly codified legal subject as embodied in the stairway's design. Aesthetic experience, used to transform the fragmented urban dweller into an autonomous legal subject, initiates the viewer into the order of law. Drawing on the notion of space of appearance, the paper questions how the stairway modulates agency and self-experience in relation to power.

Noah Grossmann's contribution takes up the issue of agency modulation and relates it to the work of Arendt and Fred Moten. He traces how Arendt (in "Reflections on Little Rock") and Fred Moten (in *Refuge, Refuse, Refrain*) look at the same photos of Black teenagers facing hostile white crowds. Arendt's essay is interpreted as opening up a simultaneity of futures that shape American society: despite the existence of liberal rights, procedures, and narratives of progress, Black individuals continue to navigate a landscape marked by racism. Moten instead focuses on Elizabeth Eckford's shaded eyes and draws on further material to describe two ongoing histories and futures into which, in his account, the teenager is to be inserted. By comparing two theorists looking at the same photographs, Grossmann uncovers a range of different, conflicting registers of the future—from progress to stalemate, from rupture to rollback—that are employed to think about racism and how it appears.

A different register of the future—promising—is taken up in the contribution by **Reinhold Görling,** who emphasizes Arendt's use of 'medium' to describe the network of human affairs that promises constitute, as well as her shift from 'space' to 'medium of appearance' in *The Life of the Mind*. While Arendt's use of 'medium' varies, she tends to employ the notion to circumscribe modes of communication in which the singular comes to appear without being overwritten by a general concept. This becomes conceivable by understanding the singular as an event that communicates itself to other events. Arendt's theory of the mind further develops this relationship by understanding appearance as an inner dialogue as well as a social relationality reaffirmed in judgment. Imagination and *sensus communis* are the central elements of this capacity for judgment. Yet, Görling argues, a problem arises in that Arendt does not pursue the dynamics of the inner dialogue any further. She highlights that appearance always simultaneously means concealment, but with regard to her dictum on the 'banality of evil' in particular, it would be important to consider the dimensions of denial and splitting, as demonstrated for instance in psychoanalysis. They interrupt the inner dialogue and conceal the self from itself.

Helena W. Crusius's essay asks what kind of political efficacy belongs not to selves but to objects, and what those things that appear between us can do. For Arendt, objects share in two paradigms of appearance: the sheer appearance of the *phainesthai* in philosophical wonder and the mediated appearance of the *dokei moi* in secular politics. But even as objects comprise the most quintessential appearances insofar as they can only be judged according to the criterion of beauty, their appearances are categorically passive—that is, the only appearances with any power are those made by the only actors capable of making their appearance, namely living creatures and sentient beings. By contrast, the object is endlessly active for Ernst Bloch, for whom what is aesthetically portrayed dialectically drives forward the utopian itself. Crusius suggests that these conflictual approaches dramatize the problem of the possibility of an effective object in terms of the declension of appearance: the dative which inheres to Arendt's object and the accusative of Bloch's show us how the active object acts, perhaps, only by tyrannical means.

Finally, **Susan Buck-Morss**'s visual-textual essay provides some meditative after-thoughts and after-images as well as a call to action. Her wager is to begin thinking in images, seriously, in a way that is sensitive to how perceptions may shift, sometimes confusingly and without an accompanying change in thought. This would allow a shift in political vision, she argues, away from the global and towards the planetary dimension.

"Which, Remarkably Enough, Does Not Get Anyone Anywhere"

Of Cameramen, Irrelevant Structures of Relevance, and the lackened Space of Appearance

Sophie Loidolt

01
Robert Musil,
*The Man
Without Qualities:
Volume 1.* Trans.
Eithne Wilkins
and Ernst Kaiser
(Capricorn Books,
1965).

"Which, remarkably enough, does not get anyone anywhere" is the heading of the first, short chapter of one of the most celebrated modernist novels, Robert Musil's *The Man Without Qualities*.[01] Musil begins by listing, in some detail, what are the somewhat irrelevant meteorological conditions of a fine August morning in Vienna. Soon after, we witness a traffic accident, which a generic upper-middle-class couple observes before the event sinks once more into insignificance. With this non-beginning, Musil anticipates a theme of the novel that also manifests itself in other strands of the plot: the failure—now relished, now tragicomic—to create and experience relevance, with even the failure itself struggling to attain relevance.

In this essay, I would like to focus my reading on these, the novel's opening pages, doing so with the assistance of Alfred Schütz and Hannah Arendt. For what Musil stages here with seemingly offhand irony is a problem of philosophical concern, from their various perspectives, to both authors: What holds the world together and makes it an oriented place for people who appear and act before one another? And what is it in the development of modernity that so unsettlingly questions this orientedness, that restructures appearance? By weaving the ideas of all three authors together, I would like to approach the question of how the concept of a space or spaces of appearance might be understood. Whereas Schütz provides structures of relevance as the decisive criterion, Arendt uses her phenomenological description to develop a normative perspective which makes it possible to trace the strengthening and slackening of 'the space of appearance' as a space of freedom. For his part, Musil claims an author's right to make appear, thereby making perceptible, from a mobile multi-perspectivism, how various spaces of appearance overlie one another and how this feels to his protagonists: as a space of appearance that allows itself to be glimpsed just before once more retreating, and whose relevance is of a completely arbitrary (and hence non-existent) character. It is a (theatrical) stage of modernity, a condition in which "the world," as Arendt would say, "has lost its power to gather [people] together, to relate and to separate them":

> The public realm, as the common world, gathers us together and yet prevents our falling over each other, so to speak. What makes mass society so difficult to bear is not the number of people involved, or at least not primarily, but the fact that the world between them has lost its power to gather them together, to relate and to separate them.[02]

It is perhaps no coincidence that Musil's first chapter should culminate in a road accident. Not only speed, increased by technology to an unprecedented degree, causes people and machines to "fall over each other." The world itself no longer stabilizes the interstices. This shall be explored in the following.

Schütz's Structures of Relevance

Let us begin with Alfred Schütz and a brief excursion into his theory of relevance, which will provide a first lens through which to examine the passages by Musil. Schütz approaches the subject of relevance from the vantage point of the theory of consciousness, combining it with questions from social philosophy, particularly that of acquired and inter-subjectively shared 'social' knowledge. The phenomenological sociologist observes that emergence and appearance in the social field correlate with certain structures of attention and weighting. While these undoubtedly are socially transmitted and formed, their sequence is subject to biographical variation, and they are experienced in the first person. Schütz distinguishes between motivational, thematic, and interpretational relevances. In short: *why* does something become a theme for somebody, *what* is the theme, and *how?* For instance, what stands out in a space to the person entering it is a matter of *motivational relevance* (in Schütz's example, it is a coiled rope in a hotel room that initially looks like a snake,[03] though, to take a different example, it may also be a

02
Hannah Arendt, *The Human Condition* (University of Chicago Press, 1998), 52–53.

03
Alfred Schütz and Thomas Luckmann, *The Structures of the Life-World* (Heinemann, 1974), 185–86.

04
Alfred Schütz,
"Some Structures
of the Life-World,"
in *Collected Papers III:
Studies in
Phenomenological
Philosophy,*
ed. Ilse Schütz
(Nijhoff, 1970), 124–25.

street scene in which one observes people flocking to a certain spot). Motivational relevance helps a person to determine their situation, which confronts them as a certain texture of significance and thereby constitutes a 'space of appearance': a space in which something is always already apprehended as something existing in a certain contextuality. Any conscious act (perception, memory, imagination, etc.) in which something reveals itself has this structure; there is no 'consciousness of something' that is not permeated with structures of relevance. Spaces of appearance—understood here primarily as mundane correlates of fields of consciousness—thus are constituted through structures of relevance that determine motivation, theme, and interpretation. Something that initially became a theme motivationally—through plans, interests, or by being affected—in the next step, that of receiving attention, acquires autonomy and thereby becomes questionable, taking on *"thematic relevancy."* This relevance guides the person's efforts to determine what is important about the theme that has now become interesting, how far they are to go in determining the object, and what is to come first—"first things first," according to Schütz, "giving thus in colloquial language an excellent definition of the thematically relevant."[04] The matter will therefore initially be one of establishing whether one is indeed faced with a snake or rather with an ordinary rope, or what happened to cause people to flock to a certain place in the streets. How something of thematic relevance is interpreted and understood, however, is a matter of *"interpretational relevance,"* the angle or viewpoint with regard to which the theme may be understood. Combined with motivational relevance, it is, moreover, interpretational relevance that determines the point at which a process of interpretation can be terminated, when a problem can be considered "solved."

Now, to raise this question to the level of intersubjectivity, it should be added that Schütz also distinguishes between "intrinsic" (i.e., self-chosen) and "imposed" relevances. Imposed relevances may be of a non-subjective kind to the extent that they disrupt, distract, or inhibit my own structures of relevance: a falling flowerpot or, more meaningfully, an event that astounds me and inexorably attracts my attention. But imposed relevances, to Schütz, also essentially include all social relevances. Human encounters are encounters between systems of relevances. Although we can never fully know another person's system of relevance, it is possible to "adjust to one another" by means of responsive, perhaps cooperative, but in any case coordinative behavior, with each person acting and reacting to the other. By such means, shared, collective relevances may develop. As long as this happens as part of a communicative exchange, we may be reciprocally under the other's "control," but we are aware of the fact.[05] This, according to Schütz, changes as the social world becomes increasingly anonymous under conditions of modernity:

> But the more the other becomes anonymous and the less his place in the social cosmos is ascertainable to the partner, the more the zone of common intrinsic relevances decreases and that of imposed ones increases. Extending reciprocal anonymity of partners is, however, characteristic of our modern civilization. We are less and less determined in our social situation by relationships with individual partners within our immediate or mediate reach, and more and more by highly anonymous types which have no fixed place in the social cosmos.[06]

In a modern world increasingly dominated by technology, in which potential distances are reduced and the scope for anonymity accordingly increases, an increasing imbalance emerges between the relevances that we choose and those that are imposed on us. Eighty years on, Schütz may seem to describe this technological dominance in slightly dated terms, yet it still strikes at the core of the matter:

> No spot of this globe is more distant from the place where we live than sixty airplane hours; electric waves carry messages in a fraction of a second from one end of the earth to the other; and very soon every place in this world will be the potential target of destructive weapons released at any other place.[07]

To the extent that it prevents me from synchronizing my system of relevances with concrete others, Schütz takes this fundamental change to the reach of human action to constitute a loss of autonomy. It is indeed impossible to achieve personal coordination with such abstractions as 'the financial markets,'

05
Alfred Schütz, "The Well-Informed Citizen: An Essay on the Social Distribution of Knowledge," *Social Research* 13, no. 4 (1946): 471.

06
Schütz, "The Well-Informed Citizen," 472–73.

07
Schütz, "The Well-Informed Citizen," 473.

'the arms race,' 'the climate crisis,' or with any system de-scribed as 'too big to fail.' Nonetheless, they determine our social and political reality, they are 'imposed' relevances in the most emphatic sense. In the essay from which these ob-servations are drawn, entitled "The Well-Informed Citizen," Schütz analyses a variety of ideal types and their different responses to imposed relevances. Whereas the "man on the street" simply accepts them unquestioningly as circum-stances with which he has to deal, the "well-informed citi-zen" is aware that these are not mere instances of facticity but rather social structures. Yet he, too, goes no further than wanting to understand and classify them, choosing what-ever frame of relevance seems fit for the purpose. "The ex-pert," by contrast, has always already selected his frame of relevance, allowing him to encounter all events as susceptible to analysis from a certain perspective. It should be stressed that Schütz does not identify these ideal types with partic-ular persons or groups of persons, instead assuming that all these types are realized in each of us. They are perspectives in which imposed relevances assert themselves in various ways: as a factual situation to be dealt with; as an explicable situ-ation susceptible to a (probably one-sided) solution; or as a situation to be judged according to a range of frames of rele-vance and interpretation. In the modern world, the well-in-formed citizen, called upon to exercise his judgement, faces a number of challenges, for which he must rely on a great deal of socially mediated knowledge. Moreover, he

> finds himself placed in a domain which belongs to an infinite number of possible frames of reference. There are no pregiven ready-made ends, no fixed border lines within which he can look for shelter. He has to choose the frame of reference by choosing his interest; he has to investigate the zones of relevances adhering to it; and he has to gather as much knowledge as possible of the origin and sources of the relevances actually or potentially imposed upon him. In terms of the classification previously used, the well-informed citizen will restrict, in so far as is possible, the zone of the irrelevant, mindful that what is today relatively irrelevant may be imposed tomorrow as a primary

relevance and that the province of the so-called absolutely irrelevant may reveal itself as the home of the anonymous powers which may overtake him.[08]

08
Schütz, "Well-Informed Citizen," 475–76.

There is something ominous about Schütz's account, suggesting an increasing difficulty of dealing with growing anonymity, increased ranges of action and their consequences. Schütz complains that politics has been trivialized by being increasingly responsive to "public opinion," a fabricated ideal type, modeled only on the entirely self-centered "man on the street." Merely reacting to circumstances means failing to understand and to change the underlying causes. Schütz, then, is concerned with opinion formation and hence with plural perspectives, which by virtue of their different frames of relevance produce differently weighted spaces of appearance. One might say that Schütz is concerned with making transparent spaces of appearance that are not merely to be accepted as the circumstances but to be understood as determined by relevance. On the one hand, this produces an enlightening effect; on the other, it places the well-informed citizen in the position of a spectator, who, by changing between frames of relevance at will (as one might change an optical lens), can pass through spaces of appearance in different configurations. Yet this is not entirely arbitrary, since imposed relevances do after all set a certain framework of facticity; nor is it independent of collective modes of perception, by means of which certain frames of relevance impose themselves as dominant. If, however, one ever wanted to proceed to action, one would not only have to decide on suitable frames of reference, they would also have to be harmonized with expert and above all with everyday perspectives:

09
Schütz, "Well-Informed Citizen," 467.

> It is this zone of things taken for granted within which we have to find our bearings. All our possible questioning for the unknown arises only within such a world of supposedly preknown things, and presupposes its existence. Or, to use Dewey's terms, it is the indeterminate situation from which all possible inquiry starts with the goal of transforming it into a determinate one.[09]

There must, in other words, exist a fixed point in the life-world from which this play of systems of relevance can be set into motion in the first place—and from which something like meaningful action is even possible. Yet it is precisely this secure anchoring in the lifeworld that can no longer be taken for granted, that has become movable. With these initial thoughts in mind, let us proceed to the analysis of the first pages of *The Man Without Qualities*.

Musil's Zooming In and Zooming Out

A literary text is capable of giving a special kind of visibility to both subjective and objective structures of relevance. Texts are able to multiply perspectives or, as in the present case, to perform perspective for themselves. By so doing, they expose structures of appearance, not by approaching them as a philosophical problem, but through their literary representation. Musil, for instance, uses the devices of 'zooming in' and 'zooming out' like a cameraman, moving between the registers of scientific abstraction and human 'common sense,' leaving us uncertain as to how to apprehend what.[10] This is something, it seems, which is no longer determined by the things themselves or by the lifeworldly context as the condition of thematization.

Beginning "over the Atlantic" in the language of science, of meteorology, we pan—taking in our sweep the planets "and many other important phenomena"—towards a place, a season, a year: "In short, to use an expression that describes the facts pretty satisfactorily, even though it is somewhat old-fashioned: it was a fine August day in the year 1913." The perspective of the lifeworld is still reasonably certain of

10   Jonathan Crary argues that the various kinds of 'focus' were only 'invented' as a result of innovations in lens and imaging technology between 1880 and 1905. This also made it possible to generate new forms of attention.
See Jonathan Crary, *Suspensions of Perception: Attention, Spectacle, and Modern Culture* (MIT Press, 1999).
Musil's technique of zooming in and out may be seen as the literary realization of such a claim and of its subjective effects. This is also the point of my comparison with Dziga Vertov's "Man with a Movie Camera," which translates the acceleration characteristic of the modern age into cinematic techniques, thereby allowing it to be experienced afresh by the audience.

being best suited to "describ[ing] the facts" while aware that it is already "old-fashioned." In this zooming in and out between the lifeworldly concern for what is important and factual on the one hand and the structure of relevance of something greater, process-driven, dynamic, and anonymous on the other, the reader continues to be productively bewildered: from the weather via the city and the walkers to the event of the accident and its interpretation. While we follow, as it were, a literary Dziga Vertov, diving into the foaming vortex of the city, we find uniqueness, unmistakability affirmed in its recognizability: an observer familiar with the city would recognize it "with his eyes shut," averring that cities have personalities and thus "can be recognised by their pace just as people can by their walk." However, should we deceive ourselves as to this ability to perceive, holistically and immediately, a city's unmistakable and unique "who," then "what does it matter? The excessive weight attached to the question of where one is goes back to nomadic times, when people had to be observant about feeding-grounds. ... This distracts attention from more important things."[11]

Musil plays with thematic and interpretational relevances, thereby making our (usually lifeworldly) motivational relevances seem questionable. Perhaps no longer appropriate? What are these "more important things," anyway? Where should one stop with interpretation? Does one not settle for insufficient exactitude ("what particular shade of red ... in terms of wave-lengths" is a nose?) and, at the same time, an excess of irrelevant individuality (why Vienna when it might just well be any other capital)?[12] And in what formations of appearance does a relevant matter show itself? Is the possibility of changing perspective and the frame of relevance at will not as shattering and yet as much of a laughing matter as the gaze into space—at least, as soon as one no longer sees the sublime there or the 'moral law within me' (Kant) but only an infinite number of possibilities and a great deal of nothingness?

The walkers to whom our focus is directed at any rate are "far from having such an impression." As members of a privileged social class, they are not that easily discombobulated: "in the exquisite underlinen of their minds—they knew who they were and that they were in their proper place in a

11
Musil,
Man Without Qualities,
3–4.

12
Musil,
Man Without Qualities,
4.

13
Musil,
Man Without Qualities,
4.

14
Musil,
Man Without Qualities,
4–5.

capital city that was also an imperial residence."[13] This knowledge of 'who one is' is secured in status. It appears outwardly—in posture, in dress, in status—while simultaneously stabilizing inward self-perception. Yet here too individualizing self-reassurance lapses into anonymity and irrelevance. The man and the woman might be Paul Arnheim and Ermelinda Tuzzi, two characters who will play major roles in the novel (and who are also constantly engaged in futile efforts to create importance and exude an air of meaningfulness around themselves). Yet it is not they, as we are told. We are thus "confronted with the enigma of who they were. If one has a lively imagination one is very often conscious of such enigmas in the street, but they become resolved in a remarkably easy manner by being forgotten, unless in the next thirty yards one can remember where one has seen these two people before."[14] The public space of a major city makes 'zooming in' a fleeting pastime. The enigma of who someone might be and how much time one can devote to resolving it can barely be kept alive until the next corner. After all, it too is irrelevant.

Then, suddenly, something happens. A pedestrian is hit by a lorry. A crowd soon gathers around the spot "like bees round the entrance to their hive." The general feeling among the bystanders is that the pedestrian has only his own lack of attention to blame. They listen to the driver's expostulations, examine the unfortunate man lying on the pavement, and make a halfhearted effort at giving first aid. Attention is heightened all round, there can be no doubt as to the relevances: after all, a human life hangs in the balance and questions of guilt and responsibility are raised. But thanks to the modern division of labor, the bystanders can rely on the swift appearance of an ambulance on the scene, bringing professional medical help. The lady and her companion move closer, step back again, hesitant in their reactions: "The lady had a disagreeable sensation in the pit of her stomach, which she felt entitled to take for compassion; it was an irresolute, paralysing sensation." Thankfully, her companion is at hand with a rationalizing, technical explanation, bringing the conversation around to lorries and their excessively long braking distances. Although she knows nothing about braking distances, the lady is somehow reassured, finding "that by this means the horrible happening could be fitted into some kind of pattern, so becoming a technical problem that no longer directly concerned her." The ambulance appears, the injured man receives first aid and is carried off, and everything looks so clean and orderly that "[p]eople walked on with the almost justifiable impression that what had occurred was an event within the proper framework of law and order."[15] This is the moment for the gentleman to make a remark about American accident statistics:

> "Do you think he is dead?" his companion asked,
> still with the unjustified feeling that she had experi-
> enced something exceptional.
> "I should think he's alive," the gentleman replied.
> "It looked as though he were when they lifted him into
> the ambulance."[16]

The opening chapter, "Which, Remarkably Enough, Does Not Get Anyone Anywhere," closes with this generically compassionate statement of compassion for the nameless fellow citizen. Did something out of the ordinary just occur? In statistical terms, certainly not. Nor even in personal terms, the affective response being too "irresolute, paralysing."[17] But was this not a public event, or at least an event that took place in the public realm and garnered appropriate attention? Do we not find a 'shared reality' actualized here?

We certainly do, albeit a reality marked by powerlessness and irrelevance. With this first chapter, Musil lifts the curtain on a stage that, as it were, collapses into itself. It is a meta-space of appearances, rendering different spaces of appearance visible. By zooming in and out, it throws light on the structures of relevance in which what appears either takes its place or disappears again. This is not a morally concerned diagnosis of the alienation of modern man, his indifference and his inability to express feelings or form relationships, etc. Rather, it is an analytic view of how the world and meaning are constituted in an everyday situation. The participants do not lack social, actional, or communicative dispositions: the occurrence (the accident) receives appropriate notice, the situation is discussed, help is offered, a functioning order is in place. The anonymous male protagonist even tries to shift from the perspective of the literal "man on the street" to that of the "well-informed citizen" (possessing expert knowledge),

15
Musil,
Man Without Qualities,
5–6.

16
Musil,
Man Without Qualities,
6.

17
Musil,
Man Without Qualities,
5.

18
Schütz,
"Well-Informed
Citizen," 467.

19
Musil,
Man Without Qualities,
6.

20
Arendt,
Human Condition, 53.

seeking to engage his lady companion in a discussion of finer technical points.[18] The only potentially disquieting thing here is the uncertainty as to whether anything actually happened and hence, *a fortiori, whether anything can happen at all*. To be more precise: whether it makes much of a difference when something moves from the category of possibility into that of reality. Why? Because, statistically speaking, it can then once more be slotted into a framework of possibility. An event thereby becomes a possible occurrence that has now indeed occurred, and this in turn diminishes the relevance of any possible event. By switching between close-up and long-distance perspectives, between concretion and anonymization, Musil allows a technique that would be familiar to the sociologist Alfred Schütz in its reliance on ideal types to penetrate into the experiential dimension of the space of appearance. The lady with "the unjustified feeling that she had experienced something exceptional" finds her way of experiencing the world already suspended between her own perspective and the distance offered by other possible (statistical, third-person, cosmic, meteorological, etc.) perspectives and hence affected by the suspicion of a wide-ranging loss of reality and relevance.[19] This, *The Man Without Qualities* tells us, is one of the effects of the modern lifeworld.

Musil Seen Through the Lens of Arendt's Critique of Modernity

Allowing Hannah Arendt as well as Alfred Schütz to assist us in our reading of Musil deepens the diagnosis of modernity beyond structures of relevance and affords a systematic perspective on what a 'space of appearance' might mean (I shall discuss the second point below). At the beginning of this essay, I quoted Arendt's finding that "the world ... has lost its power to gather [people] together, to relate and to separate them."[20] What is this supposed to mean—and, specifically, what aspect of "world" does she mean? Surely there can be no question that the world (still) appears and that the things, life-forms, and persons within it appear in some coherent arrangement. Arendt is not claiming that some kind of collective psychosis has taken hold. But the opening passages of *The Man Without Qualities* offer an unruffled explanation of what might be amiss: the lifeworld appears as a scene contemplated from a distance, one in which no real involvement is possible. This lifeworld of a modern society lacks "reality" because of a shift in perspective, which makes the world be seen from space and the individual in their function in the greater life-process of society. This is a perspective that even the individual is unable to escape: "The trouble with modern theories of behaviorism is not that they are wrong but that they could become true, that they actually are the best possible conceptualization of certain obvious trends in modern society."[21] In this context, Arendt also discusses the affinity between atomic, planetary, and social "systems" as they present themselves to us:

> [T]he reason ... why the behavior of the infinitely small particle is not only similar in pattern to the planetary system as it appears to us but resembles the life and behavior patterns in human society is, of course, that we look and live in this society as though we were as far removed from our own human existence as we are from the infinitely small and the immensely large which, even if they could be perceived by the finest instruments, are too far away from us to be experienced.[22]

Musil, it might be concluded, anticipates both this diminution of experience (*"Erfahrungsschwund"*[23]) and the paralysis of the spectrum of action. For the manifold possibilities that become palpable in his descriptions tend to be mathematical rather than motivational, tied to action. Arendt accordingly finds "world-alienation" rather than "self-alienation" to be the great problem of the modern age.[24] There are also economic reasons for this: besides all the technological developments that shift the 'Archimedean point' from the Earth itself into space (e.g., the telescope), the early modern era witnesses an accumulation of capital that results in the capitalist mode of production and its preoccupation with adding value. The "world" and all questions of politics thus come to be understood primarily in economic terms, as a great productive household. Economic theories such as that developed by Adam Smith postulate the existence of an 'invisible hand,' furthering the common good through the pursuit of private interests:

21
Arendt,
Human Condition,
322.

22
Arendt,
Human Condition,
323.

23
Hannah Arendt,
*Vita activa oder
Vom tätigen Leben*
(Piper, 1981), 412;
Arendt,
Human Condition,
323.

24
Arendt,
Human Condition,
254.

25
Hannah Arendt,
*The Origins
of Totalitarianism*
(Harcourt Brace
Jovanovich, 1973),
145.

26
Musil,
Man Without Qualities,
5.

27
Musil,
Man Without Qualities,
7–8.

Private interests which by their very nature are temporary, limited by man's natural span of life, can now escape into the sphere of public affairs and borrow from them that infinite length of time which is needed for continuous accumulation. This seems to create a society very similar to that of the ants and bees where "the Common good differeth not from the Private; and being by nature enclined to their private, they procure thereby the common benefit." Since, however, men are neither ants nor bees, the whole thing is a delusion.[25]

It is no coincidence that both ants and bees should be mentioned in the first pages of *The Man Without Qualities*. Musil describes people flocking to the scene of the accident "like bees round the entrance to their hive,"[26] and in the next chapter, which introduces Ulrich, the titular protagonist, he gives himself over to thoughts that paradigmatically anticipate Arendt's late modern man, the *animal laborans:*

The expenditure of muscular energy made by a citizen [*Bürger*] quietly going about his business all day long is considerably greater than that of an athlete who lifts a huge weight once a day. Physiologically this has been established; and so doubtless the social sum-total of little everyday exertions, as a result of their suitability for such summation, does bring far more energy into the world than do the deeds of heroes; indeed, the heroic exertion appears positively minute, like a grain of sand laid, in some act of illusory immensity, upon a mountain-top.
The idea appealed to him. But, it must be added, it was not really because he liked a life of urban respectability [*das bürgerliche Leben*] that he liked this idea; on the contrary, he was merely choosing to create difficulties for his own inclinations, which had once been different.
Perhaps it is precisely the common man [*Spießbürger*] who has an intuitive prophetic glimpse of the beginning of an immense new, collective, ant-like heroism? It will be called rationalised heroism and will be regarded as very beautiful. But what can we know of that today?[27]

Without, at this point, drawing conclusions regarding the figure of Ulrich, Arendt would surely have had something to say about the *Bürger* as well as the *Spießbürger/Spießer* ("ordinary philistines"[28]) who feel restored to comfort only in a totalitarian framework that gives them direction in their feeling of superfluousness in modernity. The premonition of monstrous violence, which is also concealed in the ant and bee metaphor, remains hidden from the novel's protagonist, perhaps remaining in a state of "delusion."[29] Blithely philosophizing in the shadow of the First World War, he can toy with the idea that, in the face of a world of uncertain meanings, it would perhaps only be logical to prefer the sense of possibility to the sense of reality.

A 'man without qualities' may on the one hand be somebody who refuses to be pinned down, who avoids situations in which his true colors might emerge. On the other hand, he may be a person in whom the modern process of anonymization is taking place and who is looking for a way to cope with it as an individual. According to Arendt's final somber analysis in *The Human Condition,* this is symptomatic for a world that has lost its power to gather and relate, in which the "experiences of worldliness escape more and more the range of ordinary human experience."[30] Instead, "the society of jobholders demands of its members a sheer automatic functioning, as though individual life had actually been submerged in the over-all life process of the species."[31] What to Ulrich is still an "interesting" speculation "may end in the deadliest, most sterile passivity history has ever known." When Musil, with delicate irony, describes this increasingly transparent space of possibility as a meta-space of appearance, this is quite appropriate to the subject, for the ironist must preserve his own light-heartedness if he is to

---

28 Arendt, *The Origins of Totalitarianism,* 368.
The translation does not render Musil's play with the terms *"bürgerliches Leben"* (bourgeois lifestyle) and *"Spießbürger"* (petit bourgeois type). The latter is translated as "common man," which could be connected to Schütz' "man on the street." But Musil's expression is more clearly judgmental and ironic, and does not simply mean the common man.

29 Arendt, *The Origins of Totalitarianism,* 145.

30 Arendt, *Human Condition,* 323.

31 Arendt, *Human Condition,* 322.

32
Arendt,
Human Condition,
323.

keep matters suspended in the air. But does that mean that all scope for action is foreclosed? That would be going too far, also running contrary to Arendt's diagnosis: "Needless to say, this does not mean that modern man has lost his capacities or is on the point of losing them."[32] The question is only whether these capacities can be actualized and preserved for long enough to form and sustain a space of appearance. Let us then consider, in the final section, Arendt's understanding of the space of appearance and what to make, from that perspective, of situations which, remarkably enough, do not get anyone anywhere.

Arendt's Space of Appearance

Arendt can help us to better understand the powerlessness of the space of appearance that Musil hints at. This, however, first requires certain conceptual clarifications before we turn to the complementary concepts of 'potentiality'/'possibility'/'*dynamis*' and 'actuality'/'reality'/'*energeia*.'

Arendt does not use the term 'space of appearance(s)' in the manner in which I have introduced it, as an appearing world that assumes a different texture according to the structure of relevance through which it is viewed. I also wish to avoid the misunderstanding that what I have spoken of so far is a 'bubble model,' in which every subject or consciousness inhabits its 'own' world, and that a world of sociability had entered the scene only with the discussion of Arendt. Rather, Schütz makes it clear from the outset that the world is public, social, and intersubjective. This basic idea can be found in the work of all phenomenologists. What Schütz's work lends itself to emphasizing and analyzing, however, is that while a shared world appears through shared structures of relevance, it can also come into view from different angles and through different structures of relevance without ceasing to be a shared world. A good many shared relevances are the result of our physical constitution. Beings altogether differently constituted physically would accordingly have different relevances and affordances. Other shared relevances are socialized through culture, technology, and language, being thereby subject to conditions of plurality and historical change. Additionally, relevances may be produced, interpreted, and politicized. This, then, is a dynamic and intersubjective process in which some things are pushed to the front and others to the back. It is a process that takes place in the field of collective ways of perceiving, historical constellations, paradigm shifts, and (not least) power relations. It therefore makes sense to speak of '*spaces* of appearance' in the plural here, for they may intersect as well as overlie or conceal one another.

Arendt, however, only ever speaks of the '*space* of appearance(s)' in the singular and in the highly specific sense of something that can occur, within the appearing world, as a *mode* of the web of human relationships. If one prefers to adhere to Arendt's terminology (which there is no obligation to do), the process described above might be fittingly described as "the 'web' of human relationships, indicating by the metaphor its somewhat intangible quality." Arendt also uses the synonymous terms "second in-between" or *Mitwelt* (with-world). This "second in-between," with which "the physical, worldly in-between along with its interests is overlaid and, as it were, overgrown," is a constantly changing web of action and speech that precedes all individual action and speech.[33] For Arendt, this is the decisive component that holds the world together, providing it with orientation. This *Mitwelt* may be subject to various modes, it may be illuminated or darkened, for instance "in times of corruption, disintegration, and political bankruptcy":[34]

> In such times, the realm of human affairs darkens; it loses the radiant, glorious brightness that is only appropriate to the public sphere, which is constituted in the togetherness of people, and which is indispensable if action and speech are to unfold fully, i.e., if those who act and speak are to appear beyond what is acted and discussed. In this twilight, in which no one knows who another is, people feel alien, not only in the world, but also among themselves.[35]

Already at this point, in the twilight of modernity, where "no one knows who another is," we might return to Musil. However, I would like to dwell on conceptual matters a little longer, for it is here that we see a first idea of the space of appearance taking shape: it is a *mode of the brightness* of the realm of human affairs, which can also exist in darkness or

33
Arendt, *Human Condition*, 182–83.

34
Arendt, *Human Condition*, 180.

35
Arendt, *Vita activa*, 170. This passage is only to be found in *Vita activa*, the German version of *The Human Condition*.

36
Martin Heidegger,
Being and Time
(Harper & Row, 1962),
56.

in twilight. But what exactly does Arendt mean by this metaphor of "brightness?" It is a medium that renders visible something that goes beyond, that represents a surplus over the appearing world. Action and speech manifest *perspectives on the world,* showing something that transcends the merely visible. How can they do such a thing? Arendt initially follows Heidegger's definition of the *logos,* of language, to which she adds action, the capacity to make beginnings. The *logos,* according to Heidegger, "lets something be seen (*phainestai*), namely, what this discourse is about; and it does so either for the one who is doing the talking (the *medium*) or for persons who are talking with one another."[36] Speech—or *logos* as a form of being together in the world—reveals the world and the speakers in a particular way. Already Heidegger notes that those who speak are the "medium" of "letting things be seen." Speech can only "let something be seen" when it is perceived by others (regardless of whether what is perceived is "correct" or coincides with what was intended; what matters is only *that* speech be perceived and that speech and action continue). If speech and action do not take place in the "space" that is the "brightness" of reciprocal being heard (attention, recognition, and uptake), they not only go wide of the mark, they may as well not have happened. Hence, they need this specific space of "brightness" that can only emerge where people come together in this quite active sense. This is a distinctive feature of Arendt's formulation of the space of appearance. In *The Life of the Mind,* where Arendt draws a clear distinction between the "appearing world" and the "space of appearance,"[37] it can be seen that this distinction follows "degrees of manifestation":

> If we consider the whole scale of human activities from the viewpoint of appearance, we find many degrees of manifestation. Neither laboring nor fabrication requires display of the activity itself; only action and speaking need a space of appearance—as well as people who see and hear—in order to be actualized at all. But none of these activities is invisible.[38]

"Degrees of manifestation" can thus be understood as degrees of necessary reciprocal actualization—necessary to being considered "existent" at all. Appearing beings, such as we are, may be oriented towards others to whom they appear and experience themselves as real only to that degree. But they and many of their activities do not depend for their existence on whether somebody happens to be taking notice at any given moment. Only action and speech and what appears through these activities require this highest degree of manifestation—the brightness of reciprocal and continuous togetherness.

It is among Arendt's principal insights that this togetherness does not always and automatically produce the same brightness. On the one hand, it is hard to prevent a space of appearance from emerging wherever people congregate—Arendt cites, for instance, the church and its efforts to keep the gathering-places of the faithful from becoming spaces of appearance, which would immediately face accusations of vanity.[39] On the other hand, the space of appearance is so fleeting that it evaporates as soon as joint speech and action cease:

---

37   Hannah Arendt, *The Life of the Mind. Volume One: Thinking* (Harcourt Brace Jovanovich, 1977), 21, 27, 29, 60.
The "appearing world" confronts each person (and species) differently, and all appear within it. This very basic concept of "world" was developed by Arendt, particularly in *The Life of the Mind,* in order to distinguish the "visible" world from the "invisible" realm (of thought) and to insist that we are at home only in the visible world. This happens by appearing in it and to one another (i.e., by being 'of' it). But this visible world, which as such might well be identified with the "space of appearance," is not what Arendt means by that term. This may be surprising, but it is due to the fact that the appearing world is not necessarily structured by language and that we share it with beings that do not speak. The logic of appearing and showing oneself—and hence also that of sociability and intersubjectivity—thus applies at a very basic level and is the domain of all living creatures, not just of humans. A web of human affairs, by contrast, and hence a historical space, can exist only at the level of language.

38   Arendt, *Thinking,* 72.

39   See Hannah Arendt, *Was ist Politik? Fragmente aus dem Nachlaß* (Piper, 1993), 164–65.

40
Arendt,
Human Condition,
199.

41
The original German
has *"aufleuchten,"*
see Arendt,
Vita activa, 198.

42
Arendt,
Human Condition,
204.

43
Arendt,
Human Condition,
200.
A merely potential
power potential is not
a power. Though
such power potential
may be potential
wherever human be-
ings congregate, it
need not necessarily
actualize itself. The
same applies to the
space of appearance:
in a merely potential
space of appearance,
nothing appears.

44
Arendt,
Vita activa, 252.

45
Arendt,
Human Condition,
200; "im Dasein hält,"
Arendt,
Vita activa,
194, 198, 199.

Its peculiarity is that, unlike the spaces which are the work of our hands, it does not survive the actuality of the movement which brought it into being, but disappears not only with the dispersal of men … but with the disappearance or arrest of the activities themselves. Wherever people gather together, it is potentially there, but only potentially, not necessarily and not forever.[40]

For the space of appearance not only to "light up" briefly and then "fade away" but to stay in existence, something more is hence required than merely the actualization of activities.[41] What is needed is a shared project that goes further. This is what Arendt calls power: "without power, the space of appearance brought forth through action and speech in public will fade away as rapidly as the living deed and the living word."[42] Power, according to Arendt, "springs up between men when they act together and vanishes the moment they disperse." This sounds suspiciously like the emergence of the space of appearance itself. Where then does the difference lie? By its nature, power is not a positive, realized force but a potential. Whenever power "springs up," this potential is realized. This does not mean that there is constant action all around but rather that everybody around would be ready to act, for instance in a situation laid down by a pact. On the one hand, Arendt stresses that power "cannot be stored up and kept in reserve" but must be actualized.[43] This is not contrary to its existence as a potential; indeed, a potential power "exists only to the extent that it is realized."[44] Power is thus a form of actualization that extends further than something fully actualized (e.g., action and speech themselves). Power can be used to project a future into time and space, to realize shared plans and enterprises. This is why Arendt consistently emphasizes that the space of appearance must be sustained by power, since it is power that keeps the space of appearance "in existence."[45] Elsewhere, Arendt distinguishes between the *space* of appearance that gathers people, the *power* that keeps it in existence as a public space, and the *force* that holds the people together once gathered:

> We mentioned before the power generated when people gather together and 'act in concert,' which disappears the moment they depart. The force that keeps them together, as distinguished from the space of appearances in which they gather and the power which keeps this public space in existence, is the force of mutual promise or contract.[46]

46
Arendt,
Human Condition,
244.

47
Hannah Arendt,
"What is Freedom?,"
in *The Portable Hannah Arendt*,
ed. Peter Baehr
(Penguin, 2000),
446–47.

What this passage makes clear is that the question is ultimately one of the *political form* that can bring to life the space of appearance as a stable entity. The point here is that an otherwise fleeting, evanescent phenomenon is condensed to form a *stage*. Although we are sometimes told that 'All the world's a stage,' stages do not simply appear like natural phenomena: they require architects, furniture, and institutions. What is more, it takes a play and it takes an audience for stages to really be stages. Arendt follows the metaphor of the stage in order to grasp the purpose of founding a polity:

> Performing artists—dancers, play-actors, musicians, and the like—need an audience to show their virtuosity, just as acting men need the presence of others before whom they can appear; both need a publicly organized space for their 'work,' and both depend upon others for the performance itself. Such a space of appearances is not to be taken for granted wherever men live together in a community. The Greek polis once was precisely that 'form of government' which provided men with a space of appearances where they could act, with a kind of theater where freedom could appear.[47]

And here we approach the heart of the matter: a space of appearance does not exist as a natural given just because we are appearing creatures in a world of appearances. Rather, it is a particular kind of stage that has to be erected, visited, played, and protected so that a way of existing that might otherwise appear only fleetingly or not at all is given a place: the possibility of *relating freely to what is given*—by judging or changing it, or perhaps simply by using words to reject it—and thereby appearing before others. This also implies the ability to freely shape the world with others, in concert or conflict with them, through words and deeds instead of force and compulsion. This is a highly specific meaning that goes far beyond the relevance-related spaces of appearance discussed earlier. The existence of relevance by no means implies that of freedom, for relevance may be created by all manner of necessities, which take effect without requiring a space of appearance. Only something that *lays claim* to appearing, that wants and needs to be perceived in order to 'be,' requires a space of appearance.

Arendt considers the Greek polis to have been the original foundation or institution (*Urstiftung*) of such a space of appearance, one that allows freedom to take the stage for its own sake. She reads the history of humanity, insofar as it is accessible to recollection, as a history of alternating light and darkness within the web of human affairs (all of this happens, to be sure, in Eurocentric orientation). As the actions of the great revolutions of the 18th century illuminate the world's stage ("for better and worse"), so we also hear of "dark times."[48] These are conditions dominated by (seemingly) inextricable necessity in which human action appears futile or as the eternal repetition of the same, or in which the revealing power of language is consciously abused and the capacity of action to form beginnings and relations is put to destructive ends:

> If it is the function of the public realm to throw light on the affairs of men by providing a space of appearances in which they can show in deed and word, for better and worse, who they are and what they can do, then darkness has come when this light is extinguished by 'credibility gaps' and 'invisible government,' by speech that does not disclose what is but sweeps it under the carpet, by exhortations, moral and otherwise, that, under the pretext of upholding old truths, degrade all truth to meaningless triviality.[49]

48 Although Arendt principally considers 'great' events and applies her analytic categories to political developments, this dynamic may equally be observed in smaller, everyday matters. Here too words and deeds may create possibilities and illuminate a shared future, just as they may destroy and darken it, see Hannah Arendt, *Men in Dark Times* (Harvest Book, 1968), viii.

49 Arendt, *Men in Dark Times*, viii.

Although the light of the space of appearance can be "extinguished," this implies the disappearance neither of the appearing world nor of the collective 'how' of appearance—the space of appearance, in its singular form, is but one possibility within the appearances that occur in human togetherness and must therefore be conceptually distinguished from the latter. But Arendt is also interested in the 'spaces of appearance' referred to and discussed earlier in the plural form: *how* the world is collectively given in various structures of relevance. In terms of both its content and its systematic structure, I would read *The Human Condition* as an analysis of how spaces of appearance (now in the plural and not in line with Arendt's terminology) historically unfold, intersect, and overlap according to the logics of work, labor, and action.[50] Without going further into Arendt's analysis, these constellations may facilitate or impede the emergence of collective action and hence the evolution of power. Only this, in turn, would permit the realization of a space of appearance of freedom in the appearing human world. But this space of appearance, according to Arendt, may not only evanesce or darken, it may even "atrophy" and "wither away."[51] The period of human history that witnesses the triumph of the *animal laborans* treats the light of publicity primarily as a means to sustain vital interests and to provide entertainment. Everything is drawn into the seemingly unending logic of production and consumption. Arendt is concerned that this will deprive the world of its remaining capacity to gather us all upon a stage, since it "harbors the grave danger that eventually no object of the world will be safe from consumption and annihilation through consumption":[52] "This alienation—the atrophy of the space of appearance and the withering of common sense—is, of course, carried to a much greater extreme in the case of a laboring society than in the case of a society of producers."[53] A laboring society, according to Arendt, is a society in which the world has largely lost the capacity for being the stage for freedom, since every stage is prone to becoming a consumer object and to evanesce in anticipation of the next spectacle.

Let us return to the starting point of these reflections, to *The Man Without Qualities*. At the beginning of this essay, I referred to a stage that opens the novel, a stage on which, remarkably enough, nothing (of relevance) occurs.

50
See Sophie Loidolt, *Phenomenology of Plurality: Hannah Arendt on Political Intersubjectivity* (Routledge, 2018), 123–48.

51
Arendt, *Human Condition*, 209, 60.

52
Arendt, *Human Condition*, 133.

53
Arendt, *Human Condition*, 204.

Following on the mutually limiting structures of relevance identified in Musil's technique of zooming in and out, another observation may now help us to dive deeper into the novel's political atmosphere. Musil shows us a stage that is "seething, bubbling," one that consists of "irregularity, change, sliding forward, not keeping in step" but, for all its dynamism, seems somehow stricken with impotence. The force-lines are drawn by machines; among them wander anachronistic 19th-century people who, while still relying on their finely embroidered undergarments, are already emitting statistical platitudes. The next moment, they are interchangeable shadows or swarm like bees around the entrance to their hive. To be sure, collective curious gazing produces little, nor is the site of an accident usually freedom's space of appearance. If there is a protagonist here, it is more likely to be the clean ambulance that arrives in time, a symbol of public order. Yet, however well administered the public order may be, there is an air of political fatigue, of loss of energy to this opening scene. Anyone familiar with the interminable pompous chatter about the "Collateral Campaign" that appears later on in the book will know that neither are revealing words uttered in the novel's salon public nor do any actions follow.[54] In the end, the protagonist retreats, not without reason, into a form of privacy that has mystical elements. Though it may be a fine August day, there is no "light" in the public sphere. And when we are told of a "seething, bubbling fluid in a vessel consisting of the solid material of buildings, laws, regulations, and historical traditions," the obvious question is how long it can last.[55] The

---

54 The "Collateral Campaign" forms a plotline in *The Man Without Qualities,* albeit one in which, as Philip Sarasin rightly observed in his brief analysis of the novel, "nobody acts and indeed nothing happens. The Collateral Campaign is an effort of leading circles in Vienna to prepare for the seventieth anniversary of Emperor Franz Joseph I's accession to the throne in 1918—'collateral' with reference to the anniversary—also in 1918 but fortunately, for Austria, only the thirtieth—of Wilhelm II, head of state of the unloved Prussian neighbor." (Philipp Sarrasin, "Der Mann ohne Eigenschaften: Robert Musils Klassiker entschlüsselt die Moderne," *Geschichte der Gegenwart,* September 4, 2022, https://geschichtedergegenwart.ch/der-mann-ohne-eigenschaften-robert-musils-klassiker-entschluesselt-die-moderne/).

55 Musil, *Man Without Qualities,* 4.

scene presented by Musil is one of suspended animation, one that may yet be stabilized. Arendt's 'atrophy of common sense' is set against the 'sense of possibility' as an alternative form of freedom—given that any attempt at action within the novel founders on the slackened space of appearance. It therefore seems more rational to come to terms with the new conditions and the limitations they impose on relevance. After all, "ant-like heroism" may be good enough. And it looked as though the unfortunate pedestrian might have survived. "But what can we know of that today?"[56]

56
Musil,
Man Without Qualities,
8.

We Need to Talk

A Museum's Response to Political Polarization in Post-Unification Germany

Martha Crowe

01
Hilke Wagner
and Kathleen
Reinhardt,
"Information Sheet:
Andreas Angelidakis,
Demos, 2016 and
4xKION, 2020."

02
"Albertinum erhält
Kunstwerk von
Andreas Angelidakis,"
press release,
Staatliche Kunst-
sammlung Dresden,
February 14, 2018,
https://
www.skd.museum/
presse/2018/
albertinum-erhaelt-
kunstwerk-von-
andreas-angelidakis/.

03
Wagner
and Reinhardt,
"Information Sheet."

As I step into the *Lichthof,* the large atrium in the center of Dresden's modern art museum, the Albertinum, I am greeted not only by the standard coat check, guest book, and gift shop, but also by a multitude of foam and vinyl blocks made to look like "leftover fragments"[01] of an ancient Greek structure. Intended to evoke an Athenian *agora,* these imitation stones visually hark back to the very foundation of Western democracy.[02] Arranged in varying formations in the open, echoey space, some blocks are utilized as seating for those passing through while others have been put to work as tables, desks, scattered surfaces. The piece, by Greek artist Andreas Angelidakis, is suggestively entitled *Demos* and aspires to "encourage interaction … [as] visitors are invited to move the pieces, to use and arrange the fragments anew [in order for them to be used] as a platform through which diverse relationships can be negotiated." The work is exhibited in the Albertinum for the stated purpose of enabling a negotiation between audience and speaker, shifting the "relationship between stage and public, participation and display."[03] The decision by the Albertinum to display the work in the *Lichthof,* through which all visitors must pass, even if they decide not to buy a ticket, makes explicit the Albertinum's self-conception as a democratic institution in a democratic state. *Demos* stands for the museum's commitment to those political values that we take to be essential to the construction of, and participation in, a modern liberal democracy: reason, liberty, and freedom.

Through the installation's theme and location, the Albertinum also communicates its aspiration to be a space open to and intended for a diverse plurality of people. The two principles of democracy and publicity are, of course, commonly held to be foundational for public institutions in liberal-democratic societies. That a modern-day museum would wish to emphasize its openness, to declare it as a key cultural and political value to visitors, is not necessarily surprising.

What is surprising however, are the lengths the Albertinum has gone to in recent years to instantiate those principles, even challenging another shibboleth of contemporary liberal German society—the imperative that mainstream political parties refuse to engage with, or to be seen to engage with, the far right, specifically, the *Alternative für Deutschland* (AfD).[04] Though this imperative does not explicitly prevent politicians from engaging with the AfD's voter base, in practice this stance has signaled to these voters that the AfD's victim narrative has some truth to it. Moreover, the "norm of non-cooperation" has been eroded, at the time of writing in early 2025, by frantic, scrambling overcompensation from centrist parties, in particular the conservative Christian Democrats (CDU), to appeal to these voters as it became clear just how many are willing to embrace far right policies.[05] The questioning of this once unbreakable taboo and the resultant shift to the right have arguably left Germany shaken and destabilized.[06]

While these power struggles and political machinations are being played out on a national stage, the Albertinum tackled the threat of the extreme right by approaching people not as voters but as members of a shared public. *Demos* was originally used by the Albertinum to host a series of events between 2017 and 2019 that enacted the principle of

04   Damien McGuinness and Laura Gozzi, "Scholz Urges Firewall Against Far Right After Election Win," *BBC News*, September 2, 2024, https://www.bbc.com/news/articles/cd05pdmzgp5o.

05   Emily Schultheis, Chris Lunday, and Nette Nöstlinger, "Germany's Merz Sparks Firestorm by Breaking Postwar Taboo," *Politico*, January 29, 2025, https://www.politico.eu/article/germany-friedrich-merz-cdu-political-tightrope-far-right-votes-afd-migration-crackdown/.

06   Jörg Lau, "A Political Gamble Backfired Spectacularly—Bringing the Far Right Closer to Power in Germany," *The Guardian*, February 3, 2025, https://www.theguardian.com/commentisfree/2025/feb/03/a-political-gamble-backfired-spectacularly-bringing-the-far-right-closer-to-power-in-germany.

openness while simultaneously questioning its utility and consequences. The events began with an open public discussion forum, held in the *Lichthof*, and developed into a series of talks, forums, and exhibitions. These events were a response to a flare-up, in 2017, of what could be called a simmering 'culture war' in the city of Dresden, involving long-held resentments, far-right rhetoric, and the tenacity of East-West divisions in present-day Germany. What began, harmlessly enough, with an opinion piece about the amount of East German art the museum had on display versus in storage rapidly escalated into what became known as a *Bilderstreit*, a term which, literally translated, means 'image conflict.' In many ways, however, 'icon controversy' better captures the historical reference to Byzantine Iconoclasm, a period known in German as the *Byzantinischer Bilderstreit*. And the debate was indeed about icons, though in the modern rather than the Byzantine sense. Not only was the controversy sparked by a fear that the museum had removed iconic GDR art from its walls, the role of the museum itself as a representative space was called into question. At its core, this conflict was about who is represented in and feels represented by modern Germany.

This text investigates the success of the museum's response in de-escalating these politically motivated tensions, asking why and to what extent the Albertinum was actually successful. As noted above, the principle of public openness makes the mere fact of a museum taking on the mantle of an 'arbiter of culture' (or of a 'culture war') by hosting participatory events for the public seem rather trite. A museum claiming to be open and a space of open exchange is almost a cliché today. And if these actions were successful, if they truly were able to mend the city's political divisions, then the case of the Albertinum would become a surprising confirmation of yet another cliché: that, if only we would all just sit down and talk it out face to face, we could resolve our greatest conflicts. This view is reminiscent of the most nostalgic evocations of classical Greek democracy, those which focus only on the free men inside the *agora*, hashing out the problems of their *polis* together as equals. It is an image that must resolutely ignore the less palatable realities of this democracy, for example, the exclusion of women and slaves, for whom participation was unthinkable.[07] The reality of these democracies makes clear that we should not take the *polis* as a political ideal.[08]

Yet this model plays an interesting role in more recent thought on our political structures. Specifically within the work of Hannah Arendt, the *polis* functions as an avenue through which the relationship between "political action, freedom, and the public realm" can be explored.[09] Though her use of the *polis* has itself been criticized as elitist, as nostalgically idealizing an antiquated system, this is to obscure its potential for clarifying the essence of politics.[10] Arendt's work on the necessity of plurality as a precondition of politics, as well as her conception of the political as arising from this plurality of people coming together "in both word and deed" to form a "space of appearance,"[11] echo the aims and enactment of the Albertinum's event series. Following this intuition, this text utilizes Arendt's conception of the *polis,* the public realm, and the space of appearance as a lens through which to investigate the series and the reasons for its resonance with people across the political spectrum. Indeed, the series offers an instantiation of Arendt's space of appearance and thus a radical approach to navigating far-right extremism. As it becomes blindingly obvious that far-right politics is no longer simply 'on the rise' but by now has most certainly 'risen', it is imperative to consider strategies for mitigating its appeal and influence. Arendt's work offers us a framework to do so, one that slots neatly into our democratic ideals while also highlighting the weakness of current representative structures. The space of appearance can show us how to move beyond the nostalgic understanding of an imagined polis and grasp the potential of what it might mean for people to come together "in both word and deed"[12]—namely, that our ability to shape and change our shared systems demands that we direct our attention not merely towards our elected representatives, but turn to face each other instead.

07
Seyla Benhabib, *Situating the Self: Gender, Community, and Postmodernism in Contemporary Ethics* (Polity Press, 1992), 91.

08
Hanna Pitkin, "Justice: On Relating Public and Private," *Political Theory* 9, no. 3 (1981): 346.

09
Roy T. Tsao, "Arendt Against Athens: Rereading the Human Condition," *Political Theory* 30, no. 1 (2002): 97–98.

10
Benhabib, *Situating the Self,* 90–92.

11
Hanah Arendt, *The Human Condition* (University of Chicago Press, 2018), 199.

12
Arendt, *Human Condition,* 199.

The *Bilderstreit*

13
I would like to extend my sincere thanks to Hilke Wagner for her willingness to meet with me and for her openness throughout our interview.

I have come to the *Lichthof* to interview the museum's director, Hilke Wagner, about the discussion series *Wir müssen reden. 'Bilderstreit' mit Blickkontakt* ("We Need to Talk: *'Bilderstreit'* Face-to-Face") and the role she played in bringing it about.[13] In 2017, art historian Paul Kaiser published an opinion piece in the local daily *Sächsische Zeitung.* Titled *Wende an den Wänden* (change/turnaround on the walls),[14] it charged the Albertinum with giving preference to West German art, sequestering the museum's collection of East German art into the depot.[15] In our interview, Wagner remarked on the aggrieved tone of the piece and that she could understand the outrage people felt upon reading it. While she did not believe that Kaiser had intended for his piece to appeal to right-wing interests, Wagner noted that "the AfD quickly understood that this was something which could be instrumentalized."[16] Very soon after publication of the piece, an AfD representative introduced a written question in the Saxon state parliament. Directly referring to Kaiser's article, the deputy requested confirmation of the claim that "only a small amount" of East German art was being shown in the Albertinum's permanent exhibit, and asked for further details as to which works exactly were on display. This was

14　The word *Wende,* used in common parlance in Germany to refer to the process of unification, can be translated as "the turn, the transition," "the change," or "the transformation." *Vor und nach der Wende* (before and after the turn) are used to distinguish pre- and post-unification. The language itself is interesting, implying a lack of agency, an occurrence missing a subject, a perhaps natural process which could just as easily occur, rather than be enacted. This differs in the other moniker *die friedliche Revolution* (the peaceful revolution), a phrase which indicates something done *by* agents, rather than done *to* them.

15　Paul Kaiser, "Wende an den Wänden," *Sächsische Zeitung,* September 18, 2017, https://web.archive.org/ web/20170926234643/http://www.sz-online.de/ nachrichten/kultur/wende-an-den-waenden-3775440.html.

16　Hilke Wagner (Director, Albertinum), my interview, September 25, 2024 [my translation].

17　Eva-Maria Stange, "Kleine Anfrage der Abgeordneten Karin Wilke, AfD-Fraktion: Drs.-Nr.: 6/10834: Thema: Abhängen von DDR-Kunst in der Galerie Neue Meister Dresden," State Ministry for Science and the Arts Saxony, October 18, 2017, https://s3.kleine-anfragen.de/ka-prod/sn/6/10834.pdf.

promptly answered by the state minister for science and the arts, who refuted the claim, stating that it "does not correspond with the facts of the matter," and providing an appendix listing in detail the 77 East German works exhibited at the time.[17]

Anlage zu Frage 2 der Kleinen Anfrage 6/10834

Derzeit ausgestellte, in der Zeit zwischen 1949 und 1989 in DDR entstandene Werke

Adler, Karl-Heinz	Schichtung von Rechteckscheiben, 1960	1
	Quadratschichtungen, 1957/1960	1
	Schichtung von Halbkreisen, 1959	1
	o.T., 1980	1
	Farbschichtung mit weißen Pünktchen, 1984	2
	Nebelraum mit weißen Pünktchen, 1984	1
	Vertikale aus dunklem Raum aufsteigend, 1984	1
	Schattenlineaturen, 1989	1
	Serielle Lineaturen 1-3, 1989	3
	Diptychon, Diagonale Verspannung, 1987	1
	Sichtung von Rechtecken mit Ausschnitt, 1962	1
	Konstruktion 1 und II. Fabrbschichtung (I=blau; II = braun), beide 1987	2
Arnold, Walter	Skulptur	1
Bonk, Hartmut	Skulptur	1
Bretschneider, Frank	Plakat AG Geige	1
Cremer, Fritz	Skulptur	1
Djurovic, Goran	Lila Gedichte, Mappe mit 14 Holzschnitten, 1984	1
Ebersbach, Hartwig	Gruppe 37,2, 1982	1
Eschefeld, Sonja	Skulptur	1
Förster, Wieland	Skulptur	6
Factor, Jan / Hans Scherecker	Bearbeitung des Parallelepipeds / Gedichte eines alten Mannes aus Prag (Textgrafiken), 1986	1
Freudenberg, Michael	Brandung, 1989	1

18
Stange,
"Kleine Anfrage"
[all typographical
errors in original].

Adler, Karl-Heinz	Schichtung von Rechteckscheiben, 1960	1
Glöckner, Hermann	Kreideschwünge, 1981	1
	sowie 7 weitere Werke, Malerei + Skulptur	7
Götze, Moritz	Everything is under control (1989), Rimski Abdul Goldfinger flieht als Königsberger Klops (1987(, Plakat Galerie am Schaufenster (1987)	3
Hegewald, Andreas	AUS REISE, 1982	1
Heinze, Helmut	Skulptur	1
Howald, Walter	Skulptur	1
Kazzer, Hans	Skulptur	1
Kerbach, Ralf	Die Unzeitgemäßen, 1-4, 1982	4
Kuhle, Wolfgang	Skulptur	1
Leiberg, Helge	Status Quo - Factory 4, 1984	1
Lücke	Krater, 1972	1
	Anayse Baselitz, 1974	1
Makolies, Peter	Skulptur	1
Müller, Wilhelm	Weiß-Grün, 1981	1
Naumann, Hermann	Skulptur	1
Ponndorf, Egmar	Skulptur	1
Schlegel, Christine	Faltrollo (1985), Hard Pop Stephan (Film), 1985 Strukturen (Film), 1984	3
Schönefelder, Baldur	Skulptur	1
Schmiedel, Wieland	Skulptur	1
Schreiber, Siegfried	Skulptur	1
Schulze, Hans-J.	Faltrollo, 1985	1
Schweiger, Detlef	Findling	1
Sommer-Landgraf, Charlotte	Skulptur	1
Steger, Hans	Skulptur	3
Stötzer, Werner	Skulptur	2
Weidanz, Gustav	Skulptur	1
Wolff, Willy	Skulptur	4
insgesamt		**77**

[01] "The facts of the matter."[18]

Wagner's appointment was also questioned, with the representative asking whether her selection was made with the
knowledge that she wished to open the Albertinum up to the
"most recent contemporary art" and whether that aim played
a role in the selection process.[19] Though this question about
Wagner does not make any mention of her West German
background, it seems to imply as much in context of the previous questions. Moreover, it slyly insinuates that Wagner is
far too focused on contemporary art and therefore has neither the interest nor the desire to engage with the shared history of Dresden and East German culture as a whole.

Thus, as the tensions in the city rose to fever pitch,
Wagner found herself to be a focal point. She was a real, tangible person upon whom decades of frustration about the process and consequences of German reunification could be un-
loaded. She describes receiving hate mail, being spat on in the
street, and even finding herself surrounded by people cursing
at her during a visit to the theatre. For her, this level of animos-
ity was shocking and traumatizing, to the point where she did
not leave the house for two weeks. She describes being "ut-
terly confused," admitting to a certain naiveté on her part at
first. The cries that she "go back to the West" and the strength
of feeling on the East-West divide drew on sentiments she, as
a relatively new citizen of Dresden at the time, did not fully
understand. However, she quickly recognized that the situation had been politically instrumentalized, as the initial criticism did not reflect the reality of the Albertinum's permanent
collection. Indeed, at the moment that the *Bilderstreit* broke
out, she actually had *more* East German art on display than
had been usual in recent years. The parliamentary question
also led to some rather bizarre moments. For example, while
tallying up the number of East and West German artworks,
Wagner had to ring up artists from the former GDR who had
fled to the West, asking: "Say, this painting ... did you do that
before or after you left the East?"[20]

Yet Wagner also readily admits that the question
drew her attention to concrete failings within the museum.
For example, when she arrived at the Albertinum, there was
no one on the team specifically responsible for East German
art. Indeed, only one staff member was allotted one day per
week to take care of the entire contemporary art collection,

19
The answer also
acknowledges the
desire to make the
Albertinum more
modern but reminds
the representative
that the director of
the museum's
collection ultimately
holds responsibility
for its program. The
response takes pains
to further note that
this freedom of art is
enshrined in the
German constitution.

20
Wagner, interview.

21
Recounted in German as *"Sie widern mich an,"* also translatable as "you make me sick." Wagner, interview.

22
Wagner, interview.

the section to which art from the GDR was assigned. So, although there was plenty of East German art on—and to—display, there was no curatorial capacity within the museum itself to engage specifically with this art in its own context. Wagner described this state of affairs as a "massive structural problem" extending far beyond a single museum. Still, at this point in 2017, the broader structural issues were the furthest thing from Wagner's mind. Instead, it was filled with frustration, even rage, as the hate letters directed at her started piling up. And so, one evening, while she was supposed to be counting the museum's collection of East German art, she found herself looking closely at one of the letters. This one simply stated: "You disgust me."[21] It was from an older man, as most of them were, and, as is more common in that generation, he had signed his name. With the name, she was able to locate a phone number and, almost impulsively, called him up. She admitted to me that, at this point, there were no "grand intentions" of dialogue and reconciliation, only the simple need to defend herself. The letter writer was "shocked," even amazed, to have actually received a call, and, according to Wagner, a "really good" conversation then developed between the two. She described the anger fading, and on the way home from the office that night she noticed that the sense of hate had left her. Wagner felt invigorated by the experience, thinking: "I have to try that again."[22]

She began by calling the rest of the letter writers whose numbers she could locate, and over and over again (with one or two exceptions), experienced the same thing as before: a conversation that left both sides relieved of the burden of rage stoked between them. Furthermore, she was learning more and more about this conflict of which she had become a focal point. Although the ostensible causes were the treatment of East German art and Wagner's status as a West German outsider, she realized the issues ran much deeper. "In the end," she told me, "it wasn't about the museum. It was about the personal experiences after the *Wende*." She noted a real sense of loss, an open wound around the issue of East German representation in contemporary culture, a feeling that their culture had been completely devalued, and this was a wound the far right had quickly picked up on and sought to exploit. By jumping on these populist themes and inflaming outrage, they had managed to achieve two goals: to portray themselves as the only champions of ordinary East German voters and to deepen the sense of division between East and West.

Wagner's analysis of her own experiences reflects the reality of the AfD's tactics. In 2019, the AfD ran political adverts in the eastern state of Thuringia, urging potential voters to take matters into their own hands and *"Vollende die Wende"* (Complete the turn/change) by voting AfD, appealing to the sense that the former GDR had been left behind in the process of reunification. Within this context, the unfounded claim that the Albertinum had moved its collection of East German art into art storage was representative of the idea that East German society as a whole, and therefore ex-East German citizens, had been forgotten in present-day Germany. Reunification, in this view, was not a peaceful synthesis of East and West so much as a rolling hegemonization by the West. Petra Köpping, an SPD politician and Saxony's minister of state for equality and integration from 2014–2019, addresses this view in her 2019 book *Integriert doch erst mal uns!* (First, integrate us!). The title, a phrase Köpping "heard time and time again in conversations with citizens,"[23] reflects the sense that modern-day Germany is a society in which East Germans perceive themselves to be foreign. A 2022 study by the University of Leipzig, which surveyed 3,546 people in Germany's eastern states, further supports these conclusions. It notes that, 33 years after the fall of the Berlin wall, one quarter of those surveyed consider themselves to be the "losers of reunification," while two-thirds reported feeling a longing for the GDR, and three-quarters identified explicitly as East German.[24]

---

23 Petra Köpping, *Integriert doch erst mal uns! Eine Streitschrift für den Osten* (Christoph Links Verlag, 2018).

24 Oliver Decker et al., "EFBI Policy Paper 2023-2: Autoritäre Dynamiken und die Unzufriedenheit mit der Demokratie," *Else-Frenkel-Brunswik-Institut,* June 27, 2023, https:// efbi.de/details/efbi-policy-paper-2023-2-autoritaere-dynamiken-und-die-unzufriedenheit-mit-der-demokratie.html.

The AfD's strategy of positioning the party as the representative of the East in present-day Germany has borne fruit, with the AfD receiving twice as many votes in the East compared to West German states.[25] In the 2021 Bundestag election the AfD received 19.1% of the vote in East Germany, as opposed to 8.2% in the West.[26] In the state elections held in the same year as the outcry against Wagner's appointment, 2017, the AfD gained 27.5% of the vote in Saxony, the state of which Dresden is the capital.[27] In the more recent 2024 elections, their share increased, with the AfD receiving 30.6% of the vote, a close second to the conservative CDU's 31.9%.[28] The presence of the AfD and its supporters within Dresden is thus not at all negligible, which goes some way towards explaining exactly how an opinion piece and parliamentary question could lead to such tumult.

Furthermore, the AfD has been accused by leading politicians of using extremist rhetoric and being responsible for the increase in right-wing violence.[29] There has long existed—almost since the party's foundation in 2013—within German political culture a refusal to engage with the AfD, so as to not signify acceptance of the party or their tactics, though this refusal has begun to ring more and more hollow of late.[30] Mainstream political parties have historically refused to form coalitions with the AfD on principle, resulting in a so-called firewall (*Brandmauer*) intended to protect the German democratic order.[31] What Wagner came to realize however, over the course of her many phone calls, was that the far right had been able to instrumentalize this approach. Through this very act of exclusion and their success in positioning themselves as the only ones listening to the

25   Frank Decker, "Wahlergebnisse und Wählerschaft der AfD," *Bundeszentrale für Politische Bildung*, December 2, 2022, https://www.bpb.de/themen/parteien/parteien-in-deutschland/afd/273131/wahlergebnisse-und-waehlerschaft-der-afd/.

26   Matthias Janson, "So haben Ost und West gewählt," *Statista*, September 29, 2021, https://de.statista.com/infografik/25874/zweitstimmenanteil-der-parteien-bei-der-bundestagswahl-2021-in-ost-und-westdeutschland/.

27   Alexander Sarovic and Dawood Ohdah, "Senioren retten die etablierten Parteien," *Der Spiegel*, September 2, 2019, https://www.spiegel.de/politik/deutschland/ergebnisse-sachsen-wahl-afd-punktet-bei-den-jungen-a-1284494.html.

concerns of East Germans, they were able to confirm the impression that mainstream modern Germany simply does not care about the East. Her phone calls disrupted this narrative somewhat—but only somewhat. This was not a conflict occurring solely at the level of individual grievances but one that reflected much broader societal tensions. What was desperately called for was a release valve—a way to defuse the mounting hostility. On the face of it, concerns had been met, the enquiry answered, and an official tally of the number of GDR artworks on display provided, one that clearly showed the claims of sequestered art to be unfounded (see fig. 1: "The facts of the matter"). Yet this response went, if not unnoticed, then certainly unfelt by the citizens of Dresden. The bureaucratic approach had been far less effective than Wagner's personal calls. The clarification regarding the museum was not enough to affect the image people had of themselves being sequestered away in broader German society, consigned to storage and left to gather dust.

As such, Wagner felt a need to attempt to approach this problem in a different manner and setting, allowing for a plurality of opinions to be voiced openly and in the presence of all. In this way, by aiming to bring people together "in the manner of speech and action,"[32] the Albertinum enabled a space of appearance to come into being. Indeed, it is only through analysis of the Albertinum's event *as* a space of appearance that we are able to fully make sense of the situation. For it is by applying this framing that a crucial element of the event can be seen most clearly—namely, that it is only by engaging with others that we are able to disrupt the imageries founding political division.

28   Paul Kirby and Jessica Parker, "German Far Right Hails 'Historic' Election Victory in East," *BBC News,* September 2, 2024, https://www.bbc.com/news/articles/cn02w01xr2jo.

29   Kate Connolly and Bethan McKernan, "German Far-Right Party AfD Accused of Fuelling Hate After Hanau Attack," *The Guardian,* February 21, 2020, https://www.theguardian.com/world/2020/feb/21/german-far-right-party-afd-hanau-attack.

30   Schultheis, "Merz Sparks Firestorm."

31   McGuinness and Gozzi, "Scholz urges Firewall."

32   Arendt, *Human Condition,* 99.

"The Space Where I Appear to Others as Others Appear to Me"[33]

33
Arendt,
Human Condition,
198.

34
Arendt,
Human Condition,
199.

35
Arendt,
Human Condition,
199.

36
Hannah Arendt,
The Life of the Mind
(Harcourt, 1978),
19–20.

37
Arendt,
Life of the Mind, 62.

38
Arendt,
Human Condition,
208.

What does it mean however, to claim that a space of appearance was created? Arendt's concept may, at first glance, appear non-complex in its explicit, literal meaning. As Arendt states in *The Human Condition*, the space of appearance in "the widest sense" refers to "the space where I appear to others as others appear to me, where men exist not merely like other living or inanimate things but make their appearance explicitly." Arendt goes on to specify that such a space "does not always exist" but comes into being when people gather together "in the manner of speech and action."[34] As such, the space of appearance might be understood to refer simply to the act of gathering people together to talk and act. To that extent, it seems fairly uncontroversial. For within the structure of our modern democracies, we of course value the ability of citizens to gather, to discuss, and to act as involved and engaged agents in political matters that concern them.

However, this reading ignores the long philosophical history which the concept draws upon, and as such fails to grasp its complex ontological, phenomenological, and political implications.[35] Arendt's use of the term 'appearance' stems from her understanding, following Kant, of the world itself as being one of appearances, whose "infinite diversity" is reflected in humanity's own diversity of perspectives and experiences. We exist in the world only insofar as we are of the world; we perceive appearances and are perceived as appearances simultaneously.[36] As there is such variety in the world and between individuals' perspectives, as diversity of interpretation is "inherent in the nature of human activities and experiences," we must collaborate to establish reality.[37] To be in a space of appearance therefore implies much more than simply existing within the view of others. Appearance in this sense is that which confirms existence, and it is the space of appearance that establishes "the reality of one's self, of one's own identity, [and] the reality of the surrounding world ... beyond doubt."[38]

Furthermore, it is also highly debatable whether Arendt's use of the word 'space' within the concept ought to be understood literally. A figurative reading, such as that offered by Roy Tsao, claims that the space of appearance is "created through the activities of action and speech themselves," and as such "can find its proper location almost any time and anywhere."[39] This reading allows for the space of appearance to be freed from any strict conception of a set space and time, and Tsao focuses here on the consequence that such a space therefore must not adhere to fixed areas and institutions, such as the *polis*. David Marshall takes the figurative reading somewhat further, separating it entirely from physical space. He argues that

> In reality, the 'space' of the 'space of appearance' was often a topos, *a place of debate* that has become a commonplace, a reference point for a culture of disputation. What is more, the figurative sense of 'space' that emerges here is a *purely relational one*. There is no abstract, Euclidean space that underlies and coordinates the topos.[40]

If we take Marshall's approach, recognizing a space of appearance thus becomes less about pinning down a specific physical location than about understanding the points of contention, conflict and need for interaction.

To complicate matters further, in her work Arendt gives flexible and sometimes contradictory definitions of "public space," the "public realm," and their relation to the space of appearance.[41] The quotation above, however, offers us a way in which to understand the distinction. Here we can distinguish between a fluid space of appearance, the metaphysical ground upon which all publics must occur, and the public realm; one of "well-organised meetings in town halls and parliaments, the established manners of debates, and the acknowledged freedoms and rights of speech."[42] From these flexible, unregulated spaces, however, a public can come into being through organization.

39   Tsao, "Arendt Against Athens," 116.

40   David L. Marshall, "The Polis and its Analogues in the Thought of Hannah Arendt," *Modern Intellectual History* 7, no. 1 (2010): 148.

41   Hans Teerds, "'The Space Between': An Architectural Examination of Hannah Arendt's Notions of 'Public Space' and 'World,'" *The Journal of Architecture* 27, no. 5–6 (2022): 764–65.

42   Teerds, "The Space Between," 765.

"The Implacable, Bright Light of the ... Presence of Others"[43]

43
Arendt,
Human Condition, 51.

44
Wagner, interview.

45
Wagner, interview.

In my time with Wagner, I was able to question her about the specifics of the first event of the series, both to get a sense of the Albertinum's intentions at the outset as well as an account of what it felt like to be in that room as events unfolded. The Albertinum aimed to provide a release valve, yes, but for whom and to what ultimate purpose? What did it actually mean to bring disparate groups together, what were they supposed to release? How did they hope to create a space for constructive dialogue without creating an opening for further polarizing tactics from the far right?

Wagner emphasized that a main concern for the first session was that it should lack any form of spatial hierarchy: no raised speaker's platform, no sense of there being a front or behind. They decided the format should be that of a "long table," with a moderator capable of approaching tense moments with a sense of humor. The invited speakers, who were sat at the table in the center of the room, were warned that they might not get a chance to speak at all—despite the fact that the meeting would have no time limit. The point was to let the public take the topics into their own hands, for it to be a chance to "come into conversation,"[44] rather than to talk *at* or lecture the audience. As for the public, Wagner had made sure the event was open to those across the political spectrum. These included the letter writers, artists who had been deemed subversive in East Germany, and ordinary Dresden citizens. In total, the audience that day numbered just over 600 people.

Looking back, Wagner recalls this first meeting as both a success and "awful." The former because "it worked, people really did feel confident in setting the agenda, and if they hadn't participated, it wouldn't have worked." The latter because "there was screaming, people ran out, some even turned their backs on me when I spoke." Yet Wagner described it as being successful in fostering a sense of "catharsis."[45] The space had allowed for an emotional experience as well as a dialogic one. What occurred in the Albertinum's *Lichthof* thus allowed for an informal organization of word and deed—a space of appearance.

[02] The seating arrangement for the first event, the long
      table provides a focal point.

[03] The event's moderator, the singular sustained
      vertical point within the gathering.

[04] "First of all, everyone who needs to say something
      must have the opportunity to do so."[46]

[05] View of the *Lichthof* from amongst the crowd—
      at eye-level.

Arendt argues that what is most important is not to reach a consensus regarding the topics of debate, but to come to understand the others' point of view as important to them, and how their beliefs and judgments reflect the selves appearing in this public. Not insisting on consensus should not be understood to equal agreement with, or even acceptance of, certain views. The Arendtian model, by allowing for plural opinions to be exchanged without insisting upon some presumed rational winner of the debate, is better suited to explore the nuances and alterability of such views. As mentioned above, the AfD has successfully managed to appeal to the frustration of many people in eastern Germany, particularly to their sense of not being heard and of their opinions as existing outside of a supposedly united Germany that was formed without their input. Thus, an effort to create a mainstream consensus, something we might call a Habermasian approach to the aim of a public space, would not succeed in persuasion or reaching acceptance. Rather, it might appear as yet another attempt by an institution or public body to convince those dissatisfied with the current state of things that they ought to accept a view which does not reflect their lived experiences. Yet if we follow Shmuel Lederman's discussion of Arendt's public sphere, it becomes clear that another analysis is possible. Lederman argues that

> acting and speaking with others in the public sphere forms a unique human experience, whose value goes beyond any specific goal to which the actors and the speakers strive; in other words, that speech and action in the public sphere with our fellow citizens are ends in themselves rather than (only) means to other ends.[47]

As such, an Arendtian approach highlights the deeper utility of the Albertinum's strategy, namely, that by removing the 'middle-man' of party politics, the discussion that took place was able to move beyond the superficiality of the original debate (counting paintings and scrutinizing artists' biographies) and actually reflect the deeper concerns the speakers held. So many of these concerns had indeed been used as "means to other ends," used to gain votes and deepen division, now attendees were confronted by their fellow citizens as "ends in themselves."[48]

46
Wagner, interview.

47
Shmuel Lederman, *Hannah Arendt and Participatory Democracy: A People's Utopia* (Palgrave Macmillan, 2019), viii.

48
Lederman, *Arendt and Participatory Democracy*, viii.

69

49
Arendt,
Human Condition,
220.

50
Hannah Arendt,
On Revolution
(Penguin Books,
[1963] 1973), 268–69.

51
Arendt,
Human Condition, 51.

The fact that this confrontation was not necessarily a pleasant one further highlights another Arendtian concept, that of the importance of plurality in her political philosophy:

> The calamities of action all arise from the human condition of plurality, which is the condition *sine qua non* for that space of appearance which is the public realm. Hence the attempt to do away with this plurality is always tantamount to the abolition of the public realm itself.[49]

Arendt's model avoids this concept of forced consensus and as such public space is considered as a space for political growth and development. This approach is far more effective in combating the rhetoric of the AfD, which attempts to utilize and increase a sense of division to further its own political aims. This approach to political discourse allows for the frustrations of those to whom the AfD and other right-wing parties wish to appeal to be expressed, heard, and addressed. Crucially, these frustrations, through exposure in the public realm, can be developed and altered far more successfully by this approach than if forced into adherence with the most rational view—as, for example, Habermas advises. Arendt writes that "opinions are formed in a process of open discussion and public debate, and where no opportunity for the forming of opinions exists, there may be moods—moods of the masses and moods of individuals ... but no opinion."[50]

Though it may be idealistic to assume that dialogue alone is capable of altering the views of these voters, I agree with Arendt that the role of public space is not to change opinion. Instead, it must allow for the development of moods into opinions, by forcing individuals to confront the underpinnings of their moods and develop them from that which is internal and private into something more public, and therefore tangible. Arendt notes that "there are a great many things which cannot withstand the implacable, bright light of the constant presence of others on the public scene," noting that it is specifically the irrelevant which disappears in this light.[51] The first "release valve" event was, therefore, able to provide attendees with a way of separating legitimate concerns from inflamed rhetoric. By gathering people together in this manner, the Albertinum and Wagner

were able to interfere with tactics aimed at creating polarization, to constitute a "web of narratives" not influenced solely
by the far right.[52]

From that first meeting an entire event series was
developed, with the topics and themes tailored to points raised
by attendees to the initial event. Artist talks, theoretical lectures, and more public discussions were organized. As audience members returned to the series again and again, the
sense of a defined public deepened. The permanent loan of
Demos was organized to allow for the *Lichthof* to be rear-
ranged while remaining non-hierarchical each time. One at-
tendee even commented that the *Lichthof* "feels like our living room, here we discuss what really moves us," a sentiment
which echoes Arendt's definition of public spaces as places
where citizens can express plural opinions and engage their
political selves.[53]

Public Things; Private Selves

The very title given to the series, "We Need to Talk," reflects
the three elements Arendt deems necessary for the constitution of public space—plurality of opinions, public things,
and speech about these things. By 'public things,' Arendt
means both material and ideal objects, so a public thing might
be anything from the village well to the constitution of a nation.[54] What is common to all such public things, however, is
their ability to be contested, engaged with, and/or of interest
to all participants in the public realm. Therefore, these things
must have an existence independent of all members while being "a subject of collective interest" to them.[55] Bonnie Honig
ascribes even greater political potential to public objects, arguing that "democracy is rooted in common love for, antipa-
thy to, and contestation of public things," which act as "sites
of attachment and meaning."[56] This does not mean, however,
that such things are necessarily imbued with any sentimental value. She understands public infrastructure to be a public thing, meaning even such prosaic material objects as pipe-
lines are necessary for common action to be possible.

The public things available for discussion in this
case were provided both by the setting itself, i.e. the museum,
its status as an institution, and its collection, and by setting
a topic and agenda for each forum. The role, valuation, and

52
Arendt,
Human Condition, 99.

53
Wagner, interview.

54
I am drawing here on
Bonnie Honig's analysis
of Arendt in *Public
Things: Democracy
in Disrepair*
(Fordham University
Press, 2017).

55
Bhikhu Parekh,
*Hannah Arendt and
the Search for a New
Political Philosophy*
(Macmillan Press,
1981).

56
Honig,
Public Things, 4–6.

57
Wagner, interview.

58
Arendt,
Human Condition, 52.

even definition of East German art were discussed. Wagner reflects today that the debate wasn't even just about East German art, it was about *the ability to define* what counted as such. She recalled how, when organizing an exhibition in honor of Karl-Heinz Adler, an artist who had been considered subversive in the GDR, she was told by an East German colleague that she was "clearly being provocative." She wanted, he claimed, "as a West German, to explain to us what good East German art is. Well, we already know that ourselves."[57] The Albertinum responded to that challenge by curating exhibitions focused on female subversive artists or highlighting the global connections between the GDR and the so-called Third World. Each exhibition, each talk that responded directly to the claims made and the anger vented in the initial discussion session, further contributed to establishing this common world of public objects.

Finally, the political underpinnings of these forums reflect the primary purpose of the public space as an arena fostering authentic politics. Thus, growing from this first 'valve event,' a space of appearance, a ground was formed upon which a public could be built. In one sense, Arendt uses the word 'public' to describe the state we find ourselves in when seen and heard by the widest audience. However, she also uses the term to denote "the world itself, in so far as it is common to us all and distinguished from our privately owned place in it."[58] As such, the term 'public' can also refer to our common world, the shared space which we enter in order to move beyond the private, confused intimacy of our inner selves. It is in the public realm that we can attempt to transcend the solitude of the soul and utilize speech to express our rational nature and develop an understanding of our shared reality.

Despite the evocative philosophical analysis of the Albertinum's events as constituting a public space, it is important to also focus on the practical. Did the events achieve what Wagner had originally hoped, could they be called a success? She says today that, even though the experience was hard personally, she has come to see that this initial outpouring of hate was not really about *her* at all, it was about a much bigger problem—one she agrees needs addressing. Her only real regret, the only thing she feels she could have done differently but that was simply not a part of this whole process, was to understand the way she was turned into a symbol. But of course, it is hard not to take personal attacks personally. And perhaps that was not a bad place to start. Feminist activists and thinkers were the first to fight for an acceptance that "the personal is political" in the 1960s and 1970s, in order to challenge the "oppressions experienced by women in the private realm."[59] And of course it would be remiss here not to observe that a classic critique of Arendt is her apparent insistence on the division between the private and public, between the political being that exists in the world common to us all, and the "sheltered existence" or "twilight" of our "private and intimate lives."[60] As the political philosopher Seyla Benhabib puts it, "'the personal is not the political': that is the message of Arendt's life and work."[61] Yet the events at the Albertinum clearly contained a personal, private element, however intertwined it may be with the more public disputes on art, culture, and who attains representation in the two. The letter writers who began this campaign were influenced, as noted earlier, by their own personal experiences and grievances post-unification. Wagner's own impulse, to pick up the phone and defend herself, was also initially a private emotion. It is hard here to draw a "crisp distinction between public and private."[62] What seems to have been achieved, however, in Arendtian terms, was bringing the light of the public to bear on these private moods.

Finally, the case of the Albertinum is not a clear narrative of triumph over the far right, of rational dialogue persuading hardened extremists to abandon their positions. Indeed, in my conversation with Wagner, she mentions that the most difficult event was the very last discussion session. This final talk was infiltrated by members of a far-right group (she is unsure which), who had tactically dispersed themselves amongst the audience. Wagner recalls noticing them at the very beginning, for by that point the attendees had become familiar, even bonded over the course of time. These new faces entirely disrupted the final event. However, despite the sour note the series ended on, Wagner views it as a clear success. Personally, because it allowed her "to understand the situation." And publicly? "It led to a reconciliation." She emphasizes that, though this was only a very small-scale

59
Renee Heberle, "The Personal Is Political," in *The Oxford Handbook of Feminist Theory*, eds. Lisa Disch and Mary Hawkesworth (Oxford University Press, 2016), 593.

60
Arendt, *Human Condition*, 51.

61
Seyla Benhabib, "The Personal Is Not the Political," *Boston Review*, October 1, 1999, https://www.bostonreview.net/articles/seyla-benhabib-personal-not-political/.

62
Benhabib, "The Personal Is Not the Political."

63
Wagner, interview.

64
Subsequent to the completion of this article, a paper has been published by Mafalda Dâmaso, examining the Albertinum's *Wir müssen reden* series. Taking a Fraserian approach, Dâmaso explores the relationship between the museum and its public and considers questions on cultural policy and audience development in polarized times:
Mafalda Dâmaso, "We Must Talk: Audience Pluralisation as a Regenerative Path to the Management of Cultural Disagreement," *International Journal of Cultural Policy* 31, no. 4 (2025): 434–50.

event, it "broke up this polarization. It showed me that, on a small scale. It's possible to break through a spiral of rage and hate."[63]

Right Back Where We Started?

My trip to the Albertinum ends, as all visits to this museum must, back in the *Lichthof.* My time here has been insightful, even hopeful at points; however, my final questions to Hilke Wagner, about the organized disruption of the final event, have dampened that impression somewhat. As I prepare to leave the building, this question of scale is at the front of my mind. After all, it's unclear whether the event series has made a lasting impact on the broader political makeup of the city. This, to be clear, was never the explicit aim of the talks and, as noted previously, the AfD's share of the vote has only increased in the time since the discussion series took place. Simultaneously, however, the ability of the far right to promulgate a narrative of victimhood *was* disrupted. The Albertinum may have only brought about change on a small scale, on the level of subjective understandings of person, culture, and representation. But this allowed for a shift in the way citizens of Dresden related to the museum and to each other.[64] In some cases, this may have been only a momentary reconsidering of mood, a momentary reappraisal of opinion. In others, it was perhaps more. It is not within the scope of this essay to quantify the what and the where of the lasting effects that the "We Need to Talk" series may have had. But we can note that it is the small-scale, even fleeting, acts of coming together that are perhaps most lacking in our political systems today. As division and polarization continue to increase, as the extreme right grows in strength and acceptability, it is necessary to approach this danger head-on, aware that it is reproduced differently and in different degrees in a plurality of people. We still need to talk.

Revolutions of the Senses
Martin Renz/Julius Schwarzwälder

01
Raymond Williams,
*Keywords:
A Vocabulary
of Culture and Society*
(Fontana, 1976), 9.

02
Susan Buck-Morss,
*Dreamworld
and Catastrophe:
The Passing
of Mass Utopia
in East and West*
(MIT Press, 2000),
236.

The same things just don't look the same anymore.

You may, for instance, come home from a war to find that the people who stayed behind "just don't speak the same language."[01] Or you may be looking for common ground with people from the other side of a recently abolished geopolitical frontier, only to discover that "looking at the same images, we did not see the same things."[02] But it is not only that two people can say the same words and mean, can look at the same object and see different things. It is more unsettling still when one and the same person, or one and the same group of people, comes to perceive exactly the same thing in a completely different way.

We call this un-unseeability. Un-unseeability concerns something that happens to people. It is not a personal quirk or an illusion, it is certainly nothing that can be revoked, and, curiously enough, for about 250 years it has been a pivotal phenomenon of modern political and even revolutionary change.

Once you see it, you can't unsee it.

Un-Unseeability: Outlines of a Phenomenon

We will approach un-unseeability by exhibiting a certain kind of image. Take a look at the logo of Toblerone chocolate.

[06]

Toblerone, of course, is well known for the resemblance of its logo to the mountain-shaped chocolate pieces that each bar consists of. While this will certainly come to mind, all that matters for our purposes is a closer visual inspection of the image. At first sight, it simply consists of a golden mountain silhouette, ostentatiously subtitled by the brand name 'TOBLERONE,' spelled out in its virtually unmistakable lettering, consisting of red capitals, gold-edged and shadowed in black. But if you look closer, you may find something else. So take another look. (Or flip the page for help.)

[07]

03
Jostin Asuncion,
"What Has Been Seen
Cannot Be Unseen,"
Know Your Meme,
November 6, 2009,
https://
knowyourmeme.
com/memes/
what-has-been-
seen-cannot-be-
unseen.

While it is clear that you have now 'found' the shape or *gestalt* of a giant bear climbing the mountain, the gravity of the perceptual shift you have just experienced might not be immediately apparent. For when you revisit the first image, you will not only be able to see a bear—you will never be able to unsee it again. The bear has become un-unseeable. This does not mean that it was invisible, though it may in fact not have come into sight immediately. Rather, the bear was (and continues to be) hidden in plain sight and, most importantly: once it is seen, it cannot be unseen.

The idea of un-unseeability gained wider attention through memes centered on the catchphrase 'what has been seen cannot be unseen.' This became an "internet axiom"[03] in the early 2000s, when it was used to describe the experience of being haunted by violent images that people saw online.

In its subsequent iterations, this pictorial phenomenon became increasingly detached from the traumatizing content to which it first referred, being applied to more harmless subjects, such as logo designs and memes of various kinds.

[08]

Though the phrasing may have stayed the same, the experience of these two kinds of phenomena is strikingly dissimilar. The difference between violent images that induce trauma and un-unseeable images in our sense comes down to the distinct ways in which they work on the viewer. Violent images burn themselves, so to speak, into your retina, with a propensity to appear when your eyelids are shut and you are looking for rest. Trauma strikes without volition; much like a permanent afterimage that makes its presence felt only every now and then, it grips and sticks to those touched by it.[04] In gore or snuff, the 'shock' comes about through the very confrontation *with* the image itself, and not through a kind of perceptual shift that occurs *within* the image. While the bear is sticky, too, it seems to stick more to or in the image than to or in your memory. You are 'forced' to see it when, and only when, you are actively looking at the Toblerone logo. The bear will hardly come to torment you at night.

Significantly, un-unseeability is also markedly different from another famous kind of perceptual shift, known as 'aspect-dawning,' which plays a decisive role in the work of the philosopher Ludwig Wittgenstein. This phenomenon is closely bound up with an image invoked by Wittgenstein, the duck-rabbit, or *hasente* in German.[05]

---

04 But even the "compulsion to repetition" *(Wiederholungs-zwang)* of the original traumatic experience in dreams and in free association is, at least in a Freudian frame, more a product of the traumatized themselves staying "fixated on" or "in obedience to" it than a kind of 'coercion,' see Sigmund Freud, *Beyond the Pleasure Principle* (W. W. Norton, 1961), 7 and 17–26.

05 We coined this portmanteau comprised of the German words *Hase* and *Ente.* If you focus on the central 'e,' you will have the phenomenon of the duck-rabbit in the spelling of the word itself.

Welche Thiere gleichen einander am meisten?

Kaninchen und Ente.

[09]

The perceptual shift elicited by the *hasente* differs more from the Toblerone logo than it might at first appear. After all, it too seems to lead its spectator to a point of no return. Once both versions are recognized, there is no going back to the state where one only saw a duck *or* a rabbit. But note that this image has the property of appearing only as *either* a duck *or* a rabbit. Once a person recognizes that the duck can also be seen as a rabbit (or vice versa), she can freely shift between the two, akin to flipping a switch that activates solely one or the other, but never both and nothing in between.

This is remarkably different from the case of the bear in the Toblerone logo, since the actual shift it engenders is contained within one singular event. It takes place once and only once, forever changing the boundaries of your perception of the logo—no flicking and no switching back and forth. There is no way to make the bear disappear except by closing your eyes, but then the mountain disappears as well.

Even if you manage to approach this state—say, by trying to look at it in a peripheral blur—you will never fully escape the presence of the bear, even and especially when attempting to negate it. While the case of the bear and of the *hasente* have in common that they make you leave a state of 'innocence'— in which one would, for instance, say "I see a duck" instead of "*Now* I see a duck"—the latter differs from the former in that it is always only one or the other aspect that forces itself upon you.[06] It is really much less a dawning than a flickering, a constant illumination or "lighting up" of either the duck or the rabbit.[07] The difference then lies in the fact that with the *hasente*, you must be able to unsee one aspect of an image to be able to perceive the other. In the Toblerone logo, you cannot see one aspect without the other, the bear without the mountain.

In this impossibility of separating the aspects of an image, un-unseeability is similar to optical illusions. But they are not the same. The difference is that the un-unseeability of the bear reveals the 'truth' of the Toblerone logo, namely the bear that is hidden in plain sight and cannot be unseen. In contrast, an optical illusion tries to hide the 'truth' of its image. Consider, for instance, the café wall illusion, which, in its most basic form, was first described in Hugo Münsterberg's *Pseudoptics* of 1894.

06
Ludwig Wittgenstein, *Philosophical Investigations* (Wiley Blackwell, 2009), 205.

[10]

It shows a pattern of black and white squares arranged in an irregularly staggered pattern, with seemingly crooked gray lines separating each row of squares. However, upon closer inspection with, say, a ruler, it turns out that the crooked lines are actually straight and run parallel to one another. In this case we are dealing with an optical illusion in that we cannot immediately perceive this image as it really is. While you may (or may not) have been able to find the bear all by yourself, we strictly require external assistance here. In terms of attempting to find out the 'truth' of the lines, the ruler trumps your seemingly private perceptual experience. The lines of the café wall are certainly not invisible—look at them—but their parallelism cannot be seen directly. In this case, our senses distort reality. In the case of the bear in the mountain, however, our perception may reveal something that has been there all along. It is not an illusion, it brings about a revelation. The subtle surprise that is brought about by the *gestalt* of the bear comes not despite but because of the fact that nothing about the image itself has changed.

07   G. E. M. Anscombe translated this phrase as "the 'dawning' of an aspect." The German is *aufleuchten,* which means 'lighting up' (something that becomes foregrounded momentarily, as when someone's eyes light up in excitement, or when some striking feature seems to jump out at you). Lighting up is an instantaneous event, whereas dawning is a gradual process; a thought cannot dawn on one in a flash. Moreover, 'dawning' is overly intellectual, as in "'it gradually dawned on me that things were thus-and-so,'" Wittgenstein, *Philosophical Investigations,* 262. Cf. Stephen Mulhall, *On Being in the World: Wittgenstein and Heidegger on Seeing Aspects* (Routledge, 1990) and Avner Baz, *The Significance of Aspect Perception: Bringing the Phenomenal World into View* (Springer, 2020). For a convincing reading of Arendt alongside Wittgenstein, see Linda Zerilli, *A Democratic Theory of Judgment* (University of Chicago Press, 2016), especially chapter 1, and, more recently, Linda Zerilli, "Wittgenstein, Arendt, and the Problem of Democratic Persuasion," in *Wittgenstein and Democratic Politics,* ed. Lotar Rasiński et al. (Routledge, 2024).

Perception: Subtitled

While the appearance of the bear-*gestalt* is a useful primer on the matter of un-unseeability, it also conceals something relevant. Our examples so far have made it seem like un-unseeability is somehow intricately linked with *gestalt*-switches. But a focus on shapes and contours distracts from an essential feature of un-unseeability: no changes in what is seen are necessary for the phenomenon to take place. To appreciate this, follow the instructions of John Berger and his co-authors in *Ways of Seeing*.[08] By showing how the phenomenon of un-unseeability may be employed as an effect, they lay bare a crucial aspect in the relation between an image and its context.

08
John Berger,
Ways of Seeing
(Penguin, 1972).
Berger's co-authors
are Sven Blomberg,
Chris Fox,
Michael Dibb,
and Richard Follis,
who are implied
when we refer to
John Berger in the
following.

Paintings are often reproduced with words around them.

This is a landscape of a cornfield with birds flying out of it. Look at it for a moment. Then turn the page.

This is the last picture that Van Gogh painted before he killed himself.

It is hard to define exactly how the words have changed the image but undoubtedly they have. The image now illustrates the sentence.

[12]

Evidently, the two images are identical, but nonetheless the image has changed. By adding a subtitle, it seems like it is supposed to take on a certain 'gloominess.' This effect is achieved by adding a photo-copied handwritten note under the image that catches the reader's attention by virtue of its graphical deviance, suggesting a kind of intimacy that distances its statement from the typed passages in which the authorial voice speaks.

None of this is to imply, however, that Berger's point is that we must in fact perceive *Wheatfield with Crows* as a sad, mournful, or gloomy painting. The interplay of image and subtitle inserts itself into the audience's perception in such a way that a 'mere' fact about the production of the image seems to stand in an intricate relation to what is depicted and what this depiction stands for. A structure of relevance is thereby constituted in which the meaning of the painting is saturated by the solitary life and suicide of its painter. Note, however, that the commentary in the main body of the text destabilizes this bond between van Gogh's biography and the meaning of the painting by refusing to elaborate how exactly the image has changed. The typewritten voice does not presuppose that readers now 'must' accept one specific way of seeing the image. (After all, this is a book on *ways* of seeing.) Instead, it demonstrates how, by making certain features of the image 'stand out,' those seeing it have to orient themselves towards this emphasis in order to 'find' their own position—feeling sad, annoyed, or something different altogether.

At this and many other points in his argument, Berger employs the phenomenon of un-unseeability to produce and exemplify an effect for his audience. What he attempts to show (not tell) is how instances of un-unseeability can be used to structure the interface of our sense impressions and the sense that we make of them—what, metaphorically, is called the 'framing' of a thing. It is not the details depicted in *Wheatfield with Crows* that matter (the night sky, some birds, a path, and a cornfield), but the way in which its framing highlights certain features for those guided by the perspective that Berger half-ironically implies. He debunks the biased perspective that such a staging of the image implies by means of an active contrast.

It is against the background of these stand-out features that you will then form your own personal judgments of the painting. You may judge the gloomy interpretation to be correct, or you may reject it as tainted by a cult of self-centered genius that reduces the meaning of a painting to its painter's suicide.[09] But in all these judgments, your point of departure will differ from your first view of the image, before you were confronted with the subtitle. There is a change in the object towards which you take your position, the aspect around which your perception revolves in acceptance or disagreement. The phenomenon of un-unseeability is here employed to produce an effect which pre-structures not the perspective you take but the basis on which you form one perspective or another in the first place. There is no 'pure,' 'authentic,' or 'innocent' perception of anything, nor has there ever been.[10]

By juxtaposing a non-subtitled with a subtitled version of *Wheatfield with Crows,* Berger shows the change in perception that the latter produces to be an effect that inserts itself into one's seemingly private perception of the image. But his point is not to suggest that there is an untarnished

09
As much is implied about the van Gogh industry in John Berger, *Permanent Red: Essays in Seeing* (Methuen, 1960), 34: "No artist's life lends itself better to this new kind of romanticism than Van [sic] Gogh's."

10
A phenomenological argument in the same vein, touching on the idea of a *perspectiva communis*, has recently been made in Emmanuel Alloa, *The Share of Perspective* (Routledge, 2024), 4: "Far from *relativizing* reality, perspective *realizes* it."

11
Berger,
Ways of Seeing, 28.

way of perceiving the image that we can return to. He enables his readers to critically assess their initial reactions to images without therefore discounting the fact that all perceptions are always embedded in existing structures of relevance. All perception is 'subtitled,' because all perception occurs in a situation that precedes it.

Oddly enough, the effect of un-unseeability plays out somewhere between coercion and voluntariness: it works by compulsion. By involving us without asking for permission, it nonetheless leaves us room to position ourselves toward it. (It does not persuade 'automatically'; we are not talking about brainwashing.) Although un-unseeability may be irrevocable, this does not mean that the purpose for which it is employed is self-evident, correct, or necessarily convincing. On the contrary, by openly employing it as an effect, Berger shows how it can be used to simulate self-evidence. Yet the intrusiveness of un-unseeability must be differentiated from its supposed claim to relevance. The point is that this implicit claim to relevance may actually be more questionable than it first appears. Berger cautions us not to mistake the self-evidence of un-unseeability for the self-evidence of a claim in whose service it is employed. By uncovering a kind of intrusive appeal that usually remains hidden in plain perception, his audience is invited to consider new, alternative ways of perceiving.

There is thus one further important conclusion that needs to be emphasized. Contrary to the language Berger employs—'ways of seeing,' 'changing an image,' and so on—the van Gogh example subtly distances us from the register of vision and draws us in the direction of a more general register of 'perception' in talking about un-unseeability. While it is true that *Wheatfield with Crows* changes by subtitling it in the way that Berger claims, this change does not happen on the level of vision. Nothing about the visual experience—shapes, colors, etc.—is tinkered with. Instead, it is our perception of the image that changes, making the image appear markedly different. Still, as the typewritten voice remarks, "it is hard to define exactly how."[11] This difficulty does not stem from an incapacity on the part of the viewer. There just is nothing 'in' the image to which you could point to spell out your newfound relation to it, nothing that could ultimately settle the question of what has changed—other of course than the stubborn, un-unseeable 'fact' that subtitles the image.[12]

The Revolution Will Not Be Unseen

There is a point in time that we believe marks the origin of the political relevance of un-unseeability. We take our cue from an epic passage in Hannah Arendt's *On Revolution*.

> The date was the night of the fourteenth of July 1789, in Paris, when Louis XVI heard from the Duc de La Rochefoucauld-Liancourt of the fall of the Bastille, the liberation of a few prisoners, and the defection of the royal troops before a popular attack. The famous dialogue that took place between the king and his messenger is very short and very revealing. The king, we are told, exclaimed, 'C'est une révolte,' and Liancourt corrected him: 'Non Sire, c'est une révolution.' Here we hear the word still, and politically for the last time, in the sense of the old metaphor which carries its meaning from the skies down to the earth; but here, for the first time perhaps, the emphasis has entirely shifted from the lawfulness of a rotating, cyclical movement to its irresistibility. The motion is still seen in the image of the movement of the stars, but what is stressed now is that it is beyond human power to arrest it, and hence it is a law unto itself. The king, when he declared the storming of the Bastille was a revolt, asserted his power and the various means at his disposal to deal with conspiracy and defiance of authority; Liancourt replied that what had happened there was irrevocable and beyond the power of a king. What did Liancourt see, what must we see or hear, listening to this strange dialogue, that he thought, and we know, was irresistible and irrevocable?[13]

---

12 After all, the idea that this is van Gogh's last painting is not only a common feature of sentimentalized accounts of his genius, it is simply mistaken, see Zachary Small, "Contrary to Popular Belief, 'Wheatfield with Crows' Was Not Vincent van Gogh's Last Painting," *Hyperallergic,* February 25, 2019, https://www.hyperallergic.com/486142/contrary-to-popular-belief-wheatfield-with-crows-was-not-vincent-van-goghs-last-painting/.

13 Hannah Arendt, *On Revolution* (Penguin Books, [1963] 1990), 47–48.

14
Arendt,
On Revolution, 43.

15
See
Hans Schavernoch,
*Die Harmonie
der Sphären:
Die Geschichte
der Idee des
Welteneinklangs
und der
Seeleneinstimmung*
(Alber, 1981).

16
See Helmut Hühn,
"Sphäre,"
in *Historisches
Wörterbuch der
Philosophie:
Band 9 Se–Sp*,
ed. Joachim Ritter
and Karlfried Gründer
(Schwabe, 1995), 1373.

Arendt's story implies that this is when the new meaning of the word revolution became un-unseeable. The word is still 'revolution,' but it no longer sounds or looks the same.

Before 1789, 'revolution' was an astronomical metaphor that likened the course of developments in the sphere of politics to the motion of celestial bodies. This cyclical motion was thought to be eternal, neither ceasing nor changing, and recurring, meaning that prior states will always be returned to. This in turn meant that it was irresistible, implying that no earthly force was great enough to divert the pre-ordained ways of the heavens. It designated a return to the eternal, original order of things—a cyclical motion that ultimately always brings about "restoration" after so and so many revolutions.[14]

The notion of 'sphere,' just like 'revolution' in the pre-modern sense, is also a remnant of astronomic imagery that was intimately tied to ideas of cosmological harmony.[15] The application of the notion to the description of human affairs began in the early 17th century.[16] In this figurative sense, it took into account one's social position and status, and was often used to indicate that someone was 'in' or 'out,' depending on how far their "sphere of activity" extended.[17]

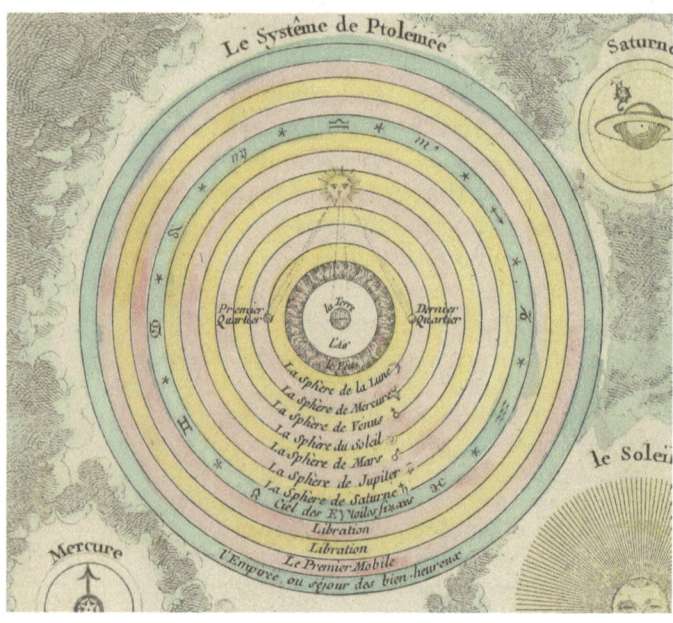

[13]　Depiction of an ancient model of the cosmic spheres from 1786.

The sphere of politics might then refer to something like an isolated upper stratum of the world to which, by divine providence, only the privileged have access.[18] The idea that politics is positioned in an exclusive spherical location thus serves as the very footing on which the pre-modern image of 'revolution' rested, which then denoted the coming-to-order of worldly affairs in their proper spherical arrangement. This is why

> coups d'état and palace revolutions, where power changes hands from one man to another, from one clique to another … have been less feared [than revolutions] because the change they bring is circumscribed to the *sphere* of government [emphasis added].[19]

Revolts, coups, and revolutions, Arendt laments, are often identified by the same attribute: their violence. Putting aside the objection that not all revolutions are violent, there is one important distinction we should make. Whereas a successful coup is prepared secretly and replaces one group of rulers with another, revolutions are brought about in public. They are situations in which the entirety of the established order collapses and a new kind of order must be established.

All of this must be taken into account when considering the dialogue that Arendt recounts. Its location—the king's private chamber in Versailles—exemplifies the pre-modern spherical logic of politics. The king's palace itself was structured in a manner that regulated access according to rank.

---

17   Antoine Furetière: *Dictionaire universel* (Rotterdam, 1708), 1950: "quand on parle de ceux qui veulent entreprendre une chose au delà de leurs forces. Il ne reüssira pas dans cette affaire, il est hors de sa sphere, elle est au dessus de ses conoissances." But already by the end of the 19th century, the term "n'évoque plus aucune image," see *Trésor de la langue française*, s.v. "Sphère," accessed March 04, 2025, https://www.stella.atilf.fr/Dendien/scripts/tlfiv5/affart.exe?19;s=1370422275;?b=0.

18   But this depends on the concrete imagistic realization. In the case of the frontispiece to John Case: *Sphaera civitatis* (Barnes, 1588), an Aristotelian treatise on political theory, the Queen is positioned outside of a spherical model of majestic virtues, governing the destiny of order like a God.

19   Arendt, *On Revolution*, 34–35.

Liancourt, the king's "grand maître de la garde-robe,"[20] was amongst the few court officials authorized to enter a location as restricted as the king's chamber without prior invitation.

Arendt's story is illuminating not only in that it contrasts the old and the new meaning of 'revolution,' but also in how the protagonists of the dialogue can be interpreted as hearing the word in the old and the new sense respectively. Their relative proximity to or distance from the events in the streets mattered to their ability to perceive the change in meaning. As Arendt explains, Louis XVI heard the word "still, and politically for the last time, in the sense of the old metaphor" and "asserted his power" by dismissing the storming as a mere revolt—at worst a change in who occupied the sphere of government.[21] And such a change in power would, in any case, be only transient, as the king's understanding of 'revolution' implied the ultimate restoration of the monarchy.

In a sense, the anecdote reenacts the feat of the Toblerone logo at the level of the word.[22] The king, as it were, fails to see the bear. Phenomenally, he is stuck with the mountain. He cannot hear the shift in emphasis of the meaning of 'revolution' towards irresistibility because doing so would imply an admission of the loss of kingly power. In a brilliantly convoluted way, Arendt then assumes Liancourt's point of view to bring out the new meaning of revolution when she asks: "What did Liancourt see, what must we see or hear, listening to this strange dialogue, that he thought, and we know, was irresistible and irrevocable?"

The answer, claims Arendt, "seems simple." Liancourt saw "the multitude of the poor and the downtrodden," who, driven by biological needs, are seen not as groups of individual people but as torrents, storms, and waves that flooded the streets and burst into the public.[23] With these images vividly impressed upon him, Liancourt's use of the word 'revolution' no longer emphasizes recurrence and order. Only one aspect remains: irresistibility. From Liancourt's point of view, the

20   Olivier Coquard, "'C'est une révolte?—Non, Sire, c'est une révolution': cet échange impliquant Louis XVI a-t-il vraiment eu lieu?," *Historia*, December 7, 2018, https://www.historia.fr/personnages-historiques/citations/cest-une-revolte-non-sire-cest-une-revolution-duc-de-la-rochefoucauld-liancourt- 1789-2058044.

21   Arendt, *On Revolution*, 47–48.

revolution is caused by the wretched masses and their public call for social justice, typically referred to as the 'social question.' His perception of the day's events would thus have accorded with exactly one aspect of the old image of the celestial bodies—the impossibility of stopping them in their course.

Liancourt reduces the revolving motion of the planets to their unyieldingness, which, in turn, prompts him to call the goings-on in Paris a 'revolution.' But this reduction of the meaning of 'revolution' to one of its aspects meant not only that the old astronomical image had become obsolete, but that a new image had already been found: the revolutionary masses in the streets, which Liancourt would have perceived to be an almost literally unstoppable force, driven by hunger and desolate misery, being pushed and pushing their way into sites both public and restricted, such as streets, squares, palaces, the Bastille. 'Revolution' now evokes an image of violent force beyond any one person's control—a "law unto itself," as Arendt puts it.[24] No longer implying an everlasting order, it is now used to describe the very overthrow of order, a dive into uncharted waters.

22 Interestingly enough, there is a modern German translation that works too well for its own good, namely *Staatsumwälzung.* Coined in Joachim Heinrich Campe's Parisian letters of 1789–1790, it captures both the old and the new meaning of revolution, depending on what syllable you stress: *Um*wälzung or Um*wä*lzung. Campe's proposal was promptly criticized by an anonymous reviewer in *Allgemeine Literatur-Zeitung,* who complained that it carried "over too much from the secondary notion of a bodily and regular movement, as e.g. the earth around its axis [our translation]." It could be said that the problem with Campe's proposal was that it functions too much like the *hasente* and too little like un-unseeability. See Joachim Heinrich Campe, *Briefe aus Paris während der Revolution geschrieben* (Schulbuchhandlung, 1790), xii, 68–72, and 121–39. His proposal can be found in Joachim Heinrich Campe: *Proben einiger Versuche von deutscher Sprachbereicherung* (Schulbuchhandlung, 1791), 39, its review in *Allgemeine Literatur-Zeitung,* 1792, vol. 1, 336; cf. Harald Kleinschmidt, "Klimatheorie, Statistik, Revolutionsbegriff: Die Transformation der Wahrnehmung der Vergangenheit in Europa zwischen dem 17. und dem 19. Jahrhundert," *Historische Zeitschrift* 138, no. 3 (2019): 630.

23 Arendt, *On Revolution,* 48.

24 Arendt, *On Revolution,* 48.

Whether you like it or not: traces of Liancourt's experience are still present whenever the word revolution is used in politics today.[25] For it was at this point in time that the word took on its "definite shape."[26] Therefore, "[w]hen we think of revolution, we *almost automatically* still think in terms of this imagery, born in these years [emphasis added]."[27] The "inundation" of the Bastille is the revolution's ultimate icon.[28] The metaphorical register of natural forces, Arendt argues, captures the widespread feeling of chaos and the loss of control, the seemingly irresistible forces that are at play in revolutionary situations.

But note how at every step of her argument, Arendt aims to undermine the intimate connection between a seeming irresistibility perceived by Liancourt in the bodily needs of the poor and the experience of revolution. On the level of textual strategy, this starts already with the brilliantly convoluted sentence structure by which Arendt virtually forces Liancourt's view onto her readers. But at the same time, she emphasizes and over-emphasizes the fact that this is merely one man's perspective. What emerges from Arendt's account is not an objective state of affairs but a way of seeing: Liancourt's paradigmatic way of seeing. Arendt makes the readers of *On Revolution* see what they would have seen had they stood in Liancourt's shoes.

25 See Karl Griewank, *Der neuzeitliche Revolutionsbegriff* (Europäische Verlagsanstalt, 1992), 187. This is of course not meant to imply that the modern meaning originated in Liancourt, as there are many precursors to him, such as Paul Ulric Dubuisson, *Abrégé de la Révolution de l'Amérique angloise* (Cellot & Jombert, 1778), who highlights the suddenness and irrevocability of the American events; see also Christopher Hill, *A Nation of Change and Novelty: Radical Politics, Religion and Literature in Seventeenth-Century England* (Routledge, 1990), 82–101. It is just that the anecdote encapsulates this shift with a unique historiographical efficaciousness.

26 Arendt, *On Revolution*, 44.

27 Arendt, *On Revolution*, 48.

28 This is a contemporary term, used for instance by Nicolas Chamfort in a description of Jean-Louis Prieur's drawing of the fall of the Bastille, as documented in Claudette Hould, ed., *La révolution par l'écriture* (Réunion des Musées Nationaux, 2005), 178: "[Le peuple] inonde cette cour d'où la mousqueterie l'écart un moment."

Yet the very setup and framing of Arendt's story favors an un-settling of Liancourt's perception. Her story starts not with what are commonly referred to as the 'big, decisive events' of July 14 but with a more delicate scene that, though legendary in its own right, certainly never gained the importance of the storming of the Bastille—which, in this intentionally under-stated telling, boils down to "the liberation of a few prison-ers."[29] She does not foreground spectacular confrontations but tells a subtler tale, that of a conversation about these bat-tles, which by definition is much harder to 'see.'

To appreciate what is at stake in this distinction, consider the following images.

29
Arendt,
On Revolution, 47.

Prife de la Baftille.
Le 14 Juillet 1789.

Prise de la Bastille.

ÉVÉNEMENT DE LA NUIT DU 14 AU 15 JUILLET 1789.

M. de Liancourt se jette aux pieds du Roi, et lui fait le récit fidel des malheurs de la Capitale.

In terms of iconicity—when literally 'seen'—the supreme spectacle of the Bastille overshadows the rather unassuming scene inside the king's chamber. It is thus not a coincidence that only one contemporary image of the chamber scene exists, and that even Jean-François Janinet, arguably one of the finest and certainly one of the most influential printmakers of the time, was incapable of fully rendering the crucial part of this scene, the un-unseeable shift in the meaning of 'revolution,' and perhaps had no desire to do so.[30]

Arendt tries to show that the iconicity of the Bastille and its later historiographic dominance do not tell the whole story.[31] In her extensive report of a report, she concerns herself not only with events and facts, but with how these events were seen and partially overlooked. From the perspective of the king, only a few prisoners were liberated—so why all the fuss? But from Liancourt's perspective, the storming of the Bastille was to become the epochal break that fused irresistibility and the new meaning of revolution to the violent image of the wretched masses. Put into the language of Berger's treatment of *Wheatfield with Crows,* for Liancourt and many

30 Janinet's potential unwillingness is pointed out in Philippe Carbonnières, *Les gravures historiques de Janinet* (Musée Carnavalet, 2011), 93–101, who notes that "without a doubt, Janinet judged the real scene to be too trivial to be represented [our translation]," as the king would hardly have been powdered as he rose from his sleep. The moderate Janinet, known for his unvarnished depictions of the revolution's cruelty and violence, remarked in 1789 that "this victory [i.e. the storming of the Bastille] [is] the most astonishing ever won since the world began [our translation]." Accordingly, print no. 18 in his series on the French Revolution, "Prise de la Bastille" (fig. 19), is the only one that is oversized. For the significance of prints in the French Revolution, see Richard Taws, *Politics of the Provisional: Art and Ephemera in Revolutionary France* (Penn State University Press, 2015), 17, as well as Anne Betrand, ed., *La révolution par la gravure* (Réunion des Musées Nationaux, 2002) and Claudette Hould and Alain Chevalier, eds., *La révolution par le dessin* (Réunion des Musées Nationaux, 2008).

31 For an overview of today's historiography of 18th-century revolutions, see David Motadel, "Global Revolution," in *Revolutionary World: Global Upheaval in the Modern Age,* ed. David Motadel (Cambridge University Press, 2021). For a historic overview of the Bastille's iconicity, see Hans-Jürgen Lusebrink and Rolf Reichardt, *Die 'Bastille': Zur Symbolgeschichte von Herrschaft und Freiheit* (Fischer, 1990).

of his contemporaries, the sub-image to 'revolution' took on a seemingly un-unseeable connection with the populace on the march.

It is for this reason that Arendt is primarily concerned with the differing ways in which contemporaries were compelled to perceive the events of this day—how they *appeared* to them. While it might still feel like revolution is firmly tied to this imagery, we only make these associations *almost* automatically. Arendt's struggle in this text is to untether the attribution of the experience of the irresistibility of revolution from the image of the rising masses.

Pathos of Freedom

This brings us to our central claim about the relationship between un-unseeability and modern revolutions. Our own sensitivity towards the phenomenon of un-unseeability today—the reason that we can find it anywhere from art to marketing to meme culture—is still connected to the effective appeal it unfolded in political history since the revolutions of the 18th century: the American, the French, and the Haitian Revolution. It is here that the phenomenon of un-unseeability, maybe for the first time and characteristically hidden in plain sight, made itself felt as a widespread and immediately relevant effect of politics.

At the center of this alternative story lies the widespread experience of un-unseeability, which appears to occur, at least in politics, suddenly during the revolutions of the 18th century.[32] This is a typical feature of revolutionary

---

32   But Arendt, *On Revolution,* 46, also notes that the revolutionaries were "old-fashioned in terms of their own time," especially when compared to the sciences and philosophy, where discoveries were typically described in the language of an un-unseeable "absolute novelty." Arendt's examples here include Galileo, Descartes, and Hobbes. In this regard, un-unseeability also resembles what Thomas Kuhn has called 'paradigm change,' though Kuhn likens this more generally to *gestalt*-switches than to un-unseeability, as described in *The Structure of Scientific Revolutions* (University of Chicago Press, 2009), 150: "Practicing in different worlds, the two groups of scientists see different things when they look from the same point in the same direction. Again, that is not to say they can see anything they please... Just because it is a transition between incommensurables, the transition between competing paradigms

situations, whose agents are "driven by events."[33] All of a sudden the same things just don't look the same anymore. This manifests itself to the historian in the "bizarre *certainty* of the arguments" and opinions observable during revolutions. The certainty with which they are uttered seems to stand in a direct relation to the speed at which they change. Today's revolutionary is tomorrow's reactionary; yesterday's view that 'the king should be imprisoned' is a sign of compromise and weakness today, when 'the king must die.' Arendt calls this experience of new things—that events outpace beliefs, opinions, and orientations—the "strange pathos of novelty so characteristic of the modern age," arguing that it first emerged in science and philosophy. However, when it became "common knowledge"[35] and

> reached this realm [i.e. politics], in which events concern the many and not the few, it not only assumed a more radical expression, but became endowed with a reality peculiar to the political realm alone. It was only in the course of the eighteenth-century revolutions that men began to be aware that a new beginning could be a political phenomenon, that it could be the result of what men had done and what they could consciously set out to do.[36]

cannot be made a step at a time, forced by logic and neutral experience. Like the *gestalt*-switch, it must occur all at once (though not necessarily in an instant) or not at all." Two incidental facts are worth mentioning: Kuhn was in direct dialogue with Stanley Cavell when they were colleagues at Berkeley, see Toril Moi, *Revolution of the Ordinary: Literary Studies after Wittgenstein, Austin, and Cavell* (University of Chicago Press, 2017), 10. Furthermore, Kuhn's *Structure* was published a year prior to Arendt's *On Revolution,* in 1962, though she finished the manuscript in 1960 and 1961 (See "Acknowledgments" in Arendt, *On Revolution).*

33 C. L. R. James, *The Black Jacobins: Toussaint L'Ouverture and the San Domingo Revolution* (Penguin, [1938] 2001), 158.

34 T. J. Clark, *Image of the People: Gustave Courbet and the 1848 Revolution* (Thames and Hudson, 1973), 10.

35 The German reads "Allgemeingut," which in this context is best translated as 'common knowledge' but also means 'common property,' see Hannah Arendt, *Über die Revolution* (Piper, [1965] 2016), 56.

36 Arendt, *On Revolution,* 46.

The un-unseeability in the meaning of 'revolution' rhymes well with the strong sense of a loss of control.[37] It is prior to any attribution of revolutionary force to what revolutionaries and spectators alike described as 'the people,' 'the mob,' or 'the masses.' In revolutionary situations, 'new' things that require new opinions and beliefs happen at an unheard-of frequency. Political un-unseeability is mushrooming, popping up in unexpected places, seemingly without causal relations yet highly effective—decades happen in weeks.[38]

The French Revolution came about not only because of unprecedented violence unleashed in the streets, but because the old structure of authority, based on the belief in an everlasting and irresistible recurrence of a pre-established, stratified order, was no longer convincing and thus ceased to be operative.[39] The breakdown of the old order was less about a lack of firepower than a lack of firing: soldiers dropped their weapons and stopped following orders.

37 See Jason Frank, *The Democratic Sublime: On Aesthetics and Popular Assembly* (Oxford University Press, 2021), 179: "As revolutionary leaders lost control of the collective demands of the crowds they themselves had incited, Arendt claims, it *seemed to them* that revolutionary actors were no longer capable of initiating or taking control of events, but were quickly overwhelmed by larger historical forces [emphasis added]."

38 The saying that 'there are decades where nothing happens and weeks where decades happen' is most often misattributed to Lenin. For the history of this misattribution, see Caroline Wazer, "Lenin Said, 'There Are Decades Where Nothing Happens' and 'Weeks Where Decades Happen'?," *Snopes,* July 24, 2024, https://www.snopes.com/fact-check/lenin-decades-quote/.

39 The German version of *On Revolution* is, once again, more extensive here, see Arendt, *Über die Revolution,* 59: "But Liancourt saw more. He saw with his very own eyes how the old order collapsed under this onslaught. The soldiers had not fired, the instruments of authority had ceased to function. This was the end that had been a long time coming. Revolutions break out and are irresistible once it has become clear that power lies in the streets [our translation]."

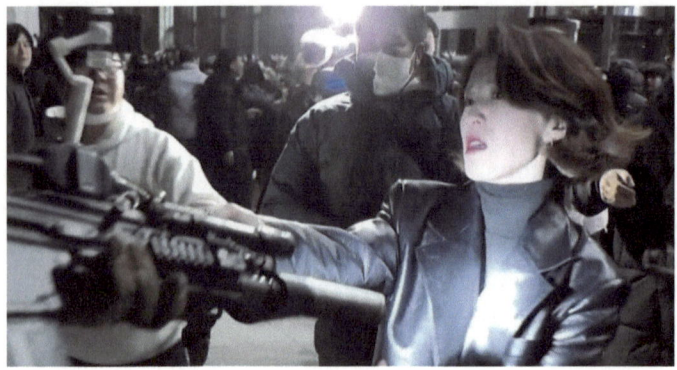

[27]
To this day (December 3, 2024) the decisive moment—will soldiers open fire on their own people? Depicted here: the parliamentarian Ahn Gwi-ryeong on her way to enter the South Korean National Assembly after it had been shut down in President Yoon Suk-yeol's attempted coup d'état.

40
See for instance Dana Villa, *Arendt and Heidegger: The Fate of the Political* (Princeton University Press, 1996), 29–30.

What we are dealing with in revolutionary upheaval is not only or even primarily a greater amount of trauma-inducing violence, but shifts in the ways of perception that undermine established authority altogether. The same orders just don't sound the same anymore.

From the perspective of revolution as a catalyst of un-unseeability, Arendt's invocation and critique of the social question during the French Revolution appear in a new light. Arendt does not have to be understood as siding with freedom *against* the social question.[40] Rather, she criticizes this very opposition by implying that the emerging publicity of the social question itself could only come about as the consequence of a newfound freedom implied in the experience of revolutionary un-unseeability. The very appearance of the social question as more pressing and relevant than political freedom is not a cause but an effect of the mob-like sub-image that became predominant in the use of the word 'revolution' in 1789. What Arendt says of conservatism is true of the social question as well: it "owe[s] its existence to a reaction to the French Revolution and is meaningful only for the history of the nineteenth[,] twentieth," and twenty-first centuries.[41]

41   Arendt, *On Revolution,* 44. See also Hannah Arendt, *The Human Condition* (University of Chicago Press, 1998), 219: "Originally, the term *le peuple,* which became current at the end of the eighteenth century, designated simply those who had no property. As we mentioned before, such a class of completely destitute people was not known prior to the modern age." Ayten Gündoğdu, *Rightlessness in an Age of Rights: Hannah Arendt and the Contemporary Struggles of Migrants* (Oxford University Press, 2015), 67–75, also foregrounds passages in Arendt in which the social question is treated as a politicizable issue.

What is at stake, then, in Arendt's rejection of identifying the French Revolution or politics with the needs of the poor is not her disavowal of the social question as such, but an answer to the question of how it could become a political issue at all.

Political Paradigm Shifts

We can now tackle one further aspect that precedes the question of how something as extensive as the social question could become a political issue, namely: what does it mean, at that point in history, for a political issue to appear as such without any new 'thing' needing to come into play? To repeat, un-unseeability is not simply an instance of aspect dawning, for there is no going back behind it. Nor is it an illusion that distorts one's perception, because the new state of perceptual affairs that un-unseeability brings about is real. Nor is it a traumatic reaction to the ensuing violence, since its effect is not brought about by involuntary memory alone, much in the same way that revolution is not brought about by violence alone.[42]

Instead, when un-unseeability became politically relevant, it changed the meaning of politics itself. Politics was no longer a sphere, it became a potential *medium* of reality. This medium concerned the question of what actions, attitudes, and events people perceive to be relevant and immediately effective. Politics became that highlighting force which makes persons, matters, and spaces 'stand out' as relevant to 'everyone' in comparison to other concerns that are ignored or not considered generally relevant. The new meaning of politics-as-medium could hardly be exhausted by addressing it in terms of strict binaries such as visible/invisible—who gets to enter and to act in a territorially delimited sphere and who does not. On the contrary, its workings now concerned degrees of visibility or hiddenness.

The emergence of un-unseeability in politics was experienced as the arrival of unprecedented and irrevocable 'newness.' Amongst these novelties was the admission into politics of the poor, "appearing for the first time in broad daylight," along with their demands—the social question.[43] When the sphere of politics had opened up to the crowds of Paris, their influx made it expand until it burst like an overblown balloon. The formerly highly restricted 'sphere'

42
See Arendt,
On Revolution, 35.

43
Arendt,
On Revolution, 48.

of politics became so enlarged that it started to disintegrate. Politics itself was no longer an affair of the few but—at least potentially—of all. Much in the same way that waves of people sloshed and spilled into the location where power was concentrated, power now sloshed and spilled out of that location in a way that, potentially (and only potentially), it became ubiquitously accessible.

Politics became mediatized. During the French Revolution, spaces that were never thought of as relevant in any way attained political self-awareness. People in these spaces acted under the impression that they could effectively influence and shape their reality. These spaces now included not only the royal court or the meeting places of liberal aristocrats and reformed clerics but also newly established spaces of assembly where the poor of Paris came together, such as barricades and baker's queues.[44] It is almost impossible to overstate the degree to which these new spatial arrangements seemed significant and positively alien to contemporaries. Just consider the fascination displayed by one of the most influential historians of the French Revolution, Thomas Carlyle.

> If we look now at Paris, one thing is too evident: that the Baker's shops have got their Queues, or Tails; their long strings of purchasers, arranged in tail, so that the first come be the first served, were the shop once open! … In time, we shall see it perfected by practice to the rank almost of an art; and the art, or quasi-art, of standing in tail become one of the characteristics of the Parisian People, distinguishing them from all other Peoples whatsoever.[45]

44 Both the barricade and the baker's queue gave rise to highly complex metaphorical and representational dimensions. For the former, see T. J. Clark, *The Absolute Bourgeois: Artists and Politics in France 1848–1851* (Thames and Hudson, 1973), 9–30, and Frank, *Democratic Sublime*, 123–52. For the latter, see Jean-Claude Boulogne, "Faire la queue: une allusion historique," *Canal Académies*, October 27, 2008, https://www.canalacademies.com/emissions/un-jour-dans-lhistoire/les-allusions-historiques/faire-la-queue, and René Scherer, "la queue de robespierre (sur le langage de la terreur)," *L'homme et la société* 63/64 (1982): 46–47.

45 Thomas Carlyle, *The French Revolution: A History in 3 Volumes, Volume I: The Bastille* (Chapman and Hall, 1837), 232.

Carlyle is quick to point out that this "talent" of "spontaneously standing in queue, which distinguishes … the French People from all Peoples, ancient and modern," proves that that the people out in the street, while often terrifyingly violent, should not be considered "dull masses." The French 'mob,' to Carlyle one of "the liveliest phenomena of our world," constituted itself in spaces where people came together and discussed their interests. Dispersed queues of women waiting for bread, aggravated by "laggard men [who] will not act," could turn into a forceful and decisive march on Versailles—seemingly by no *one*'s order but rather by everyone's accord.[46] Remarkably, it is not a person but a space that engenders these actions.

That politics became mediatized does not mean that the place of power just moved to a different location. It did not simply wander from the palace to "the street."[47] Power was no longer connected to a physical location or the physical body of the king; instead, it became a potential of spaces—understood virtually, not bound to specific physical locations. What Carlyle's account brings to the fore is the novel political potential of bakers' queues, generally, as a space of appearance.

But formal institutions such as the National Assembly explicitly understood themselves as virtual spaces, too. This is well exemplified in the 'Tennis Court Oath,' which, on June 20, 1789, established the National Assembly. Locked out of their designated meeting location in Versailles' *Salle des Menus-Plaisir*, the representatives of the Third Estate followed a proposition of Dr. Guillotin, later famed as the

46 Carlyle, *French Revolution*, 250–52. It is pointed out in Joan B. Landes, *Women and the Public Sphere in the Age of the French Revolution* (Cornell University Press, 1988), 109, that this march was not solely about bread. As "marchers asserted their right as women to participate in public affairs," this was also a struggle about the inclusion of women in the bourgeois public sphere. This struggle was all the more pressing since a considerable amount of the driving ideas of the French Revolution were masculinist in character, such as Rousseau's doctrine of "separate spheres," which formally introduced the domestic-public dichotomy along gendered lines, see Frank Turner, *European Intellectual History from Rousseau to Nietzsche* (Yale University Press, 2014), 208–25.

47 Arendt, *Über die Revolution*, 59, see also Hannah Arendt, *On Violence* (Harcourt, Brace & World, 1970), 49.

inventor of the *guillotine,* to gather in a nearby indoor court, where they swore "not to separate and *to reassemble wherever necessary* until the Constitution is established [emphasis added]."[48] Accordingly, the National Assembly henceforth was neither bound to a specific physical location nor reducible to its members, which might change over time. The potential continuity of such spaces of appearance depends upon their recognizability, which may be formalized. When they are actualized, they must look like spaces of this type and participants' behaviors must be widely considered typical for such a space. (Think of the conditions under which you would and would not say that people are queueing up in front of a shop or the conditions under which you would and would not take seriously an assembly that proclaims itself to be the National Assembly.)

Accordingly, politics was no longer extraneous to the concerns of ordinary people. It became the medium through which they—at least potentially—could actualize their newfound freedom in everyday or mundane contexts.[49] People in these spaces experienced themselves and their doings as efficacious and relevant, even when they and their observers *argued* that they were driven by misery. This was an important part of what 'freedom' came to mean. Freedom in this sense is not synonymous with 'volition,' the ability to 'do as one pleases,' or "liberation," the purely negative license for people to engage, as Arendt puts it, in a "more or less free range

48   Philippe Bordes, *Le Serment du Jeu de Paume de Jacques-Louis David* (Réunion des musées nationaux, 1983), 14. The painter of the best-known image of the tennis court oath, Jacques-Louis David, rose to fame in 1785 through his *Oath of the Horatii.* It remains up to speculation in how far the earlier image inspired the events that are depicted in the later one, but the deputies seem to have raised their right arms to take the oath, just like David's Horaces.

49   It is worth emphasizing that it is more than an abstract theoretical claim to say that politics is a medium—it is a historically specific judgment. Politics was not always a medium or a sphere. Even today, politics is often discussed as if it concerned a 'sphere,' as when politics is reduced to established political institutions, such as parliament. This overlooks that parliaments may under specific circumstances not deserve the name of 'political' places, for instance when they are unable to agree on legislation or when the relevant debates of the day take place outside it.

of non-political activities which a given body politic will permit and guarantee to those who constitute it."[50] Instead, it refers to the shared spirit or conviction that human beings can
work together to create their own laws and decisively shape
and influence the reality they face. Freedom meant that actors
could conceive of themselves as able to plan and to constitute
un-unseeable new beginnings.[51]

The insight into the ability of humans to act together
to constitute such un-unseeable new beginnings implied
changes not only in political spatiality but also in the general
understanding of political time. Its unfolding becomes conceivable as primarily linear once un-unseeability becomes a
political phenomenon. Though itself of ancient origin, the
idea of a linear account of time, coupled with the possibility
of the acceleration of history through an intensification of
events,[52] gained new potency when Joseph Priestley, in his

50
Arendt,
On Revolution, 30.

51
This is also what
Arendt has in mind,
see Arendt,
On Revolution, 29:
"Crucial, then, to
any understanding of
revolutions in the
modern age is that
the idea of freedom
and the experience
of a new beginning
should coincide."

52 Incidentally, the language of 'necessity' implied by the
historiographic dominance of the French Revolution has
done lasting harm to the European revolutionary tradition,
since it tended to create a belief in the necessity of the
course of history which could, at best, be sped up or slowed
down by political actors. This was noted by Buck-Morss,
Dreamworld, 58: "[Lenin] was a maverick among Marxists in
his belief that political movements could speed up the
course of history." Contrasting the French and the American
Revolution, Arendt considers the historiographic dominance of the latter a part of the gigantic "tragedy" that is
the French Revolution, see Arendt, *On Revolution,* 132,
cf. 66, 125. But this is not primarily because she takes it to
have failed. As a form of drama, tragedy broadly refers to a
conflict between a protagonist and a superior force or a
situation that does not allow for perspicuity. The protagonist's mistaken judgment, which Aristotle calls *hamartia* ('to
miss the mark,' as a javelin thrower might), leads to pity and
fear in the viewer. But in the case of the tragedy of the
French Revolution, pity and fear intensify precisely because
the protagonists bring about the very problem they try to
deal with by mistakenly believing the social question to be
based in necessity. The dominance of the French Revolution
in revolutionary historiography also induced such a tragic
dimension, misperceived as necessity, in the way later revolutions played out. In this sense, the French Revolution,
especially in its violent episodes, is deeply traumatic. But
less so in the Freudian sense we used above, where trauma
is operative mostly in laboratory conditions of the imagination (in dreams, or on the analyst's couch), and more as
outlined in Jean Laplanche, *Die allgemeine Verführungs-
theorie und andere Aufsätze* (edition diskord, 1988), 204–07,

wildly popular *A Chart of Biography* (1765), popularized a pathbreaking visual conception of history: the timeline. This made it possible to see, "'at one view,'" history as a constant stream that gained speed in special periods when the arts and sciences flourished—such as Priestley's own time, which he took to be singularly productive.[53] Yet for Priestley himself, "the timeline was a 'most excellent mechanical help to the knowledge of history,' not an image of history itself."[54]

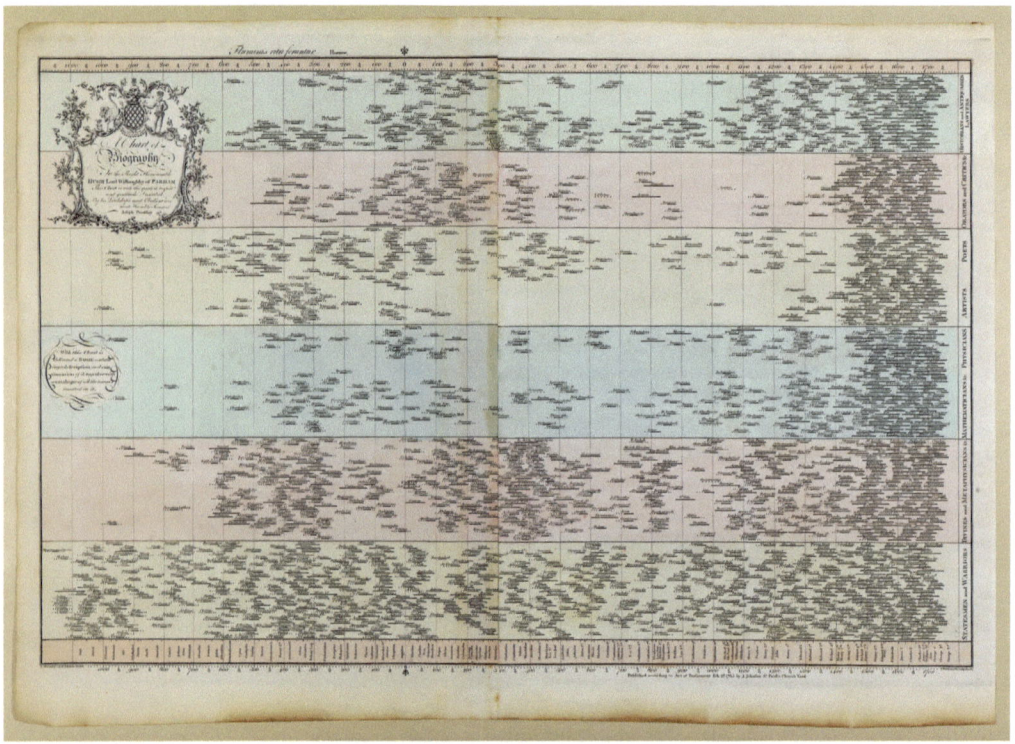

[28]

in reference to the concept of afterwardsness (*Nachträglichkeit*), which describes a prior event being re-interpreted in light of a later one. All heirs to the French Revolution find themselves compelled to repeat its script, which in turn means that the 'original' script itself is constantly re-interpreted and rewritten. We are indebted to Lisa Pfeifer for acquainting us with these passages in Freud and Laplanche and for helping us understand the differences between them.

However, with the break in order that revolution signifies, the mediatization of politics, and the experience of new beginnings as constituted in human action, history itself was increasingly understood in the image of a linear timeline, and more radically so than Priestley's graphic innovation implied.[55] Immediately after the fall of the Bastille, Revolutionaries even started calling 1789 'year I of Liberty' in pamphlets and treatises, letting the stream of time begin anew. Though institutionalized by the National Convention in 1792, this practice started spontaneously. It offered a unique opportunity to mark as epochal the break from what people had already started calling the 'ancien régime.'[56] Developments in this linear movement were generally no longer understood as expressions of a pre-given order of things, but as comprised of un-unseeable and irrevocable events. The break in order and the "perception of sudden change in all areas of life"[57] signified by 'revolution' entails the potential of new beginnings, which is to say: the potential of experiencing a kind of irrevocability that is identical to how un-unseeability temporally marks a point of no return.[58] But at the same time, it must be noted that this break can only happen against the background of whatever is already established. There is no break without a background of continuity against which it happens. It is always the *same* things that no longer look the same.

53 Daniel Rosenberg and Anthony Grafton, *Cartographies of Time* (Princeton Architectural Press, 2010), 118–26. Priestley's chart rewards closer examination and is available digitally at "The Chart of Biography," University of Oregon, accessed March 1, 2025, https://pages.uoregon.edu/infographics/dev/timeline/pages/index.html.

54 Rosenberg and Grafton, *Cartographies of Time,* 20.

55 Cf. Rosenberg and Grafton, *Cartographies of Time*, 126.

56 While the recurring days and months of a calendar "merely organize the regularity of everyday life, it is only the enumeration of years, whose counting is open towards the future, that offers the permanent possibility of innovation." See Reinhart Koselleck, "Anmerkungen zum Revolutionskalender und zur 'Neuen Zeit,'" in *Die Französische Revolution als Bruch des gesellschaftlichen Bewußtseins,* eds. Reinhart Koselleck and Rolf Reichardt (De Gruyter, 1988), 64.

57 Rolf Reichardt, "Révolution, révolutionnaire," in *Handbuch politisch-sozialer Grundbegriffe in Frankreich 1680–1820, Heft 22: Opinion publique, Révolution, Contre-révolution,* eds. Jörg Leonhard, Hans-Jürgen Lüsebrink, and Rolf Reichardt (De Gruyter, 2021), 99.

Let us, in closing, return to the general phenomenon of un-unseeability. You can now see that throughout our chapter, as we ventured deeper and deeper into politics-as-medium, the imaginatively shared perception of a thing—the Toblerone logo, *Wheatfield with Crows,* the word 'revolution,' a revolutionary world—became increasingly more essential to the thing. And the deeper we progressed into politics-as-medium, the more the description of a thing became inextricable from the thing that is being described. This is the specific "density of reality" which Arendt claims to be present *only* in politics.[59] It comes out in the assumption of relevance and immediate effectivity that claims to something being 'political' entail. In simpler terms: of the two claims that a) 'this revolution' is irresistible, b) 'this image' is a painter's last and thus presumably gloomy, only one claim becomes more threateningly real as more and more people take it to be true.

If you now think back to how Berger emphasized un-unseeability as a potential effect of perception by comparing a non-subtitled to a subtitled version of *Wheatfield with Crows,* you come to realize what it means for un-unseeability to have entered and embraced politics-as-medium. The difference between Berger's and Arendt's un-unseeabilities boils down to the different stakes involved in missing out on them. In the former case, you risk having a slightly narrow-minded perspective on a painting of some art-historical significance. In the latter, you risk contributing to being trapped in a world of violence and chaos.

58   According to Reinhart Koselleck, *Futures Past: On the Semantics of Historical Time* (Columbia University Press, 2004), 49: "Since then, revolution obviously no longer returned to given conditions or possibilities, but has, since 1789, led forward into an unknown future. The nature of this future is so obscure that its recognition and mastery have become the constant task of politics."

59   'Density of reality' is our translation of what is called *Wirklichkeitsdichte* in Arendt, *Über die Revolution,* 57, which in Arendt, *On Revolution,* 46, is called "a reality peculiar to the political realm alone."

Paradise Lost
Art, Caviar and Irreconcilable Differences
Raha Golestani

A "contested space"[01]—this is how Vali Mahlouji, a London-based curator and art advisor, describes the Shiraz Festival of Arts, which took place in Iran annually from 1967 to 1977. For Mahlouji, proof of the festival's enduringly controversial nature lies in the silence that has shrouded its artistic territory, rendering it an unfairly neglected object of study, an obscure lacuna in pre-revolutionary Iranian history.[02] Mahlouji's project, *The Archeology of the Final Decade*, aims to disrupt this silence by researching, collecting, and recirculating the fragmented, underexposed, and, in many cases, even banned materials related to the festival.

While Mahlouji observes the silence surrounding the festival, the discourse of the Shiraz Festival of Arts can equally be characterized as congested—a cacophony of competing and dispersed voices, narratives, and interpretations that overwhelm its space.[03] The irreconcilability of these narrations has, in part, to do with the ephemeral nature of a performing arts festival, as opposed to a static art object. As Hannah Arendt puts it: while the "arts of making" result in products that persist beyond the creative process, the performing arts, as products of action, are not sustained by a

01   Vali Mahlouji, "Perspectives on the Shiraz Festival: A Radical Third World Re-Writing," in *Iran Modern*, eds. Fereshteh Daftari and Leyla S. Diba (Asia Society, 2013), 87.

02   Vali Mahlouji, "The Shiraz Festival Complexities," interview by Jian Ghomeshi, *Roqe Media*, November 26, 2021, podcast audio, 6:09, https://open.spotify.com/episode/4JaCz5UvZFXa2zevAHyVxl.

03   Mathew Randle-Bent calls Mahlouji the most prominent voice in contemporary discussions of the festival. Mathew Randle-Bent, "'Indigenous Avant-Gardes': The Shiraz Arts Festival and Ritual Performance Theory in 1970s Iran," *Arab Stages* 14 (2023): 2–3.

tangible presence and depend on further acts to ensure their existence and prolong their relevance. Their preservation, Arendt argues, can only occur through the same means that enabled their appearance. They must be re-enacted.[04]

This fragile dependence on further actions seems particularly pronounced in the case of the Shiraz Festival of Arts, which ended abruptly with the 1979 revolution. The festival's material traces were scattered; some were destroyed or removed from public view, some would make it outside the country, while the whereabouts of other fragments remain unclear.[05] To re-stage its space, one must make do with a few low-quality videos of performances and documentaries, pictures, old interviews, festival catalogs, and magazines found in different public and university libraries abroad, written accounts as well as mostly oral histories. However, it is not only the lack of a conclusive archive that complicates the festival's afterlife. Rumors, conspiracies, and speculation have surrounded this iterative space not only as it unfolded but also in its aftermath.

Due to their shared dependence on a publicly organized space and an audience, Arendt identifies a strong kinship between the performing arts and politics.[06] This affinity is driven ad absurdum in the case of the Shiraz Festival of Arts. The troubled nature of this space has much to do with the Shiraz festival's proximity to the 1979 revolution. In her memoirs, Farah Diba, the former queen of Iran who initiated the Festival, recalls how it became associated with the revolution in its afterlife: "Some people later would even claim that the festival paved the way for the Islamic reaction and was, therefore, one of the causes of the overthrow of the monarchy."[07] The historian Houchang Chehabi, who has written extensively on the festival's place in the "revolutionary mythology," claims that it served as a *cause célèbre* in revolutionary discourse.[08] It was even condemned by Khomeini himself,

04   Hannah Arendt, *Between Past and Future: Six Exercises in Political Thought* (The Viking Press, 1961), 153.

05   Mahasti Afshar, "Festival of Arts, Shiraz-Persepolis, 1967–1977," *Iran Namag* 4, no. 2 (2019): 12.

06   Arendt, *Between Past and Future*, 154.

07   Farah Diba, *An Enduring Love: My Life with the Shah, A Memoir* (Miramax, 2004), 233.

who at the time was in exile in Najaf (Iraq). In this light, the festival was later often depicted as an aesthetic mistake with massive political consequences that further alienated the people from the monarchy.[09] Alongside such frequent attributions of direct causality, some interpreted the festival's entanglements with the revolution as a case of (aesthetic) intuitions foreshadowing (political) transformations[10]—a safety warning for how revolutions might be closer than they appear. Either way, having not survived the revolution in one piece, the festival was never able to escape its shadow.

Nonetheless, the festival was not seen exclusively through a revolutionary frame. It would come to mean very different things to very different people: a symbol of decadence and promiscuity, *Westoxication*,[11] "an oppressive regime's public relations scheme"[12] but also "one of the leading theatre festivals in the world,"[13] "a third world re-writing,"[14] and a "culturally democratic space, albeit within an autocratic regime."[15]

08   Houchang Chehabi, "The Shiraz Festival and Its Place in Iran's Revolutionary Mythology," in *The Age of Aryamehr: Late Pahlavi Iran and Its Global Entanglements*, ed. Roham Alvandi (Ginko, 2018), 186, 190.

09   Gholam Reza Afkhami, *The Life and the Times of the Shah* (University of California Press, 2009), 404.

10   Arby Ovanessian, interview by Shirin Sami'i, *Iranian Oral History Project Harvard*, Paris 1983, 26–27, https://fis-iran.org/fa/oral-history/ovanesiyan-arbi/ [my translation].

11   For a broad account of the festival's association with Westoxication, see "Occidentosis and the Shiraz Arts Festival," in *Pahlavi Iran and the Politics of Occidentalism: The Shah and the Rastakhiz Party*, Zhand Shakibi (I.B. Taurus, 2020), 283–301.

12   Chehabi, "The Shiraz Festival and Its Place in Iran's Revolutionary Mythology," 182.

13   Micheal Kirby, "An Editorial: The Shiraz Festival: Politics and Theatre," *The Drama Review: TDR* 20, no. 4 (1976): 2.

14   Mahlouji, "Perspectives on the Shiraz Festival: A Radical Third World Re-Writing," 88.

15   Joshua Charney, "The Shiraz Arts Festival: Cultural Democracy, National Identity, and Revolution in Iranian Performance, 1967–1977," (PhD diss., University of California San Diego, 2020), 15.

While these different visions disagree on the implications of the festival—particularly on the extent to which its fleeting and limited space of appearance succeeded in or fell short of embodying "a kind of theater where freedom could appear"[16]—this essay distances itself from normative readings of both the festival and of Arendt's notion of space of appearance. The opaque nature of this specific space of appearance disarms such dichotomies as free versus unfree, aesthetics versus politics, public versus private, and postcolonial versus Orientalist. Rather than imposing binary interpretations, it is more illuminating to shift the focus to the conditions informing its prism-like nature and the spectrum of responses it generates and sustains. How does the example of the Shiraz Festival of Arts invite such contradictory interpretations? What is the secret to its indeterminacy? How can a performing arts festival take on such political significance, to the point of being forced into an explanatory role for a revolution in its reception?[17] And what does its lingering space of appearance reveal about the complex dynamics between art, politics, and power in pre-revolutionary Iran? Does this space ultimately tell a story about underestimating the political relevance of art or about its instrumentalization for the sake of keeping up appearances?

Back to the Future

The Shiraz Festival of Arts took place over a period of about ten days each summer from 1967 to 1977. It was centered on dance, theater, performance, and music and accompanied by film screenings, exhibitions, symposia, and panel discussions. Instead of the capital, Tehran, the festival was held in and around Shiraz, a location chosen for its greater historical and cultural significance. Shiraz was the city of wine and poetry, famous for being the birthplace of poets such as Hafez and Saadi. Shiraz also provided proximity to monuments such as Persepolis, Pasargadae, Naghsh-e Rostam, Delgosha Garden, and Saraye Moshir, as well as the desert. This unique setting brought art, particularly theatre, out of closed quarters into the open air.[18] During the festival, the whole city would become activated. Monuments like Persepolis hosted larger performances, while smaller performances were staged in cafes,

16
Arendt, *Between Past and Future*, 154.

17
Vali Mahlouji, "Meta-Political Aspirations and Praeternatural Investigations: The Festival of Arts, Shiraz-Persepolis," *Academia.edu*, 2014, 3.

18
Afkhami, *The Life and the Times of the Shah*, 417.

shops, and Pahlavi University. Expanding the already extensive and unconventional public space of the festival, a good
deal of its program was broadcast on national TV.

The international festival was "an unusual hybrid"
aimed at reconciling 'apparent opposites,' namely, the avant-
garde arts of the West and the marginalized traditions of the
East.[19] The festival's mission, formulated in its constitution,
reads: "Given Her Majesty Shahbanu Farah's special attention and interest in promoting art and honoring authentic
national arts, and to elevate the level of art in Iran—honoring the work of Iranian artists, introducing foreign art and
artists to Iran, and acquainting art lovers and enthusiasts
with the artistic expressions of the world—a new organization named the 'Shiraz Arts Festival Organization' is being
formed."[20] This unlikely combination was meant not only to
"shake up people's attitudes"[21] but also to help Iranian artists
overcome an inferiority complex.[22] By putting Iranian artists
on the same stage as Western giants, the festival proposed
a postcolonial alternative to dominant, Eurocentric views
of culture in what Mahlouji calls an embodiment of Homi
Bhabha's "third world re-writing."[23]

However, the festival was not free of Orientalist
tropes. This was evident in the festival's polarized curating
tendencies: East versus West, traditional versus avant-garde,
irrational versus rational, past versus future, authentic versus progressive. In this dynamic, through the gaze of the
Other, the Iranian artists became aware of themselves in a
new light. This confrontation sometimes created anxieties
concerning the loss of self and local traditions in the face of

19   Catherine Gunther Kodat, *Don't Act, Just Dance:
      The Metapolitics of Cold War Culture*
      (Rutgers University Press, 2015), 114.

20   *Shiraz Arts Festival According to SAVAK Documents*
      (Center for Reviewing Historical Documents, 2002), 4.

21   Diba, *An Enduring Love*, 232.

22   Farah Diba, "For the Love of Her People, an Interview With
      Farah Diba About the Pahlavi Programs for the Arts in Iran,"
      interview by Donna Stein in *PERFORMING THE IRANIAN
      STATE: Visual Culture and Representations of Iranian
      Identity*, ed. Staci Gem Scheiwiller (Anthem Press, 2013), 76.

23   Mahlouji, "Perspectives on the Shiraz Festival:
      A Radical Third World Re-Writing," 88.

Western art forms. It would, at times, reinforce self-exoticization and lead to an "invention of tradition" further encouraged by the festival's exotic and historic setting.[24]

The Shah used the same setting for the 2,500[th] anniversary celebrations in October 1971, when the Pahlavis staged a reintroduction of Iran onto the global scene. The notorious "Desert Bash" even made it into the 1980 edition of the *Guinness Book of World Records* as the most extravagant party on record.[25] The celebration aimed to establish a symbolic connection between the Pahlavi regime and the ancient glory of the Achaemenid Empire. During the Persepolis celebrations, the Shah famously held a speech on Cyrus' tomb chamber at Pasargadae, proclaiming in a shaky voice: "Rest in peace, [Cyrus,] for we are awake." The festival would later often be associated and studied in relation to this "self-Orientalizing spectacle," which aimed to assert that Iran had remained true to its cultural heritage while transcending beyond its confinements.[26]

24
Eric Hobsbawm, "Introduction: Inventing Traditions," in *The Invention of Tradition*, eds. Eric Hobsbawm and Terence Ranger (Cambridge University Press, 1983), 2.

25
Abbas Milani, *The Shah* (Palgrave Macmillan, 2011), 321, 338.

[29] Performance of Karlheinz Stockhausen's *Mantra* at the 1972 Shiraz Festival at Saraye Moshir, with the composer handling the electronics from the crowd, while Aloys and Alfons Kontarsky perform on piano.

The festival's program would come to be adorned by the names of Western artists and groups such as Peter Brook, Jerzy Grotowski, Robert Wilson, Iannis Xenakis, the Maurice Béjart ballet, the Merce Cunningham Dance Company, John Cage, Karlheinz Stockhausen, Arthur Rubinstein, Abbey Lincoln, and Max Roach. Some would become regulars, returning multiple summers to create large-scale commissioned pieces inspired by the unique setting of Shiraz. The festival also prioritized South-South connections, exposing Iranians to certain art forms for the first time: Indian Raga music, Bharatanatyam and Kathakali, Qawwali from Afghanistan, Balinese Gamelan, Japanese Nō, Kabuki, and many more.[27] They listened to the music of Ravi Shankar and Ram Narayan and were exposed to Shūji Terayama's experimental theater.

[30]   Dancers from Maurice Béjart's company appear in a photo taken at the Shiraz Festival of Arts.[28]

26   Talinn Grigor, "Orientalism & Mimicry of Selfness: Archeology of the Neo-Achaemenid Style," in *L'Orientalisme architectural entre imaginaires et savoirs*, eds. Nabila Oulebsir and Mercedes Volait (Publications de l'Institut national d'histoire de l'art, 2009), 273, 280.

27   Mahasti Afshar, "Festival of Arts, Shiraz-Persepolis, 1967–1977," 5.

The festival also served as a space to preserve and cultivate local and folkloric Persian traditions. Every night at Hafezieh, it featured performances of traditional Persian music by such artists as Faramarz Payvar, Jalil Shahnaz, Mohammad-Reza Lotfi, and Shajarian. Experimental theater was also promoted, with works by Abbas Nalbandian and Bijan Mofid, while reviving traditions such as Naqqāli, Ruhowsi, and Ta'zieh. Ta'zieh, in particular, was endangered at the time since "because of the ritual's religious character and, more importantly, its history of use in the context of political protest, the practice of ta'ziyeh had been outlawed by the Pahlavi regime since the 1930s."[29]

Unique works emerged from this context, using the intercultural setting to reverse the Babelian confusion. In 1972, Robert Wilson staged *KA MOUNTAIN AND GUARDenia TERRACE: a story about a family and some people changing.* Wilson chose seven foothills for the play, which was performed continuously for a week, twenty-four hours a day, lasting a total of 168 hours. He initially worked with 100 participants, but the number eventually grew to 700. In Wilson's own words:

> At the base of the first hill I erected a sort of tower of Babel that had seven levels. Walking up this scaffolding structure, one could sit and converse with a wide range of people: artists, housewives, teachers, scholars, shepherds, etc. People were talking about anything and everything: politics, art, how to make a pizza, and how to build a house. There was an elderly storyteller from the bazaar telling stories from the past and a housewife from New Jersey conversing with local women from the city of Shiraz. It was a real cross-cultural view of the East and West. …

28   The exact time, place, and specific performance are unknown. It is unclear but possible that the dancer Patrice Touron signed the image. These unknown details reflect the fragmented nature of the festival. The photographer Abbas Hojatpanah notes that all his negatives remain in Iran, and this image is among the few photos he could find from the ballets, but he could not identify further details.

29   Lindsay Goss, "You Are Invited Not to Attend: Answering the Call for a Cultural Boycott of the Shiraz Festival of the Arts," *PERFORMANCE PARADIGM* 14 (2018): 19.

30
Robert Wilson,
"KA MOUNTAIN
AND GUARDenia
TERRACE: A Story
About a Family
and Some People
Changing, A 168-Hour
Play For The 1972
Festival of Shiraz,"
in *Iran Modern*, 95.

31
A. C. H. Smith,
*Orghast at Persepolis:
An International
Experiment in Theatre*
(The Viking Press,
1972), 45.

32
Milani, *The Shah*, 348.

33
Robert Gluck,
"The Shiraz Festival:
Avant-Garde Arts
Performance in 1970s
Iran," *Leonardo* 40,
no. 1 (2007): 20–28, 216.

I cannot imagine anyone today taking such a risk and commissioning a piece like this. There was no censorship, no one telling me I could not do what we did.[30]

Intercultural works and collaborations between Iranian and visiting artists were also encouraged, as seen in *Orghast,* a production between directors Peter Brook, Arby Ovanessian, Geoffrey Reeves, and Andrei Serban with poet Ted Hughes. In *Orghast,* they worked with languages such as Avesta, Greek, and Latin to unearth a "language belonging below the levels where differences appear."[31]

Despite these large-scale and ambitious gestures of reconciliation—reversing the Babelian confusion or digging below the level where differences appear—the Shiraz Festival of Arts is primarily remembered as a site of tension, both during its performances and almost 50 years after its final act. To this day, its unstable space of appearance exhibits immersive interpretive flexibility and hermeneutical openness. In being able to appear so differently to different people, its example speaks of the unique and complex interplay between aesthetics and politics. If we were to imagine these two abstract categories as bound in a contractual relationship—as if in a marriage between two leading powers of pre-revolutionary Iran—then the festival was a singular product of their irreconcilable differences.

Scenes from a Marriage

To understand the diverse nature of responses given to the Shiraz Festival of Arts, one is forced to look into the broader context of artistic expression and authoritarian rule in the pre-revolutionary period. Abbas Milani describes the period between 1965 and 1975 as "a discordant combination of cultural freedoms and political despotism—of increasing censorship against the opposition but increasing freedoms for everyone else."[32] Inconsistencies in the allocation of freedom across these two spheres were grounded in an assumption of the autonomy of the aesthetic sphere, where "artistic expression co-existed in an ultimately untenable balance with political repression."[33]

This discrepancy was rooted in the power distribution in the public sphere between Queen Farah Diba and Mohammad Reza Shah Pahlavi.[34] Mohammad Reza Shah ascended to the throne in 1941 after his father, Reza Shah, was forced to abdicate during the Allied occupation in World War II. Although Iran had claimed neutrality, it was occupied by the Allies due to suspicions of Nazi sympathies. In the early 1950s, Prime Minister Mohammad Mosaddegh nationalized Iranian oil, asserting Iran's right to control its resources and challenging British interests. In response, a 1953 coup organized by the CIA and British intelligence ousted Mosaddegh and consolidated Mohammad Reza Shah's power. His reign, which coincided with a dramatic increase in oil revenues in the 1970s, was marked by the continuation of his father's Westernization policies and his ambition to transform Iran according to his vision of the 'Great Civilization.' In 1975, he established a single-party system with the Resurgence Party, abandoning any pretense of democratic governance.[35]

Farah Diba, the former queen of Iran, was (and is) renowned for her patronage of the arts and culture and for being the driving force behind numerous festivals, museums, and educational institutions. However, it was not only Diba's passion for the arts that characterized her. During this period, Diba emerged as the epitome of good taste. Diba would become famous as a demure and modest fashion icon, wearing the latest hairstyles and haute couture. Yves Saint Laurent designed her wedding dress, and she often wore tiaras designed by Van Cleef & Arpels or Harry Winston.

Diba is frequently depicted in her public persona as "the ideal complementary force to the Shah." For instance, former British ambassador Anthony Parsons described her as "beautiful, artistic, compassionate, and intelligent," emphasizing the different responses evoked by Diba and the Shah: "Where he inspired awe and fear, she inspired love and affection."[36] William Shawcross offered a similar account, portraying Diba as someone who does everything with a pinch of style, "a warm-hearted, rather cultured figure who was much easier with her role than the Shah with his ... She retained something that the Shah had never had—an ability to appear spontaneous and in touch."[37]

34
Diba was introduced to the Shah in 1959 while studying architecture in Paris, and they were soon married. Although Diba was primarily expected to produce a male heir to the monarchy, she would become a cultural force in her own right and be assigned the role of regent.

35
Houchang Chehabi, "Iranian History, 1945–79," in *Iran Modern*, 15.

36
Anthony Parsons, *The Pride and the Fall, Iran 1974–1979* (Jonathan Cape, 1984), 25.

37
William Shawcross, *The Shah's Last Ride* (Simon and Schuster, 1988), 95.

Diba's approachable demeanor, her patronage of the arts, and her soft 'appearance' were often criticized as constituting the glamorous and shiny façade of the Shah's rigorous politics. Perceived as "a symbol of cultural premium placed on appearance and illusion,"[38] Diba was accused of distracting from the social realities of Iran[39] and, in essence, of aestheticizing politics. The Shah and Diba each exerted influence over a different area of the public sphere. In this power dynamic, Diba's activities were often depicted as secondary to those of her husband, and similarly, aesthetics as a mere complement to political power:

> Iranians like to feel they are more European than Oriental, and Farah takes seriously her husband's promise to make Iran the most sophisticated country in Western Asia. She works at it. To match the economic great leap forward of her husband, she has created film and music, and theater festivals, and she has animated this sense of pride and purpose among Iranian artists and musicians.[40]

On the other hand, the Shah, in various accounts, is often characterized by his ignorance of the arts.[41] In a 2014 interview, when asked about her husband's involvement in the Shiraz Festival of Arts, Diba stated: "He didn't see those kinds of things. ... I was the one going to the festival. ... He didn't have time. He had other things to do."[42]

38   Annie Pfeifer, "'Our White Hands,' Iran and Germany's 1968," in *Iran and the West: Cultural Perceptions from the Sasanian Empire to the Islamic Republic,* eds. David Bagot and Margaux Whiskin (I.B. Tauris, 2018), 113.

39   "Abroad, which clothes Farah Diba wears and the name of her hairdresser are well known. But does the world also know that the Iranian army has been waging a brutal campaign against the population of the southern province of Fars?" Bahman Nirumand, *Persien: Modell eines Entwicklungslandes oder Die Diktatur der Freien Welt* (Rowohlt, 1976), 120.

40   Kourosh Abbassi and Tina Ghazimorad, producers, "Shahbanou," 1:12:12, 2016, YouTube, https://www.youtube.com/watch?v=32Uu7SJMUYA.

41   See, for example, Chehabi, "The Shiraz Festival and Its Place in Iran's Revolutionary Mythology," 169.

When Diba, inspired by French festivals such as Nancy and Royan, proposed the idea of the festival to her husband, the Shah was quite content to leave the matter up to her.[43] The irrelevance of the cultural sphere, coupled with the 'feminization' of aesthetics as concerned with appearances (and supposedly unlike politics in that respect), helps explain how it was left to Diba. Some accounts also suggest that it was her reward for tolerating the Shah's extramarital affairs:[44] "One of the things he gave his wife to keep her pacified was a free hand in the fields of her interest. In due time, Farah became a power unto herself."[45] Within the international press, the German daily *Neue Hannoversche Zeitung* similarly employed an infantilizing tone in describing Diba's activities: "The Shiraz Festival is the queen's plaything, and no one is allowed to take it away from her."[46]

Diba's supposedly harmless involvement in her 'fields of interest' and cultural 'hobbies' was seen as aligning with the Shah's reformist 'White Revolution,' which promoted women's rights and education. However, while the desirability of women playing a public role in the Pahlavi era was proclaimed, this opening of the public space to women often remained symbolic and limited.[47] This is evident in an interview conducted by Oriana Fallaci,[48] who had provoked the Shah by alluding to his well-known affairs and womanizing nature:

42   Farah Diba, "Farah Pahlavi," interview by Bob Colacello, *Interview Magazine*, January 8, 2014.

43   Afkhami, *The Life and the Times of the Shah*, 415.

44   Milani, *The Shah*, 362: "The Shah simply smiled, ordered Alam to keep quiet and pay the bill, and said, 'You know I have to live a little too.' Alam clearly understood the Shah's implied message. 'Her Majesty must be allowed to do anything she wants, and her entourage engage in any shitty work so that the Shah hears less grumbling.' Here then was the political price the Shah was paying for his philandering."

45   Afkhami, *The Life and the Times of the Shah*, 54.

46   Reinhard Beuth, *Neue Hannoversche Zeitung*, 1977, cited in *Shiraz Arts Festival According to SAVAK Documents*, 380.

47   Talinn Grigor, *Building Iran* (Periscope, 2009), 176.

48   Oriana Fallaci was an Italian author and journalist who conducted various bold interviews with (controversial) world leaders such as Indira Gandhi, Henry Kissinger, Muammar Gaddafi, and, ironically in the Iranian context, both Mohammad Reza Pahlavi and Khomeini.

49
Mohammad Reza
Pahlavi,
"Interview With
Mohammad Reza
Pahlavi,"
in *Interviews with
History,* Oriana Fallaci
(Liveright, 1976),
271–72.

50
Grigor,
Building Iran, 176.

51
Abbas Milani,
*Eminent Persians:
The Men and Women
Who Made Modern
Iran, Volume 1:
1941–1979*
(Syracuse University
Press, 2008), 167.

52
Grigor,
Building Iran, 184–86.

I don't underrate them [women]; they've profited more than anyone else from my White Revolution. ... And let's not forget I'm the son of the man who took away women's veils in Iran. But I wouldn't be sincere if I stated I'd been influenced by a single one of them. Nobody can influence me, nobody. Still less a woman. Women are important in a man's life only if they're beautiful and charming and keep their femininity and ... This business of feminism, for instance. What do these feminists want? What do you want? You say equality. Oh! I don't want to seem rude, but ... You're equal in the eyes of the law but not, excuse my saying so, in ability. No. You've never produced a Michelangelo or a Bach. ... You've produced nothing great, nothing![49]

Since the Shah had excluded both aesthetics and women from influential roles, overlooking their potential power, aesthetics during this period underwent a process of 'feminization.' This 'feminization' stemmed from its intertwinement with the figure of Diba and the assumption that aesthetics, like women, was politically inconsequential and irrelevant. Ironically, both turned out not to be harmful for PR purposes, instead helping Iran imagine and present itself as a sophisticated 'Great Civilization.'

This 'feminization of aesthetics' offered Diba a means of exercising indirect political power through culture, by allowing the appearance of things that the politics of the day would typically constrain.[50] Together with their partitioned exercise of power in the public realm, Diba and the Shah personified the tension between two never directly articulated paradigms that coexisted in Iran in the late 1960s and 1970s in response to a rapidly changing geopolitical situation.[51] This tension is often framed as a clash between two modes of modernity. The art historian Talinn Grigor, for instance, distinguishes Diba's "feminized version of modernity" from the Shah's "masculinist paradigm of Western modernism." While the Shah's policy involved bulldozing cultural heritage sites to make way for Western-looking buildings, Diba's version of modernity focused on preservation, and she became known for halting many of these aggressive modernization projects.[52]

[31] Mannequins displaying the attire
of the royal couple at the Museum of Royal Clothes
in Niavaran Palace, Tehran.

The Shiraz Festival of Arts would become Diba's most pro-vocative legacy. While often discussed as the site where the rift between the Pahlavis and the public became visible, it also marked the space where the contrast between the visions endorsed by each of these two figures became most appar-ent.[53] A posthumously published private remark by the Shah frames the festival as the object of an ongoing marital conflict:

I don't understand what use this festival is to us. Its costs are outrageous, and I doubt it has any benefits. They invite low-profile artists who nobody knows, stuff caviar down the throats of a few foreign journalists, and shower them with various gifts. Then, when they return to their countries, they spit on us and criticize us… But, well, the Shahbanou is very insistent.[54]

This division was also reflected in the institutional order of the festival. It fell under the supervision of Reza Ghotbi and the NIRT (National Iranian Radio and Television) rather than the Ministry of Arts and Culture, which was subject to stricter censorship. Joshua Charney describes the festival as embodying multiple paradoxes, as "An artistically liberated zone within an autocracy, and a celebrator of Iranian traditions during an era of Westernization."[55] The festival became known as an enclave, as a paradise[56] garden in the midst of a desert.

In this logic, the festival's singular dynamics and its restrained, feminized space of appearance were perceived as confirming Arendt's verdict that "Freedom, wherever it existed as a tangible reality, has always been spatially limited."[57] The festival's location in Shiraz, once described by Diba as an "oasis of nature and culture,"[58] limited in time to eleven

53 "In the eyes of some ministers and advisors to the king, the Shiraz Festival symbolized too great a desire for openness to the outside world. Thus Minister of Court Asadollah Alam, whose culture and intelligence I much admired, reproached me in his memoirs for my 'misplaced liberal ideas.' Many others like him saw a divergence between my husband's political line and the one I followed." Diba, *An Enduring Love*, 234.

54 Houchang Nahavandi, آن روزها (Sherkat-e-Ketab, 2005), 166 [my translation].

55 Charney, "The Shiraz Arts Festival: Cultural Democracy, National Identity, and Revolution in Iranian Performance, 1967–1977," 3.

56 'Paradise' derives from the Avestan *paridaēza,* an ancient Persian concept of an enclosed garden. Dating back to the first millennium BC, these gardens were an integral part of Persian architecture, as evidenced by sites such as Pasargadae and Persepolis. Mehrdad Fakour, "GARDEN i. ACHAEMENID PERIOD," in *Encyclopaedia Iranica,* 2012, https://www.iranicaonline.org/articles/garden-i.

57 Hannah Arendt, *On Revolution* (Penguin Books, 1965), 275.

58 Diba, *An Enduring Love,* 228.

fleeting interventions each summer, could be seen as aligning with Arendt's metaphor of "oases in a desert"[59]—existing inside an autocratic system while somehow operating outside its rules. As Arendt argues, tyrannies are not necessarily marked by sterility; rather, the "arts may flourish under these conditions if the ruler is 'benevolent' enough to leave his subjects alone in their isolation."[60]

Whether the festival could be perceived in such a subversive light was itself hotly debated, both during and after the event. Some argued that it was not only the 'benevolence' of the rulers that informed the festival's relative openness but also the co-optation of public space with a view to projecting a positive image internationally. Yet it is precisely the presumption of the festival as an autonomous aesthetic sphere—one able to transcend the unstable structures in which it was embedded—that Houchang Chehabi underlines as the source of its vulnerability[61] and, we might add, of its political power. This might indeed help explain the festival's disproportionate provocations, which manifest in a space of appearance that continues to be troubled even today.

Trouble in Paradise

Tensions surrounding the festival took various forms, ranging from confrontations and negative press coverage to boycotts and threats. Over time, they intensified, extending beyond domestic debates and taking on a more international character. The festival's ambitious project of curating intercultural works in visible public spaces came up against differing expectations and sensibilities, as well as conflicting views on common sense, taboos, and social dos and don'ts.

One notable controversy was the festival's staging and televising of Ta'zieh. Critics argued that the theatricalization of Ta'zieh, rather than preserving the tradition, was detrimental to its essence, which depended on improvisation and community participation.[62] Another uneasy moment would arise in 1971 when Iannis Xenakis presented the specially commissioned *Polytope of Persepolis* at the festival's opening ceremony. This one-hour open-air spectacle, featuring light, sound, and movement amid the ruins of Persepolis, was accompanied by 150 children, each carrying a torch, who walked through the space and finally stood in formation to spell, in Persian,

59
Arendt,
On Revolution, 275.

60
Hannah Arendt,
The Human Condition
(The University of
Chicago Press, 2018),
203.

61
Chehabi,
"The Shiraz Festival
and Its Place in
Iran's Revolutionary
Mythology," 192.

the phrase "We bear the light of the earth." Xenakis, who claimed that the piece was "a tribute to Iran's past and her great Zoroastrian and Manichean revolutionaries,"[63] was surprised to find that the work drew different associations from the Iranian audience. One newspaper printed the blunt headline: "Xenakis Attempts to Burn Persepolis."[64] For many Iranians, Xenakis' piece evoked Alexander the Great's conquest of Persepolis, and the imagery fed into the discourse of Westoxication during the Pahlavi era.

Gharbzadegi (غرب‌زدگی), often translated as 'Westoxication' or 'Occidentosis,' was a term coined by Ahmad Fardid and popularized by Jalal Al-e Ahmad in an essay in which he describes it as a disease afflicting Iran. Published in 1962 and written in the aftermath of World War II and the traumatic coup against Mossadegh, the essay reflects growing anti-colonial sentiments. It echoes broader cultural anxieties characteristic of its period, criticizing the East's inferiority complex, uncritical imitation, and acceptance of Western norms.[65]

The Shiraz festival's programming and expenditure on Western artists were criticized as manifestations of Westoxication, misplaced priorities,[66] and "elitist exclusivity."[67] As the Iranian composer Alireza Mashayekhi remarked:

62 For more on the debates surrounding Ta'zieh look at Babak Rahimi, "Staging Ta'ziyeh: Aryanism, Heritage, and the Shiraz Arts Festival, 1967–1977," virtual lecture, September 27, 2023, posted on October 9, 2023 by the Mossavar-Rahmani Center at Princeton University, YouTube, 1:00:20, https://www.youtube.com/watch?v=leUR-rk8dBs.

63 Iannis Xenakis, *Music and Architecture* (Pendragon Press, 2008), 316, 219, 223.

64 Cited in Charney, "The Shiraz Arts Festival: Cultural Democracy, National Identity, and Revolution in Iranian Performance, 1967–1977," 91.

65 Al-e Ahmad's concept of Westoxication was incorporated into the rhetoric of the Islamic Republic after the revolution. However, Hamid Dabashi and other scholars argue that his ideas should be distinguished from their later use, as he did not witness the revolution or its aftermath. See Hamid Dabashi, *The Last Muslim Intellectual: The Life and Legacy of Jalal Al-e Ahmad* (Edinburgh University Press, 2021), 128, 165.

66 Chehabi, "The Shiraz Festival and Its Place in Iran's Revolutionary Mythology," 168.

67 Afkhami, *The Life and the Times of the Shah*, 418.

"In a country that has no tradition in Classical music and no acquaintance with contemporary music, the festival had the appearance of an invasion. Sociologically, at a time when we needed a modest electronic studio, we should not have spent a fortune to invite big foreign names."[68] Gholam Hossein Saedi echoed this sentiment:

> In another context, the festival might have been received differently, … but in that context, it felt like a humiliation. … During the opening in Persepolis, when, for example, Peter Brook was supposed to come, the poor village people would gather and look from out-side and see that some cars and Rolls-Royces and BMWs arrive. People with fancy crazy clothes, guards everywhere … they would sit in their houses and ask themselves, where did all these people go? It had become a Mount Olympus in its own right and humi-liated the people.[69]

The festival's most provocative moment came in 1977 with the play *Pig, Child, Fire!*, performed by the Hungarian *Squat Theatre*. Famous for their controversial works, the *Squat*'s "appearance in a display window of a shop on a busy street in Shiraz felt like their greatest provocation to date."[70] The play was staged in a shop window on Ferdowsi Street, al-lowing passersby to catch a glimpse of the play. The audi-ence was seated inside the shop, gazing outside towards the street, which became "an extension of the stage or a living background."[71] Gholam Reza Afkhami, in his biography of the Shah, later wrote: "In hindsight, it would have been politically wise not to have shown it."[72] The reaction to the play spiraled

68 Bob Gluck, "Conversations with Alireza Mashayekhi, Iranian Composer: A New East-West Synthesis," based on conversations via email in December 2006 and January 2007, https://econtact.ca/14_4/gluck_mashayekhi.html.

69 Gholam Hossein Saedi, interview by Zia Sedghi, *Iranian Oral History Project Harvard,* Paris 1982, https://nrs.harvard.edu/urn-3:FHCL:627504, 22 [my translation].

70 Pamela Karimi, *Alternative Iran: Contemporary Art and Critical Spatial Practice* (Stanford University Press, 2020), 215.

71 Anna Koós, "Squat Theatre: Staging Life/Living on Stage," *AJ: A Journal of Performance and Art* 35, no. 3 (2013): 24.

72 Afkhami, *The Life and the Times of the Shah,* 420.

out of control, reaching newspaper headlines. A *Keyhan* newspaper headline on the play read: "Avant-garde Art or Showing Sexual Acts on the Street?"[73] William Shawcross's account reflects the spread of rumors about the play:

> It reached a climax in 1977 when another troupe of actors took over a shop in the main street of Shiraz, hard by the mosque, and performed in the shop and on the pavement a play that involved a full frontal rape and lewd acts between naked, consenting actors. Such a performance would have led to scandal and the arrest of the actors in any English or American provincial street. Performed in Shiraz, it aroused enormous anger and offense.[74]

[32]   Poster for Squat Theatre's controversial play *Pig, Child, Fire!* performed at the 1977 Shiraz Art Festival.

This account is dismissed by several scholars, including Mahasti Afshar, who personally attended the play and described these claims as exaggerated and untrue.[75] Nevertheless, the alleged rape scene further fueled the narrative of a broader cultural invasion by the festival.[76] The reports enraged the clergy, who were also offended by the festival's overlap with Ramadan, seeing it as another manifestation of its anti-Islamic ethos. Soon, Ayatollahs Mahallati and Dastgheib launched attacks on the festival, threatening to shut down the bazaars and mosques in protest. According to a report issued by the Bureau for Intelligence and Security of the State (SAVAK),

73   "Avant-garde Art or Showing Sexual Acts on the Streets?," *Keyhan*, August 23, 1977.

74   Shawcross, *The Shah's Last Ride*, 28.

75   Mahasti Afshar, جشن هنر شیراز-تخت جمشید، ۱۳۴۶-۱۳۵۶ (Iran Namag, 2023), 150.

76   Bijan Saffari, interview by Shirin Sami'i, *Iranian Oral History Project Harvard*, Paris 1983, https://nrs.harvard.edu/urn-3:FHCL: 627504, 25–29 [my translation].

On 25/09/1977, Mr. Seyyed Abdolhossein Dastgheib, during a speech at the Jameh Mosque of Shiraz, stated, 'I heard something. Pig feast! Pig feast! It has a strange name. Those who go here, male and female together, are inferior to pigs. Damn them. Its founder is a pig. Curse them.'

The news duly reached Khomeini in exile, who condemned the festival from Najaf: "You do not know what kind of immorality has recently begun in Iran... They showed sexual acts in front of all the people! And [the gentlemen] remained silent."[77]

Beyond domestic debates, the Shiraz Festival of Arts also became the subject of international controversy, peaking in 1976 with a boycott led by Iranian poet Reza Baraheni and critic and playwright Eric Bentley. For them, the festival functioned "as a deliberate effort on the part of a repressive government to deflect accusations of human rights abuses while fostering a national image of prestige and sophistication."[78] These sentiments had already provoked confrontations with artists participating in the festival. The "pleasure paradise"[79] was proving to be 'difficult.' During a panel talk with Jerzy Grotowski, a group of students challenged him: "You are a socialist person coming from a socialist country. If you believe in this idea, why are you destroying this belief by coming to an Imperialist country and performing a performance here?" To which Grotowski supposedly answered: "If you think like this, give up theatre and take up a gun."[80]

These confrontations would take on a more public and international character in 1976, when Baraheni, who had been imprisoned himself, highlighted the oppression in Iran under the Shah's secret police and the increasing number of political prisoners: "I would urge all artists who believe in freedom for others as well as for themselves to boycott Iran."[81] Baraheni met with Cunningham and Cage, ultimately convincing them to boycott the festival.[82] Baraheni and Bentley argued that the gains of a cultural boycott as "an attempt at the institutionalization of embarrassment" would be tangible, especially for a regime concerned with keeping up appearances.

77
Shiraz Arts Festival According to SAVAK Documents, 395, 391, 404 [my translation].

78
Goss "You Are Invited Not to Attend," 11.

79
Negar Azimi, "Good Intentions," in *Frieze* 137, March 2011.

80
Shamohammadloo and Bozorgmehr, interview by Masoud Najafi Ardabilli cited in Masoud Najafi Ardabili, *Grotowski in Iran,* (Peter Lang, 2019).

81
Reza Baraheni, "We Who Have Been In the Shah's Prisons Are Grateful to Marion Javits," interview by Nat Hentoff, *The Village Voice,* February 2, 1976, 15.

82
Reza Baraheni and Gregg E. Gorton, "Iran Boycott; An Exchange," *The New York Review,* November 25, 1976.

[33] Performance by Merce Cunningham Dance Company
at Persepolis during the 1972 Shiraz Arts Festival.

83
Victor S. Navasky,
"Boycott. The Moral
Question. The Polit-
ical Question. The
Practical Question,"
The New York Times,
August 15, 1976, 2–4.

84
Arendt,
On Revolution, 275.

85
Kirby, "An Editorial:
The Shiraz Festival:
Politics and
Theatre," 2–3.

The public call for a boycott elicited varied responses from participating artists, revealing broader perceptions concerning the entanglements of aesthetics and politics that extended far beyond Shiraz. Here, the very idea of the arts as "oases in a desert"[84] was directly questioned. While artistic spaces may never be untouched by their political circumstances, must they inevitably be complicit in the same unjust structures they inhabit, be it in Shiraz or elsewhere? Or is it possible to imagine these spaces not as ignorant of their surroundings but as potentially subversive? What is more fatal: the aestheticization of politics or destroying the only sites where subversion might seek refuge?

Many artists rejected the boycott for different reasons. Critic Michael Kirby articulated a recurring argument: "The purpose of the boycott of Shiraz (and the boycott of the Olympics by the African nations) was political. I do not believe in mixing theatre (or sports) and politics."[85] Merce Cunningham echoed this position: "My work is not concerned with politics ... and I have always felt it should be free to be shown in any place that is made open to it, whether that is a gym in a Detroit high school or an open-air theater in Shiraz."[86]

While some argued by insisting on the autonomy of the aesthetic sphere, Xenakis, who was in talks to establish an art center for fundamental research in audio-visual arts in Shiraz, took a different approach. In an open letter to *Le Monde,* he depicted the boycott as hypocritical:

> Today when it is impossible to name one single country that is truly free and without multifaceted compromises, without any surrender of principles. 'Democracy' is a fallacy, an artificially sweetened mythology in the mouths of all regimes … Must I couple every country with its own cancer?[87]

The third argument against the boycott was that participation in the festival would be more subversive than staying away. This view stressed the "political power in the misuse of what a regime declares an urban space to be."[88] The festival is often credited with fostering critical works that could evade censorship to some extent. Plays such as Bijan Mofid's *City of Tales* (1968), Abbas Nalbandian's *A Modern, Profound, and Important Research into the Fossils of the 25ᵗʰ Geological Era* (1968), and Esmaeel Khalaj's *Killing Friday* (1973) were made possible by the festival's relatively open conditions under NIRT. In her diaries, Diba accordingly emphasizes her view of the festival as a space where the opposition could appear,[89] reinforcing the idea that it was a "liberal space within a dictatorship."[90]

Despite the relative openness, outsiders did not miss the festival's heavily governed nature. Carolyn Brown, a member of the Merce Cunningham Dance Company, recalls how the artists would each receive their "'guide,' a euphemism for the male uniformed guard with a lethal-looking gun who guarded our trips to the toilet, to the stage, to wherever we might need to go."[91]

Other artists critically engaged with the political reality of the country they were visiting using the advantages of their "outsider's pass."[92] *Fire* by the *Bread and Puppet Theatre* is often cited in this context. The group, having become more familiar with the situation in Iran, is said to have

86
Cited in Navasky, "Boycott," 2.

87
Xenakis, *Music and Architecture,* 311, 233.

88
Jacques Rancière and Mark Foster Gage, "Politics Equals Aesthetics," in *Aesthetics Equals Politics: New Discourses across Art, Architecture, and Philosophy,* ed. Mark Foster Gage (MIT Press, 2019), 14.

89
Diba, *Enduring Love,* 233.

90
Mahlouji, "Perspectives on the Shiraz Festival: A Radical Third World Re-Writing," 91.

91
Carolyn Brown, *Chance and Circumstance: Twenty Years with Cage and Cunningham* (Alfred A. Knopf, 2007), 501–02.

92
Goss, "You Are Invited Not to Attend," 18.

93
Mahasti Afshar,
جشن هنر شیراز-تخت
جمشید، ۱۳۴۶-۱۳۵۶،
163.

94
Mel Gordon,
theater critic and
director, cited in
Robert Coe,
"Boycott Takes
Pizzaz Out of
Shiraz Festival,"
Soho Weekly, 1976,
cited in Goss,
"You Are Invited
Not to Attend," 22.

95
Smith,
Orghast at Persepolis,
259–260.

96
Goss,
"You Are Invited
Not to Attend," 24.

97
*Shiraz Arts Festival
According to SAVAK
Documents,* 434, 441,
443, 453.

read a statement protesting the repression of political opponents in Iran before each performance.[93] In addition to the subversive character of the art itself, the very presence of the outsider's gaze was discussed as a cause of temporary freedom, as noted in this account, where going to Shiraz becomes almost a heroic act: "'Western journalists do a lot of good,' says Gordon, an ex-SDS [Students for a Democratic Society] member. 'It's like an oasis for Iranians who are not free to discuss politics the rest of the year.'"[94] Peter Brook further argued that the presence of foreign artists enabled a negotiation with dominant powers:

> The desert island in which one can work outside a complex, largely repressive social machine does not exist. ... Before leaving Tehran, I was able to have an hour and a half alone with the Queen, when I seized the opportunity to say what had to be said on every level of Persian life, starting with the censorship, without frills, without beating around the bush, directly to a person who, within a restricted field of movement, has got more influence than anyone in the country. ... We exploited the situation given to us to draw home to them what we consider should be said at least as much as they could exploit the external aspects of our work to fit in with their general world-publicity.[95]

Those in favor of the boycott argued against this compromise, citing the high price for appearing at the festival, including self-censorship, as well as the cannibalistic nature of such a space of appearance, which ultimately might subsume even the most subversive content into its overarching logic. Instead of striving for fleeting moments of political freedom, these critics suggested that the more fitting response would be to disappear completely through "the artistic act ... of not making art."[96]

The last planned iteration of the festival, which would have seen Pina Bausch and Yoshi Oida come to Iran, never took place. For months, it was surrounded by clouds of uncertainty. Posters were printed but never distributed to avoid further provocation.[97] Amid growing protests and security concerns, the event was ultimately canceled. In the words of Bijan Saffari: "What was happening in the streets was much more compelling, and people would no longer pay for tickets to go watch theater ... The main show had spilled into the streets instead of remaining in the theater hall."[98]

Looking back at the festival after its appearance and disappearance confronts us with multiple paradoxes. Its divisive space resists the relief of closure, constantly oscillating between grief and grievance, subject to melancholic sighs of what-ifs but also scapegoating cries. Feminized and confined to harmless aesthetic aspirations, appearances make for the best hideouts. While often famous for concealing 'realities,' their dismissal as superficial and inconsequential can ironically transform them into a domain of subversion. The festival's example provides us with a manual for where to hide things best: on the surface.[99]

98
Saffari, interview, 18.

99
Cf. Hugo von Hofmannsthal, *Buch der Freunde* (Insel Verlag, 1922), 56.

When Constantinople Was a Center of Central Europe (We Were Best Friends)

Merve Yıldırım

01
This text is based on sections of my master's thesis research at Goethe University Frankfurt.

02
Karl-Heinz Ziegler, "Deutschland und das Osmanische Reich in ihren völkerrechtlichen Beziehungen," *Archiv des Völkerrechts* 35, no. 3 (1997): 259. All translations from German and Turkish are my own unless otherwise noted.

Looking back at the friendship between Germany and Türkiye, before the establishment of their respective modern states and constitutions, the first written documentation of this relationship can be traced to the Habsburg Emperor Matthias.[01] In 1616, he apostrophized his counterpart Sultan Ahmet as "the Turk, our neighbor and friend" to ratify the peace between the then neighboring empires.[02] Over the next decades and centuries, this mention was followed by other mutual declarations, treaties, and diplomatic gifts with or in the name of friendship. Although this concept of friendship remained a constant amid their otherwise differing trajectories, one particular moment stands out. Exactly 300 years after the first official reference by Emperor Matthias, moving towards a point of concrete manifestation, an attempt was made to give this abstract friendship a home and a material foundation in Constantinople: the construction of a *Haus der Freundschaft/Dostluk Yurdu* (House of Friendship).

Conducting such an effort in the midst of the Great War may seem unexpected and certainly bold. The project exemplifies the paradox of seeking to provide stability to something often lacking permanence, physicality to something inherently relational, and appearance to something not necessarily visible. Yet, given the specificity of a German-Turkish friendship and the unprecedented nature of such a building, its intended construction appears more experimental than anything else—an effort to enact the proximity, similarity, and familiarity between two entities that had historically lacked all three.

It was in order to give material permanence to a longstanding friendship that, in 1916, the *Deutsch-Türkische Vereinigung* (German Turkish Union, hereafter 'Union') commissioned the *Deutscher Werkbund* (German Association of

Craftsmen) to organize a competition among selected architects for a building to represent the ties between the German and Ottoman Empires. But within two years, both empires had been defeated, changing the financial conditions and possibilities as well as the political intentions and goals. As a result, the construction of the House of Friendship never made it past the laying of the foundation stone. Today, all that remains is a street sign marking the planned building site. And yet, what does this sign still signify to anyone other than a short street, a mere 85 meters long?

Against this background, it becomes clear that the project needs to be understood not only as a material point of intersection of the history, politics, and culture of the two empires on a horizontal level but also, vertically, as their attempt to transfer the idea of their abstract relationship from a state level to the general public. Stimulated by a concrete object to be experienced and sensed, official relations were supposed to be "fueled by the will of the citizens of both nations to come close and remain close."[03] Although the House never materialized, even today the 'friendship' seems to be more than just a (forgotten) memory, as former German Chancellor Olaf Scholz emphasized on the occasion of the devastating earthquake in southern Türkiye in 2023: "we are true friends."[04]

Perhaps the lasting nature of this friendship makes it more surprising that no 'house' for this 'friendship' has ever been attempted again, and that the history of what would have been a shared space remains largely overlooked and neglected. Indeed, especially since the 1961 bilateral recruitment agreement, which established Turks as the largest minority group in Germany, ties between the two countries have only deepened.[05] The House of Friendship would have symbolically integrated not only two cultures, but also (parts of) Europe and Asia into a new front "facing a whole world."[06] But the memory of Constantinople—today's Istanbul—as a center of such a union against the West was either successfully suppressed or gradually lost its appeal. And at this point, the question arises: was Constantinople really the only place and 1916 the only time to project a house dedicated to German-Turkish friendship between Germany and Türkiye, and, if so, why?

03
Deutscher Werkbund and Deutsch-Türkische Vereinigung, *Haus der Freundschaft: Ein Wettbewerb deutscher Architekten, mit einer Einführung von Theodor Heuss* (F. Bruckmann, 1918), 5.

04
Die Bundesregierung, *"Kanzler kompakt: Wahre Freunde helfen einander,"* posted February 18, 2023, https://www.bundesregierung.de/breg-de/suche/kanzler-kompakt-erdbeben-2166198, 2:16.

05
Bundeszentrale für politische Bildung (bpb), "Bevölkerung mit Migrations-hintergrund," April 24, 2024, https://www.bpb.de/kurz-knapp/zahlen-und-fakten/soziale-situation-in-deutschland/61646/bevoelkerung-mit-migrationshinter grund/.

06
Werkbund and Vereinigung, *Haus der Freundschaft*, 47.

Building a Friendship

Sultan Muhammed V.

[34] Emperor Wilhelm II in Turkish
Field Marshal uniform at Dolmabahçe
Palace in Istanbul (October 15, 1917).

[35] Sultan Mehmed V was appointed
Prussian Field Marshal by the
Emperor (1916).

07
'Germany' refers here
to the German nation-
state established
in 1871 as well as to
its predecessors.

In order to follow the paths that led the German and Turkish empires to each other as *friends* and the exceptional endeavor to materialize their friendship in a 'house' within a specific time and place, it is important to understand the conditions that each empire faced on the eve of the Great War. As we have seen, the friendship between Germany[07] and the Ottoman Empire can be traced back to earlier centuries, when the word "friend" was first used by the Germans to address the Turkish partner in a treaty. This agreement was reaffirmed in subsequent treaties, but it was in the *Friendship and Trade Treaty* of 1761 between Prussia and the Ottoman Empire that the word "friendship" first appeared in the title of a treaty. Thus, the reference to friendship shifted from a mere personal address and title to a term that characterized and named the official state relations between the two sides. 'Friendship' was now established as a contractual framework and political reality. The economic connection this shift brought paved the way for a new geopolitical space that was to enter the global dynamic. Although the treaty's impact was initially discernible primarily in terms of trade and travel, it set the direction for the expansion of affordances, that is, the increasing potential actions and possibilities within the established space and environment[08]—in *legal* terms of friendship.[09]

The relationship further intensified with the proclamation of the German Empire in 1871 and, even more importantly, the accession of Emperor Wilhelm II in 1888, as did the meaning and value of this specific bilateral friendship. During his reign, the emperor would make three visits to the Ottoman Empire, the first in the year following his coronation. After his first visit to Constantinople, the existing *Friendship and Trade Agreement* of 1761 was expanded to include the German Empire and further augmented as the *German-Turkish Friendship, Trade and Shipping Treaty* of 1890.[10] These agreements solidified into a framework for economic and political cooperation while maintaining their reference to friendship.[11]

08   Originally developed by psychologist James J. Gibson, the theory of affordances is a concept in the field of perception that describes the potential actions that an environment or object offers to an individual. In the context of space and architecture, affordances refer to the ways in which the design and features of a built environment enable or constrain the behavior of its occupants.

09   From a legal perspective, it is noteworthy that, considering the Ottoman Empire's sharia-based legal system—which traditionally categorized territories as *Dar al-Islam* (under Islamic rule) and *Dar al-Harb* (outside Islamic governance and potential conflict zones)—Güneş Işıksel highlights how friendship served as a strategic framework to legitimize sustained peaceful relations with non-Muslim states. For an overview of the meaning and practice of friendship in the Ottoman Empire specifically, see Güneş Işıksel, "Hierarchy and Friendship: Ottoman Practices of Diplomatic Culture and Communication (1290s–1600)," *The Medieval History Journal* 22, no. 2 (2019): 12–13.

10   Ziegler, "Deutschland und das Osmanische Reich," 261, 270.

11   Around this time, the rhetoric of friendship in international treaties was frequently employed to formalize alliances and colonial arrangements, often serving to obscure underlying power asymmetries and strategic interests. For a concise overview of the use of friendship rhetoric in international treaties, see Heather Devere et al., "A History of the Language of Friendship in International Treaties," *International Politics* 48 (2011).

12
Ziegler,
"Deutschland und das
Osmanische Reich,"
269.

13
İlber Ortaylı,
*Osmanlı
İmparatorluğu'nda
Alman Nüfuzu*
(İletişim Yayınları,
2014), 94.

14
The fountain,
originally intended
to be completed for
the 25th anniversary
of Sultan Abdülhamid
II's accession (Sep-
tember 1, 1900), was
officially inaugurated
on Emperor Wilhelm's
birthday (January 27,
1901). See Meryem
Müzeyyen Fındıkgil
Doğuoğlu, "19. Yüzyıl
İstanbul'unda Alman
Mimari Etkinliği
[German Architectural
Activity in 19th-century
İstanbul]" (PhD diss.,
İstanbul Teknik
Üniversitesi, 2002),
244.

Wilhelm II's visits to the Ottoman Empire in 1889 and 1898 were crucial in transforming diplomatic relations into a more personal alliance. It was due to the personal relationship and trust between the emperor and Sultan Abdülhamid II that the friendship gained a new symbolic quality.[12] During his second visit in 1898, Wilhelm II was received "not with diplomatic displays of friendship, but with out-of-control displays of friendship," as the Turkish historian İlber Ortaylı points out.[13]

[36] Before the opening ceremony of the German
Fountain on Emperor Wilhelm's birthday
(January 27, 1901).

The spectacle of this public display and performance suggested the kind of alliance aimed for: an emotional affinity between peoples rather than merely a political relationship between two imperial rulers. The same visit also marked the donation of the German Fountain, built in the historic center of Constantinople, which foreshadowed the House of Friendship in its materiality, locality and meaning.[14] The fountain not only symbolically broke ground for this friendship's public presentation and reception, it also inaugurated a spatial aesthetic targeting the perception of the local public. Since the abstract and symbolic relations of friendship find a material point of reference in the fountain, it serves as a site of encounter, inviting every (Turkish) passerby into a metaphoric space of friendship.

What We Talk About
When We Talk About Friendship

Of course, these visits were neither based on nor motivated by personal, emotional affection. Instead, they were the result of a powerful pro-colonial lobby influencing both the emperor and the bureaucracy, and supporting their quest to expand Germany's cultural, economic, and political influence.[15] As such, this period marked the beginning of what has been described as a *Drang nach Osten* (Drive to the East), moving away from Bismarck's cautious strategy of balancing and toward a more assertive imperial influence—especially in the Ottoman Empire.[16] Representative of this course was the initiation of strategic infrastructure projects during this period, notably the Berlin-Baghdad railway, which facilitated access, movement, and transportation in the region. While stabilizing the integrity of the Ottoman Empire, the concessions granted effectively allowed the railroad to become an instrument of informal empire-building, extending German influence, presence, and profits. The orientation towards the East, however, was not simply a positive action, motivated by imperial ambitions or "colonial desire."[17] It was also a reaction to external pressure following the establishment of the Triple Entente between France, Britain, and Russia in 1907. Along with Germany's ambition of gaining parity with other colonial powers, further strengthening of economic and political-diplomatic ties with the Ottoman Empire was a strategic response to the isolation created by the Entente.

Conversely, for the Ottomans, the motivation behind official rapprochement with Germany was driven neither by expansionism nor by isolation; rather, it was a response to the encirclement and the subsequent concentration of Western interests upon the future of the Ottoman Empire. The central powers' discourse on the Ottoman Empire, as encapsulated in the *question d'Orient,* occurred in the context of the strategic and political challenges faced by the Empire as a result of significant territorial losses and increasing foreign intervention in its affairs.[18] Realizing that it could no longer remain neutral or divert foreign interests by playing them off against each other, Türkiye adopted a policy of friendship in order to break its own encirclement and decided to approach Germany as the least threatening actor—the one with the

15
Suzanne L. Marchand, *German Orientalism in the Age of Empire: Religion, Race, and Scholarship* (Cambridge University Press/German Historical Institute, 2009), 336.

16
Malte Fuhrmann, *Der Traum vom deutschen Orient: Zwei deutsche Kolonien im Osmanischen Reich 1851–1918* (Campus Verlag, 2006), 152–54.

17
Malte Fuhrmann, "Anatolia as a Site of German Colonial Desire and National Re-awakenings," *New Perspectives on Turkey* 41 (2009): 124.

18
Mustafa Gencer, "Osmanlı-Alman Münasebetleri Çerçevesinde 'Şark Meselesi,'" in *Türkler Ansiklopedisi*, vol. 1, eds. Hasan Celal Güzel, Kemal Çiçek, and Salim Koca (Yeni Türkiye Yayınları, 2002), 45.

19
Gencer, *Osmanlı-
Alman Münasebetleri*,
50–51.

20
Ortaylı, *Osmanlı
İmparatorluğu'nda
Alman Nüfuzu*, 81.

fewest colonies.[19] Within this framework of peaceful policy, the sultan took an open and welcoming stance towards the German alliance.[20] Shared by many circles, this sentiment was not merely strategic but was also actively reinforced through narratives of cultural affinity in the Ottoman press, which idealized Germany as a natural ally: "The courage, bravery, and high qualities of the Ottomans are also found in the Germans. These two peoples were created practically identical to each other. Ottomans remember the German name with respect and affection."[21]

Unlike other powers, the German Empire claimed not to be interested in Ottoman territory, instead purporting to be concerned for its preservation and strengthening. The Ottomans hoped that German support would aid them in the belated modernization of their military and infrastructure, whose deficiencies were among the reasons for the Empire's relative fragility and weakness. Meanwhile, Germany, as a 'belated Great power,' aimed to expand its economic outreach to compensate for its 'delayed' entry into colonial ventures.[22] Thus, the alliance and collaboration between the two empires served their respective interests: the Ottomans sought modernization as part of their nation-building process and (financial) stability, while Germany, in search of its proverbial *Platz an der Sonne* (place in the sun), pursued geopolitical power and (economic) opportunities in the East. In this context, the term friendship reflects a tense if not paradoxical affair: while Germany positioned itself as a guardian of Ottoman territorial integrity, its deepening economic entanglement and infrastructural dominance ensured a growing dependence on German capital and expertise. As asymmetries deepened, friendship revealed its dual aspect—the intention to protect could easily turn into a desire to control.

21   *İkdam*, 2 Cemaziyelahir 1316 [October 18, 1898], 1, quoted in
      Ortaylı, *Osmanlı İmparatorluğu'nda Alman Nüfuzu*, 94:
      "Osmanlıların cesaret ve mertlik ve yüksek nitelikleri
      Almanlarda da vardır. Bu iki millet birbirinin adeta aynası
      olarak yaratılmıştır. Osmanlılar Alman ismini saygı ve
      muhabbetle anarlar."

22   Gregor Schöllgen, "Dann müssen wir uns aber Mesopotamien
      sichern! Motive deutscher Türkenpolitik zur Zeit Wilhelms II.
      in zeitgenössischen Darstellungen," *Saeculum* 32, no. 2 (1981):
      137, 145.

Increasing debt and other economic constraints meant that the Ottoman Empire came increasingly under foreign influence and control, intensifying the hegemonic ambitions not only of the Allied Powers but also of the German Empire.[23] To avoid threatening the balance of power or rousing Turkish suspicions, by displaying any apparent colonial activity toward the Ottoman Empire, Germany characterized its *Drang nach Osten* policy as a *friedliche Durchdringung* (peaceful penetration, or *pénétration pacifique*).[24] By forgoing territorial acquisition and material expansion, Germany claimed to avoid "sinking back to the level of territorial nations," instead asserting its superiority through the "perpetual expansion of the German idea."[25] As part of this new conception, it sought "moral conquests"[26] in the Ottoman lands by exporting "spiritual and material culture."[27] Targeting Turkish "hearts and minds,"[28] Germany hoped to pursue economic and power-political advantages without assuming direct rule, administrative control, or other responsibilities of a colonial power. *Kulturpolitik,* as Suzanne Marchand describes it, "in theory aimed at conversion without force, friendship without binding ties, and benevolence without short-term reward."[29]

---

23 Cenk Reyhan, "Türk-Alman İlişkilerinin Tarihsel Arka Planı (1878–1914)," *Belleten* 69, no. 254 (2005): 224.

24 The actors of this movement have been referred to as "peaceful imperialists." For an in-depth study see Jürgen Kloosterhuis, *"Friedliche Imperialisten": Deutsche Auslandsvereine und auswärtige Kulturpolitik, 1906–1918* (Peter Lang, 1994). For a more detailed account of the development of *pénétration pacifique* within the Ottoman Empire, see Fuhrmann, *Der Traum vom deutschen Orient,* 142–94.

25 Paul Rohrbach, *Der deutsche Gedanke in der Welt* (Langewiesche, 1912), 8: "Zurücksinken auf die Stufe der Territorialvölker" and "immerwährende Ausbreitung der deutschen Idee."

26 Rohrbach, *Der deutsche Gedanke in der Welt,* 217.

27 Rohrbach, *Der deutsche Gedanke in der Welt,* 225.

28 "Deutsch-türkische Vereinigung," *Deutsche Levante-Zeitung,* April 1, 1914.

29 Suzanne L. Marchand, "Orientalism as Kulturpolitik: German Archaeology and Cultural Imperialism in Asia Minor," in *Volksgeist as Method and Ethic,* ed. George W. Stocking Jr. (University of Wisconsin Press, 1996), 300.

30
Malte Fuhrmann,
"Deutschlands
Abenteuer im Orient:
Eine Geschichte
semi-kolonialer
Verstrickungen,"
in *Türkisch-Deutsche
Beziehungen:
Perspektiven aus
Vergangenheit und
Gegenwart*, eds.
Claus Schönig,
Hatice Bayraktar
and Ramazan Calik
(De Gruyter, 2020),
13–14.

This informal cultural imperialism, intended to secure investments and increase trade, relied on concrete and material gestures that were both accessible and visible to the target audience. Cultural policy—which encompassed the foreign school service and the foreign press policy as well as private organizations, associations, and journals—sought to influence the local population through representative buildings such as embassies, churches, monuments, and schools, and by exhibitions and events.[30] Within the framework of friendship, culture became a means of extending influence beyond official borders without altering them—in other words, facilitating spatial expansion. Up to this point, the effective 'space' of friendship remained confined to individual actors or entities engaged through various agreements and the resulting military, trade, or diplomatic ties. However, for this network to expand beyond formal agreements and manifest in the broader public of both empires—and, by extension, their territories—it was necessary to enact its presence within society, reaching those who were not de facto subjects of friendship.

Against this background, the German-Turkish Union was established in February 1914 by Ernst Jäckh, a leading member of the *Arbeitsausschuss für Mitteleuropa* (Working Committee for Central Europe), following an invitation from German Secretary of State Gottlieb von Jagow.[31] The Union brought together nearly all major financial and industrial companies with interests in the Eastern Mediterranean region in order to centralize, practice and maintain German-Turkish friendship.[32] With this step, what had previously been rather an abstract friendship, a contractual reality and metaphoric space, took on a more tangible form. With the institutionalization of the friendship, the German-Turkish Union emerged as an official actor in its own right, a third political authority with the power to shape relations and curate this friendship.[33]

31   Sabine Mangold-Will, *Begrenzte Freundschaft:
Deutschland und die Türkei 1918–1933*
(Wallstein Verlag, 2013), 247.

32   Fuhrmann, "Deutschlands Abenteuer im Orient," 28.

33   A few years later in 1917, its Turkish counterpart, the
Türk-Alman Dostluk Cemiyeti (Turkish-German Union) would
be founded in Constantinople.

Friendship: A Space between Two

What began as an official declaration of friendship not only created (the perception of) a common space supported by two empires, it became an instrument for uniting and directing disparate interests. Although these interests were related to the same shared space of friendship, they were targeted at different spheres of influence and action that could conflict with, counteract, or play off each other. Within this space, economic, infrastructural, and technological asymmetries or political, cultural, and religious differences did not hinder this friendship; on the contrary, asymmetries and differences opened opportunities for power-political spaces and resources that each side could offer, negotiate, or make accessible to the other. The concept of friendship enabled the development of a shared space even while maintaining the boundaries of the individual entities and the antagonisms between them. Yet when access is not negotiated or willingly offered but instead assumed or asserted, a space of friendship risks being reversed. Since friendship suggests a trust built up over time and is supported by a common past rather than a future, its rhetoric could ultimately be exposed as a mere language of persuasion and disguise if that trust was betrayed.

  The core around which this particular friendship evolved, the reason for its resilience and increasing strength and stability, was military cooperation. The challenges faced by the Ottoman Empire—between 1875 and 1878 alone, state bankruptcy, two changes of sultan and a defeat by Russia—led Sultan Abdülhamid II to seek civilian and military advisors from Germany.[34] German military missions to the Ottoman Empire began as early as 1882. By the time of the second mission, well before any conception of the House of Friendship, this alliance was already being described as the "(corner)stone of German-Turkish Friendship-building."[35] Although still a metaphor, the allusion to a relationship that was being projected, taking shape, and becoming tangible foreshadowed the later material and real dimension. But in another sense, the image acquired spatial reality even sooner. By 1914, the abstract space of friendship was translated into military borders, as military cooperation evolved into a brotherhood in arms with the Ottoman Empire's entry into the war alongside

34
Elke Hartmann, "Das Dilemma der Reform: Die Arbeit der deutschen Militärmission im Osmanischen Reich in der Zeit Sultan Abdülhamids II. zwischen Kulturdifferenz und Interessendivergenz," in *Osmanen in Hamburg: Eine Beziehungsgeschichte zur Zeit des Ersten Weltkrieges*, ed. Yavuz Köse (Hamburg University Press, 2016), 71.

35
Dr. rer. pol. Schaefer, "Zur Gründung der Deutsch-Türkischen Vereinigung," *Tägliche Rundschau*, January 3, 1914: "ferner bildet die Militärmission einen Eckstein des deutsch-türkischen Freundschafts-gebäudes."

36
Werkbund and
Vereinigung,
*Haus der
Freundschaft*, 5.

37
Werkbund and
Vereinigung,
*Haus der
Freundschaft*, 8.

38
Werkbund and
Vereinigung,
*Haus der
Freundschaft*, 5.

39
Ernst Jäckh,
*Der goldene Pflug:
Lebensernte eines
Weltbürgers*
(Deutsche Verlags-
Anstalt, 1954), 130.

40
"Wettbewerbe,"
Deutsche Bauzeitung
50, no. 74
(September 13, 1916):
387.

41
Kloosterhuis,
"Friedliche
Imperialisten," 265.

Germany. The joint effort to defend the common space not only tested its limits and boundaries, but also gave them physical expression.

For the general public, these borders and military frontiers were still far away, and the contractual ties of a space just beginning to be contoured and defined were still too abstract. But how to bring something close that in fact just is not? How to make a metaphor concrete, and how to materialize space and, possibly even friendship in a *house?* Now that we are beginning to grasp the abstract space of this friendship, which began as a friendly address and later became a contractual framework and even a defended territory, let us turn to its projected physical manifestation as a 'house.' As we approach the time and place of the House of Friendship, it should come as no surprise that its conception was closely linked to the discourse of war and that it was launched as a project to deepen and consolidate the wartime alliance.[36] Against the political and historical background of Turkish-German friendship outlined above, let us examine the architecture as an example of its unique aesthetic appearance.

Shaping a Building

The idea for the House of Friendship was to accommodate "[t]he high purpose of spiritual give and take between the two nations,"[37] to create a "center point"[38] for German-Turkish collaboration. As a part of cultural policy, the project originated from the private initiative of the German-Turkish Union, with Jäckh as its self-appointed "author."[39] Nonetheless, it was "in any case to be regarded as a political matter for the *general* German public."[40] The idea was promoted extensively in the press and by prominent personalities, quickly gaining widespread support and popularity in society at large, with members of the Union alone collectively donating two million marks.[41] In addition to individual supporters, Jäckh's connections in the state and in business were also instrumental (most notably Robert Bosch), as was the emperor's donation of one million marks. On the Turkish side, the sultan contributed a property as large as five thousand square meters in the *center* of the then-capital, Constantinople. Once again, a metaphor began manifesting as the cultural policy aimed at winning the "hearts and minds of the Turks" gradually materialized: the project was to be located "not in the foreign neighborhood of Pera or Galata, but in the heart of Turkish life."[42] The site chosen from among those suggested to the Union was situated on Divan Yolu, near the fountain gifted by the German emperor. It was surrounded by Cistern Square and the site of the future Turkish parliament building, a project in which Germany was expected to play a role.[43] Even though neither building was ever completed, the significance of this planned spatial arrangement extends beyond mere physical proximity. Read symbolically, Germany's involvement in the construction of the 'body of government' reflects its vision of influence and presence in Türkiye's nation-building.[44] Rather than imposing direct authority, built interventions—particularly the design and construction of spaces of control and governance—could become a means of embedding and consolidating the long-term projection of power through presence.

A German counterpart of sorts to the House of Friendship in Constantinople, on the other hand, was initially set up in the rooms of a student dormitory in Berlin's Grunewald before a planned move to a more prestigious and spacious location at the corner of Unter den Linden and Wilhelmstraße in April 1918.[45] One could certainly argue that the realization of a Turkish space in Berlin progressed more quickly, but its scale remained modest and temporary—perhaps more akin to 'Apartments of Friendship.' By contrast, the 49 by 96 meter plot in Constantinople was not only significantly larger but also far from empty. To make room for the project, the demolition of two mosques, a school, and dozens of houses and workplaces was quickly initiated. It seems that any obstacle, regardless of scale and matter, could be overcome, as the sultan's adjutant-general Mehmed Zeki Paşa candidly admitted: "Do you realize that if our government provides you with a building site in Stambul for your Dostluk Yurdu, this is against our laws? Islamic law does not allow foreigners to own land in Stambul. But you are no stranger to us, you are our best friend."[46] While accommodating friends is important, what does a place designed to accommodate friendship look like, what are its form and function?

42
Werkbund and Vereinigung, *Haus der Freundschaft*, 5.

43
Jäckh, *Der goldene Pflug*, 330.

44
Fuhrmann describes the binary process of a "coincidental appropriation by German imperialism and Turkish nationalism" as fundamental to the idea of colonizing Anatolia. See Fuhrmann, "Anatolia as a Site of German Colonial Desire," 143–44.

45
Jäckh, *Der goldene Pflug*, 334.

According to the building program, such a building was to house libraries, lecture halls, exhibition rooms, a theater, a cinema, an outpatient department, a telegram room, a café, and apartments. At the request of the Union, the task of finding a suitable architect for the project was delegated to the Werkbund.[47] Jäckh, who was at the forefront of both organizations, hoped thereby to enhance the Werkbund's prestige and increase its opportunities.[48] The Werkbund was entrusted with a key role in shaping the House of Friendship, both in terms of its architectural design and also in defining the symbolic terms of German-Turkish friendship and thereby making a geopolitical statement. As such, this project was not only central to the Werkbund, it was to be foundational in the ideological and aesthetic construction of an imagined supranational space known as *Mitteleuropa* (Central Europe).[49]

The selection of architects took place at the *Werkbund*'s annual meeting in Bamberg in June 1914, where Jäckh also delivered his lecture *Der Werkbund und Mitteleuropa*. In relation to the *Werkbund*'s political agenda, Jäckh outlined the project's political role and aesthetic design as a key component of German foreign policy. Accordingly, in his speech, Jäckh imagines the friendship between the German, Austrian and Ottoman empires as a larger geopolitical force that aesthetically demonstrates clear distinctions and boundaries, asserting that "After all, the borders of a future Central Europe, the greater Central Europe, are also indicated in this

46 Mehmed Zeki Paşa to Jäckh, April 2, 1917, quoted in Jäckh, *Der goldene Pflug*, 329: "Ist Ihnen auch klar, daß, wenn unsere Regierung Ihnen in Stambul einen Bauplatz für Ihren Dostluk Yurdu zur Verfügung stellt, dies gegen unsere Gesetze geschieht? Das islamische Recht ermöglicht keinem Fremden Grundbesitz in Stambul. Aber Sie sind ja kein Fremder für uns, sondern unser bester Freund..."

47 A German association of artists, architects, designers, and industrialists, founded in 1907 in Munich. Its purpose was to establish a partnership between traditional craftsmanship and industrial mass production, promoting quality in design and contributing to the creation of a new cultural and aesthetic identity in Germany. The *Werkbund* was a significant force in the early 20th century, influencing the development of modern architecture and design, and laying the groundwork for what would later become the Bauhaus movement.

48 Karl Ernst Osthaus-Archiv Hagen, DWB1/211, "Protokoll der Vorstandssitzung," June 13, 1916.

way."[50] This idea of an affinity between aesthetics and (geo)politics further underscores the significance of architecture in its spatial manifestation.[51] The project should be understood not as a passive representation of relations but rather as active participation in shaping them, giving spatial form to something hitherto undefined.

Against this background, Jäckh presents a harsh critique of the "Europeanization" of Stambul, a neighborhood known today as Fatih. While acknowledging the contributions of French and Italian architects, he also accuses them of having "deindividualized, deadened, deformed" and indeed "raped" Constantinople.[52] Here, the distinction extends beyond architecture, highlighting a deeper political contrast. As the historian Malte Fuhrmann observes, Germany's tendency to identify with the allegedly subjugated Other was a defining characteristic of German colonial ideology, shaped by a 19th-century self-image of having been subject to French colonialism.[53] This affinity for the Turks, evident in the romanticization of Turkish architecture, was not merely a reflection of political rhetoric but an active effort on the part of Germany to align itself aesthetically with Türkiye, reinforcing and justifying Germany's political distinctness from other European states by framing them as the ultimate *Other*.

49   Originally emerging in the nineteenth century, *Mitteleuropa* gained strategic importance during the Great War as part of a vision for a German-led supranational order. While Friedrich Naumann, *Mitteleuropa* (Reimer, 1915) popularized the idea, Ernst Jäckh had already articulated this vision in an earlier Werkbund lecture, framing design as a geopolitical instrument in the envisioned integration of Central Europe and Asia Minor. For broader context on the early 20th-century imperial and geopolitical frameworks relevant to the House of Friendship, see Kenny Cupers, *The Earth That Modernism Built: Empire and the Rise of Planetary Design* (University of Texas Press, 2024), chap. 4.

50   Ernst Jäckh, *Werkbund und Mitteleuropa* (Gustav Kiepenheuer Verlag, 1916), 20.

51   Cupers argues that Ernst Jäckh should be understood "as a geopolitician in his own right," emphasizing his role in linking modern design with German political ambitions and geopolitical strategies.
       See Cupers, *The Earth That Modernism Built*, 229.

52   Jäckh, *Werkbund und Mitteleuropa*, 22.

53   Fuhrmann, "Deutschlands Abenteuer im Orient," 15.

The *Werkbund*'s and, by extension, the entire German attitude toward the protection, preservation, and defense of Turkish architecture reflects the German policy of preserving the territorial integrity of the Ottoman Empire, which set Germany apart from other European states. On an international level, this was accomplished by contextualizing the project within 'Central Europe,' as opposed to the 'West.' This distinction is further addressed at the urban scale and, more subtly, through architectural styles. The geopolitical contrast established with Central Europe is followed by a socio-cultural differentiation between the 'Turkish' architectural landscape of Stambul and the 'European' neighborhood of Pera. Finally, an art-historical contrast is indicated by the juxtaposition of the "Mohammedan mosque" as a symbol of Islamic architecture and the "Greek temple" as a symbol of Western architecture. At the height of this discourse, Jäckh strategically employs the stark contrast between deeply rooted cultural-religious expressions to support his argument. He presents the "organic" Turkish and Werkbund approach to architecture as one that "grows from within" in direct opposition to the "representative" Greek/Western temple, which had developed "from the outside in." In conclusion, he states: "The German Werkbund's sense for the organic finds a like-minded note in the Turkish sense of building."[54] The term "organic" here implies the development of a natural and authentic style or (building) culture, as opposed to a forced and synthetic one that is external to the circumstances. Ultimately, the term aims to validate a sense of place while recontextualizing historical continuities. Again, all levels of comparison presented by Jäckh serve to construct, justify, and legitimize an innate proximity to—and unity with—the Ottoman Empire by excluding the West *aesthetically*.

Regardless of the final design, the building process itself became an instrument for the aesthetic creation and performance of a distinct common culture and space. Yet space cannot simply be created, nor did it need to be. These projects were framed as a reconstruction of what was already shared, whether in borders or buildings. Ultimately, individuals were to believe in these structures by inhabiting them. Perhaps even more important than the project itself were the actions and interactions related to it that sustained the divide the building itself was meant to define. In this respect, Jäckh's approach to the site visit was as a means of distinguishing approvingly "that no European had undertaken a Constantinople building project in the way we Germans had."[55] But as already mentioned, the project was to concern the whole of German society, and Jäckh's assertion of Germany's unique affinity with the East was not sufficient in itself. The *Bulletin of the German-Turkish Association,* published in *Deutsche Levante-Zeitung* on July 16, 1916, presents "11 Hints for Travelers to the Orient," suggesting understanding, appropriate behavior, and sympathetic attitudes towards Turks on account of their cultural seniority: "The cradle of our culture was in the East. It is only since the end of the Middle Ages that we have gone our own way. So enter the Orient as you would your grandfather's house, filled with awe and gratitude!"[56]

The image of the Orient itself as a "house" is striking in the context of the construction of a House of Friendship, "house" in each instance signifying the concretion of an abstract idea, its appearance in space. Less obvious, perhaps, are the political implications of how this idea was realized. Although the House of Friendship symbolized a shared spatial vision for both Germany and Türkiye, there was a tension in the project between Germany's vision of imperial expansion and the Ottoman Empire's desire for preservation. However, the rather passive involvement of Türkiye should not be misunderstood as a lack of agency. It was not the Ottoman Empire that had to construct an innate proximity to Germany; rather it was Germany that, in seeking more than proximity, had to devise a narrative to legitimize its presence. For such a spatial narrative, architecture can serve as a common ground, a supposed "a-historical reference that enables the translation of difference into similarity."[57] The House of Friendship provided a potent metaphor for that common ground—yet one that still had to prove its worth by being realized. And for that, it had to be *designed.*

55
Jäckh,
*Werkbund
und Mitteleuropa,* 22.

56
"Mitteilungen der
Deutsch-Türkischen
Vereinigung e.V.
(Bulletin of the
German-Turkish
Association),"
*Deutsche
Levante-Zeitung,*
July 1, 1916:
"Die Wiege unserer
Kultur stand im
Osten. Erst seit
Ausgang des Mittel-
alters sind wir eigene
Wege gewandelt.
Tritt deshalb ein in
den Orient wie in
das Haus deines
Großvaters, erfüllt
von Ehrfurcht und
Dankbarkeit!"

57
Gülsüm Baydar,
"The Cultural Burden
of Architecture,"
*Journal
of Architectural
Education* 57, no. 4
(2004): 25.

[37] Students playing chess and checkers at the German-Turkish
Friendship Dorm in Berlin (November 10, 1917).

Friendship by Design

58
Gropius was invited
but could not
participate due to
military service,
see Werkbund and
Vereinigung, *Haus der
Freundschaft*, 8.

59
Werkbund
and Vereinigung,
*Haus der
Freundschaft*, 46–47.

At the same *Werkbund* meeting in Bamberg, the architects who would participate in the competition were chosen in a confidential vote, as a result of which invitations were sent to Peter Behrens, German Bestelmeyer, Paul Bonatz, Hugo Eberhardt, Martin Elsaesser, August Endell, Theodor Fischer, Walter Gropius, Bruno Paul, Hans Poelzig, Richard Riemerschmid and Bruno Taut.[58] These architects were then required to submit their designs within two months, by October 15, 1916, to be judged about a month later. The competition was judged openly by the architects themselves and was won by Bestelmeyer, with Behrens coming second and Riemerschmid third. However, due to both the close involvement of the emperor and significant changes in plot size, Bestelmeyer's design underwent several adaptations, until finally, despite mounting political uncertainties, the foundation stone was ceremonially laid on April 27, 1917.[59]

Though the Union initially planned to wait until the end of the war, the chosen date—the anniversary of Sultan Mehmed V's accession to the throne—was ultimately set under pressure from the Turkish government, which sought to strengthen its prestige.[60] While neither the emperor nor the sultan attended the ceremony, officials of both empires did, alongside representatives of the Union. The emperor did visit the construction site later the same year, on October 16, testifying to the importance of this project. The visit was closely followed by the press as well as being filmed by Turkish and German crews in an effort to publicize the message of a successful and productive cooperation.[61] The primary goal of these media efforts was to promote the wartime alliance and bolster a supposedly unbreakable friendship.

60
Kloosterhuis,
*"Friedliche
Imperialisten,"* 631.

[38]
Sultan Mehmed V
receives Emperor
Wilhelm II
(October 15, 1917).

[39]
Jäckh presents
the building plans
to Emperor
Wilhelm during
his visit to the
construction site
(October 16, 1917).

Within this context, the war was not taken to jeopardize the realization of the project but rather to enhance its symbolic function as the spatial representation of a friendship, public appearance and promotion of the House were accordingly further cultivated. An exhibition was organized in Berlin, presenting all eleven design proposals.[62] The exhibition was accompanied by a catalog featuring an introduction by Theodor Heuss, a co-founder of the *Werkbund*, who would later become the first president of the Federal Republic of Germany. A testimony on how the materialization of friendship might have looked can be found in this 1918 catalog, which presents all the proposals. But maybe Heuss's comments are even more telling than the individual architectural projections of friendship depicted in the catalog. What his judgments reveal are aesthetic expectations of the building, which reflect expectations of the appearance of the friendship itself. Seen from this perspective, these comments refer less to the House of Friendship itself than to the project and the projection of friendship as a space of appearance.

Heuss begins with a fundamental question: should the architectural statement be artistic or political? Unlike an embassy, he argues, which tried to "represent" the state it "serves," the House of Friendship was meant to be a "self-portrayal" not of the state but rather of a "nation." Yet the building was nonetheless to be representative in character, capable of expressing German national identity. Here another question posed by Heuss becomes more pressing: "Do we have an architecture that clearly expresses the German essence?" While acknowledging that "the building will have to

61   The film was shown for fourteen days in Turkish cinemas, see Jäckh, *Der goldene Pflug*, 330. The German film material is available at Filmschatzarchiv, *Isanbul–Konstantinopel 1917: Kaiser Wilhelm II Visits Turkey's Capital*, YouTube, posted May 24, 2012, https://www.youtube.om/watch?v=HTMGwFVMr8I. The Turkish film material has been incorporated into a short documentary produced by the state television channel TRT 2: TRT 2, *Tarihin Ruhu | Kayzer'in İstanbul Ziyareti | 15. Bölüm*, YouTube, posted July 10, 2019, https://www.youtube.com/watch?v=jEpr7TmbONA.

62   Tobias Schlunk, *Das 'Haus der Freundschaft' und der Genius loci: Martin Elsaessers Beitrag in dem Architekturwettbewerb des deutschen Werkbundes für ein deutsch-türkisches Kulturhaus in Konstantinopel 1916* (Wasmuth Verlag, 2018), 46.

blend in with the cityscape," this expectation is set against a broader claim: that through this building, "German architecture will be given its first opportunity to demonstrate its skills in an outstanding location in Türkiye."[63] While various architectural styles were associated with Germany, the pursuit of a distinct and unified national style revealed a lasting sense of inferiority with regard to the well-established architectural traditions of France and Italy. German architects were expected to foreground their national identity in their work. As they operated within the *Werkbund,* their designs were inevitably institutionalized and tied to the *Werkbund*'s broader political ambitions for Germany and, by extension, Central Europe.

With a third question, reminiscent of Jäckh's speech in Bamberg, Heuss asks to what degree architects should concern themselves not only with the urban context and environmental aspects of the setting for their designs, but also with the question of "whether and to what extent impulses from Oriental architecture should and wanted to be adopted."[64] Heuss follows up an assessment of the state of German architecture with a suggestive evaluation of its Turkish counterpart. Acknowledging the rich architectural history of the "Islamic Orient," he declares that it had become creatively "sterile" and dependent on "Western Europe," particularly through the influence of French architects. Not only had its buildings become "boring" and fallen prey to an "academic schematism" alien to "the Orient, its character and tradition," but Heuss also notes that the Turks had remained unconcerned with this development, as evidenced by their deliberate surrender to "Westernization"—at least until now. Suggesting that a turn may now be underway, he identifies the aim of what he calls "Orientalizing" designs as "to show the Turks in a great attempt what can be developed from the formal ideas of their past."[65]

63
Werkbund and Vereinigung, *Haus der Freundschaft,* 6–11.

64
Werkbund and Vereinigung, *Haus der Freundschaft,* 6.

65
Werkbund and Vereinigung, *Haus der Freundschaft,* 6–7.

[40]

This was surely a noble aspiration but in retrospect appears rather tragicomic, as it created a double bind both for the participating German architects and for the Turks who later trained with some of them.[66] Ought their designs to appear Turkish in a German manner, or rather German in a Turkish manner? In other words, was it "right and possible to come to the Turks in a 'German' house in such a 'Turkish' way"— the question remains as to how the architects navigated the commission and instructions from the German side while simultaneously addressing the Turkish context.[67] Underlying this negotiation is a deeper tension posed by Heuss earlier. His curious initial question—should architecture be making an "artistic" or a "political" statement—raises the issue of whether the political should visibly manifest in the design. However the brief to express national character in a façade might be interpreted, the aesthetic was inextricably bound up with the political through the House's projected role and

66   For a third of the participants, the competition served as a gateway to future professional opportunities in Türkiye. While Bruno Taut and Paul Bonatz took on influential teaching roles, others such as Hans Poelzig and Martin Elsaesser contributed to the architectural development of the newly founded Turkish state. See Burcu Dogramaci, *Kulturtransfer und nationale Identität: Deutschsprachige Architekten, Stadtplaner und Bildhauer in der Türkei nach 1927* (Gebr. Mann, 2008).

67   Werkbund and Vereinigung, *Haus der Freundschaft,* 41.

place in shaping an amicable space between Germany and Türkiye. Seen from this angle, this project is less about the political manifesting aesthetically than about an aesthetic constituting politics: Germany seeking to appear as Türkiye's best friend.

Needless to say, the term friendship was from the start more an instrument for achieving a desired end rather than a mere description of a state of events, and the House in this respect was a "curtain act," to borrow the words of the architectural historian Suha Özkan.[68] Behind the curtain, the peaceful performance of friendship was little more than a play of war. As part of this display, Germany encouraging the sultan to declare jihad was framed as an act of friendship, strategically constructed to help win the war 'as friends.'[69] War, in Jäckh's imagination, seemed to be a comparatively small step before "the German victory in this world war" provided an opportunity "to organize the new world politics and a new world culture."[70] But before abandoning the notion of friendship entirely, let us hold on to this sentimental idea for just a few more paragraphs. In the end, what would such a building really have looked like?

The House of Friendship

Setting aside Jäckh's confession—"I have always held with the Apostle Paul's letter to the Corinthians: '...To the Jew I have become a Jew..., to the Greek a Greek, to the Roman a Roman...' So: a Turk to the Turks!"[71]—the architects' approaches raised further political questions instead of providing aesthetic answers, thereby revealing the negotiation of power through representation. Hence, Martin Elsaesser's

68
Suha Özkan, "Türk-Alman Dostluk Yurdu Öneri Yarışması, 1916," *O.D.T.Ü. Mimarlık Fakültesi Dergisi* 1, no. 2 (1975): 178.

69 For the related "Revolutionary propaganda through Turkey," see Max Freiherr von Oppenheim, *Denkschrift betreffend die Revolutionierung der islamischen Gebiete unserer Feinde*, ed. Steffen Kopetzky (Das kulturelle Gedächtnis, 2018), 17–19. For a detailed discussion of the Ottoman declaration of Jihad during the Great War and its strategic aspects, see *Jihad and Islam in World War I: Studies on the Ottoman Jihad on the Centenary of Snouck Hurgronje's "Holy War Made in Germany,"* ed. Erik-Jan Zürcher (Leiden University Press, 2016).

70 Jäckh, *Werkbund und Mitteleuropa*, 6.

71 Jäckh, *Goldener Pflug*, 323.

72
Werkbund
and Vereinigung,
*Haus der
Freundschaft*, 26.

73
Werkbund
and Vereinigung,
*Haus der
Freundschaft*, 33.

74
Werkbund
and Vereinigung,
*Haus der
Freundschaft*, 15.

75
Werkbund
and Vereinigung,
*Haus der
Freundschaft*, 35.

76
Jäckh,
*Werkbund
und Mitteleuropa*, 21.

77
Werkbund
and Vereinigung,
*Haus der
Freundschaft*, 5.

design was questioned by the jury as to whether it "hit the right tone in picking up Persian motifs,"[72] while Bruno Paul "said himself that he drew a building that could just as easily be in Munich and Berlin as in Italy," aiming to convey its purpose "as unobtrusively as possible."[73] Peter Behrens's proposal was discussed as "American" or "Turkish,"[74] and Hans Poelzig's "imperiously cheerful" design prompted concerns about "whether such a grand gesture is not too self-willed, self-confident and grandiose when the German will to friendship asks for hospitality in a foreign country."[75]

As these questions remained unanswered, the House of Friendship—a building never built, never materialized—also never became the intended symbol of friendship it was meant to be. Instead, it became a metaphor for a friendship that never got beyond the laying of its foundation stone. The building was intended not to reflect any kind of existing friendship, but rather to serve as a medium for the construction of a specific German-Turkish friendship that others would experience, witness, and produce. Not only would every future visitor and passer-by add to the evidence of its existence, but the discourse around the House—including the competition, activities, practices, and preparations surrounding it—was a testimony already. Even before its realization, the project was already reshaping perceptions of landscape and geography, envisioning Constantinople as "the oriental center of our Central Europe."[76] And although Germany's plan for a Central Europe was never realized, its projection was the driving force of a friendship that, for a while, itself constituted such a space. Once so close as to constitute a center of Europe, Istanbul, the former Constantinople, now looks across the Bosporus to Asia again. Though perhaps Heuss's words will hold true and the friendship will prove more enduring:

> As long as [the German-Turkish] friendship does not have the character of an accidental combination (comparable to the English-Romanian, the Serbian-French 'alliance' of those years), they have the greatest interest in ensuring that official state relations are fueled by the will of the citizens of both nations to come close and remain close.[77]

[41]   The foundation ceremony (April 27, 1917).

Ultimately, we did not see a building, but through it, mechanisms of building and constructing relations that are still lasting.[78] And while their friendship did not require a building to exist, the 'House'—much like the idea of Central Europe—needed friendship to be realized. Yet its failure to materialize affirms friendship as a projected space of appearance rather than a physical space with borders or walls. Even without the built structure, the very projection and creative process generated, for the project's duration, the perception of a spatial reality that never physically existed. Thus, the architectural designs and styles need and perhaps should not be discussed—just as the House of Friendship seemed able to make something present without ever being visible itself. To look at the proposals might actually distract us from seeing how friendship was being made to appear. And yet something of the House becomes visible in hindsight: its evanescent presence at the foundation ceremony is difficult to unsee.

78   Only last year both countries celebrated the "centenary of the friendship treaty," see Anadolu Ajansı, "Cumhurbaşkanı Erdoğan, Almanya Başbakanı Scholz ile ortak basın toplantısı düzenledi," YouTube, live-streamed October 19, 2024, https://www.youtube.com/watch?v=nVDh7AgWwxE.

While the foundation stone was also the project's tombstone, the event—marking the beginning of construction—now also reveals that something had died and was buried here too. But, looking back on the friendship between Germany and Türkiye should not trap us in the past. Rather, it invites us once more to consider Turkish-German relations as an inherently *aesthetic affair* and to appreciate the countries' historic friendship as a distinctive instance of unresolved style.

[42]

Proceeding Through Steps
The Political Aesthetics of Legal Subjectivity in the Amtsgericht Mitte, Berlin

Dorothea Douglas

K. went over to the stairway to get to the room where the hearing was to take place, but then stood still again as besides these steps he could see three other stairway entrances, and there also seemed to be a small passageway at the end of the yard leading into a second yard. It irritated him that he had not been given more precise directions to the room, it meant they were either being especially neglectful with him or especially indifferent, and he decided to make that clear to them very loudly and very unambiguously. In the end he decided to climb up the stairs, his thoughts playing on something that he remembered the policeman, Willem, saying to him; that the court is attracted by the guilt, from which it followed that the courtroom must be on the stairway that K. selected by chance.[01]

01
Franz Kafka, *The Trial* (Echo Library, 2007), 42–43.

02
Adolf Klein, "Die Rheinische Justiz und der rechtsstaatliche Gedanke in Deutschland," in *Recht und Rechtspflege in den Rheinlanden,* eds. Adolf Klein and Josef Wolffram (Wienand, 1969), 116–18.

In the popular imagination of the West, courts feature as one of the quintessential spaces in which the modern individual appears as a subject capable of action. Here, the citizen steps into the space of a legal *topos,* which all members of society are able to inhabit while paradoxically remaining unique, singular. Historically, this spatial particularity materializes pointedly, uncomfortably where public spaces are split, recodified, and functionally differentiated, often concurrently with processes of state-building. For the fractured legal and political orders of the German territories of central Europe, an early point of convergence within this process came with the adoption of the Napoleonic Code in the territories left of the Rhine. Introducing the separation of powers and the institution of public prosecutors, the Code fundamentally reconfigured trials, which had previously been based on written correspondence, as public oral proceedings requiring the participation of lay persons.[02] This expansion of the law's contiguous spaces created a need for buildings which were not only physically separate from those of other branches of state power, they would also require dimensions which could accommodate both differentiated groups of jurists and the newly involved public. On top of this real spatial need, these sites were expected to integrate the laity into court proceedings as active participants.

03
Werner Schubert, "Das Bürgerliche Gesetzbuch von 1896," in *Kodifikation als Mittel der Politik: Vorträge und Diskussionsbeiträge über die deutsche, schweizerische und österreichische Kodifikations-bewegung um 1900,* ed. Herbert Hofmeister (Böhlau, 1986), 11–28.

[43]   View from inside the staircase between floors one and two.

04
See also Hans Schulte-Nölke, *Das Reichsjustizamt und die Entstehung des Bürgerlichen Gesetzbuchs* (Klostermann, 1995), 279–284; Hans-Peter Haferkamp, *Das BGB* (Böhlau, 2023), 108–112.

While the publicness of trials developed in parallel across the fragmented legal orders of pre-imperial nineteenth-century Germany, consolidation of the polity in 1871 reframed calls for a unified jurisprudence as part of nation-state-building. The political goal of imperial unity (*Reichseinheit*) teetered precariously on the technical feasibility of legal unity (*Rechtseinheit*). Codification initially focused on criminal law, finding early achievement in the 1877 passage of the *Reichsjustizgesetze*.[03] These laws enshrined the Napoleonic Code's spatial necessities—being public, representative, and separate—as a mandated standard. Civil jurisprudence would only be standardized in all territories of the *Reich* with the introduction of the *Bürgerliches Gesetzbuch* (BGB), which was passed by the *Reichstag* in 1896; coming into effect on January 1, 1900. The BGB was the product of a 25-year quarrel amongst Germany's political factions, which was ultimately settled in favor of liberal-bourgeois interest. Notably, contemporaries characterized the BGB for its un- (though not a-) social bent, which largely privileged the basic rationale of the market.[04]

161

05
For a concise delin-
eation of jurisdiction
see: Otto Kästner,
"Die Architektur
deutscher Land-
gerichte zwischen
1900 und 1920"
(PhD diss.,
Goethe University
Frankfurt, 2012),
19–20.

Importantly, the introduction of this novel legal standard anticipated built sites of jurisprudence which were mono-functional and specialized. Civil jurisprudence was newly divided by the dyad of *Land-* and *Amtsgerichte,* with juris-diction established along the lines of litigious value and the length of potential sentencing. The purview of *Amtsgerichte* extended to cases with a litigious value of up to 300 marks and a commination of up to six months. Cases exceeding these markers moved to the higher civil courts of *Landgerichte.*[05] Particularly the *Amtsgericht'*s daily workings were taken up by non-contentious matters, such as the registration of property and family relations. Additionally, the land register, mat-ters of estates, and various registries of social and profes-sional unions were kept here. In contrast to the administra-tive, correspondence-based proceedings of only a hundred years earlier, banal and ordinary legal matters were now gov-erned under the same mandate of publicness which had re-written criminal proceedings. Particularly in this mundane function, *Amtsgerichte* served as a novel space for civilian and state interaction.

At this historical moment, the state was particu-larly dependent on the citizen being able to enter into contact with its administrative sites as a legal subject (*Rechtssubject*). State actors conceived of this novel figure, imagined to be lib-eral and economically rational, as navigating the new, nation-wide civil law apparatus autonomously, in pursuit of their own interests. A keen sense that the seamless inhabitation of this role required sites in which it could be rehearsed and real-ized permeated government. As I will show, architecture, by virtue of its potential for kinetic experience, was understood as a crucial tool for impressing this particularized understand-ing of the self upon the citizen. Stairwells, the final vestiges of representative space within an increasingly streamlined ar-chitecture of administration, were particularly important in this regard. Describing a continuous volume of a building's mass, main stairways served as receptors, condensers, and ushers to the public. As consciously configured spaces of dy-namic movement, staircases lent themselves to flourishes of *Gestaltung* by planners. A notable high point of this praxis was reached in the construction of the massive *Amtsgericht* wing at the *Justizpalast* in Berlin-Mitte, located on Littenstraße.

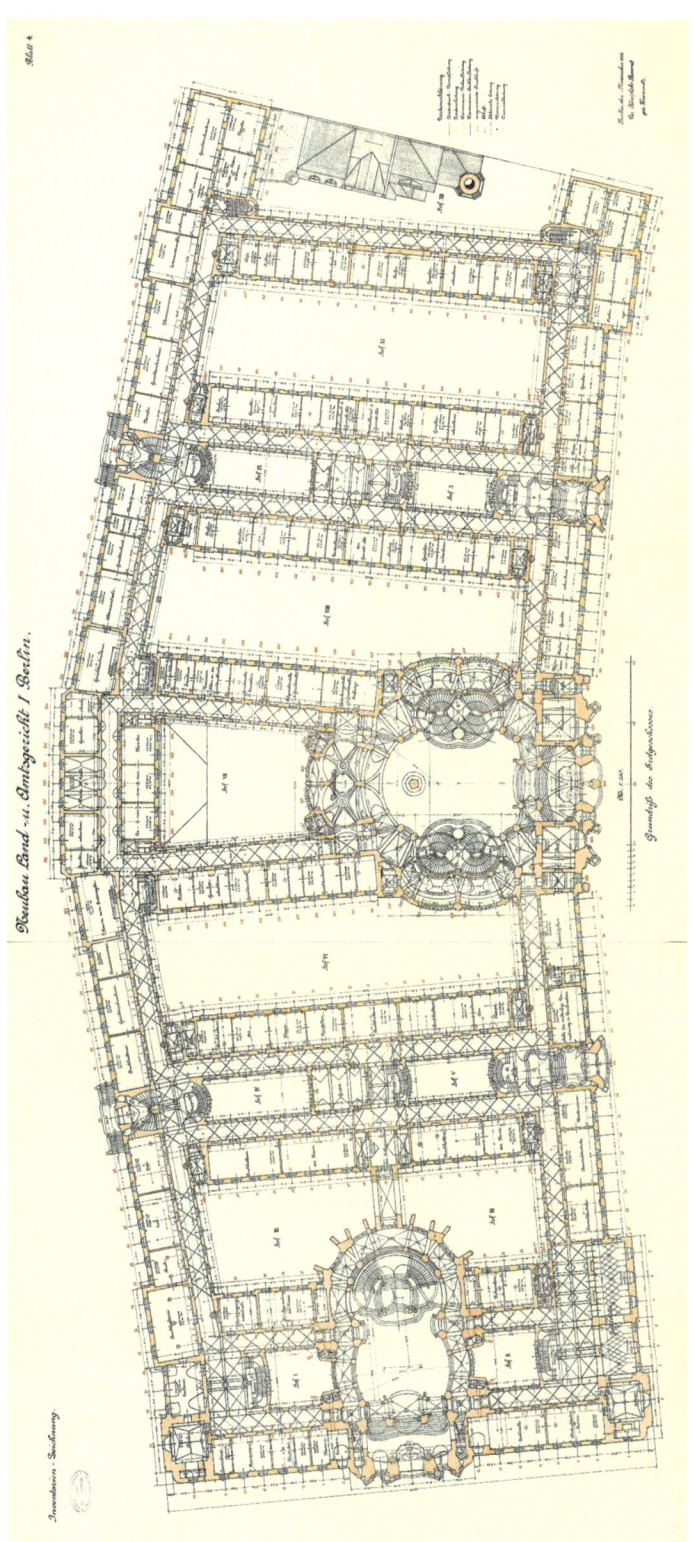

[44] Ground floor plan of the *Land- and Amtsgericht Mitte.*

163

06
For an overview see Albert Spitznagel, "Geschichte der Psychologischen Rhythmusforschung," in *Rhythmus: Ein interdisziplinäres Handbuch*, eds. Eckart Altenmüller, Katharina Müller, and Gisa Aschersleben (Huber, 2000), 1–40; Boris Roman Gibhardt, "Einleitung: Zum Widerstreit historischer und systematischer Ansätze in der Rede von Rhythmen," in *Denkfigur Rhythmus: Probleme und Potenziale des Rhythmusbegriffs in den Künsten*, ed. Boris Roman Gibhardt (Wehrhahn, 2020), 9–20.

07
For an introductory overview on Schmarsow see Roland Meyer's entry in Susanne Hauser, Christa Kamleithner, and Roland Meyer, eds., *Architekturwissen: Grundlagentexte aus den Kulturwissenschaften* (transcript, 2011).

08
Volker Kähne and Klaus Lehnartz, eds., *Gerichtsgebäude in Berlin: Eine rechts- und baugeschichtliche Betrachtung* (Haude u. Spener, 1988), 97.

As we will see, one way of understanding this spatial arrangement's peculiar emergence at the nexus of imperial legal standardization and Prussian architectural rationalization is by considering contemporaneous experimental theories of the sensory body's cognitive potential, theorizing a mode of sensory aesthetic experience capable of bestowing psychological and physiological harmony upon the body. This concern for embodiment's epistemic ability—a predicate to much avant-garde thinking in Germany at this time—characterized turn-of-the-century German art history's search for architecture's anthropological and psychological 'last elements.'[06] Aiming at disciplinary demarcation, thinkers strove to derive essential meta-categories of art from historical observation, which could in turn describe (and judge) artistic production across time and place. Within the field of architectural theory, the German art historian August Schmarsow played a pivotal role in moving the discursive 'constant element' of historical observation from ornament toward the shaping of space as modelled void.[07] This paper seeks to examine how this paradigm of spatial perception functioned within the larger societal aim of relating subjects to the novel legal order and questions the political potential these spaces rendered.

Amtsgericht Mitte

Along the eastern side of Littenstraße, across from the ruins of Berlin's old Franciscan monastery, the *Amtsgericht Mitte* is housed in a monumental neo-baroque building from the previous turn of the century. The building was completed in two stages between 1896 and 1904 and still houses both a *Land-* and an *Amtsgericht*. The building of the *Landgericht*, a four-winged *corps de logis* completed in the first stage of construction, faced Gruner Straße and was partially demolished in 1968 to allow for the widening of the street.[08] Today, only the building of the *Amtsgericht* remains, housing both courts. From the frontage along Littenstraße, the building extends to the tracks of the *S-Bahn*, which runs along the back of the building. In its original comb-like structure, these two fronts were connected by seven bisecting tracts, making a total of 12 internal courts.

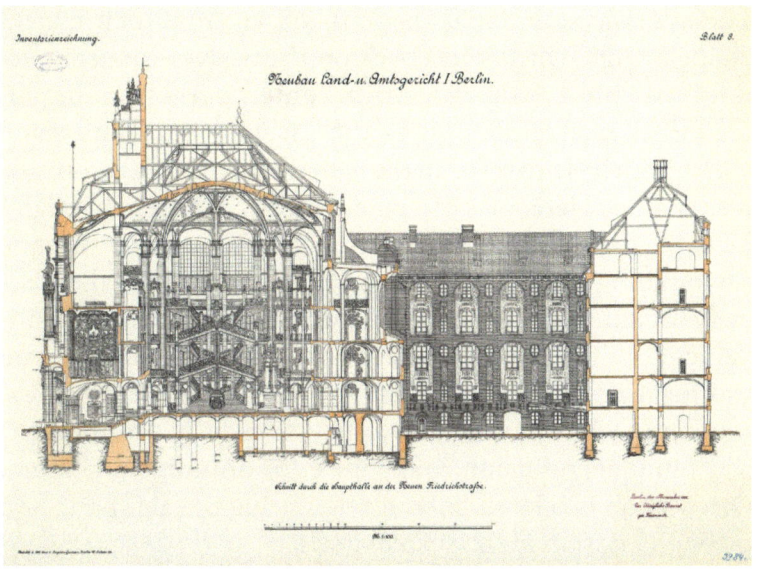

[45] Cross section of the stairwell pavilon
      at Neue Friedrichstraße (now Littenstraße).

Even today the view from Littenstraße shows the length and slight concavity of the building's main façade, two formal problems neutralized outwardly through the central pavilion housing the main staircase. A compact structure in which the building's ornament is condensed, the pavilion's façade is marked by three oblong windows. Along with the building's double towers and first-floor pillar-herm, the ornate central section streams upward, counteracting the horizontal breadth of the main façade. The building's portico undulates in several folds, plotting a B-shaped antechamber in horizontal section. From here the visitor is taken into the building's main cavity through a sloped vestibule.

In vertical projection, this interior is dominated by four galleries, which span the circumference of an oblong central air space (*Luftraum*). The viewer climbs to a shallow O-shaped plateau underneath the gallery system and descends from here into the negative of the *Luftraum*. At ground level, a monumental tabernacle once stood as a singular freestanding monument, looming up into the third-floor gallery, punctuating the chamber's axis of symmetry. The staircase's two main stairways lie left and right of this axis, foregrounding the gallery system with which they fuse, leading into the adjoining wings of the building.

165

09
Schmalz aimed to conduct light into the space so that "schon bei den ersten Schritten in der Vorhalle [the viewer would be drawn with] vollen Blick auf die Hauptlichtquelle, das Fenster."
Otto Schmalz, "Das neue Land- und Amtsgericht Berlin-Mitte," *Zeitschrift für Bauwesen* 56, no. 4–6 (1906): 270–76.

10
The *Dezernat*'s first director, Karl Friedrich Endell, was explicit about this frugality, particularly as a directive for lower courts. Karl Friedrich Endell, "Ueber Geschäftshäuser für Amtsgerichte und Landgerichte, sowie über die zugehörigen Gefängnisse," *Centralblatt der Bauverwaltung* II, no. 10 (1882): 89–91.

11
Similar entities existed in other German states. The Prussian Dezernat was functionally split into an eastern and western department.

The stairways' unusual shape is drawn from their conch-shaped runs, which wind back on themselves to form a re-doubled spiral staircase. At its center, a freestanding diamond-shaped landing gives the ensemble its figure eight curve, which is mirrored in the galleries and the pavilion's external walls. Here, massive pillars carry the gallery's weight, allowing the wall to give way to large window areas. Within the building context, the swell of the stairways is dramatically backlit, their dynamic profile cast in stark relief.[09] This principle of undulation is transposed onto the parapet and waiting halls, forming pockets of repose inside of the space's transitory whirr. This flamboyant dynamism makes the stairways uniquely difficult to navigate for uninitiated visitors. Orientation is offered only in referencing the air space, not by one's location in the system itself.

The Administration of Space

It is important to contrast the building's eclectic dynamism with the efficient, rigid, and centralized authority that planned it, the *Dezernat für Justizbauten*. An early subdivision established in the Prussian Ministry of Public Works (*Preußisches Ministerium der öffentlichen Arbeiten*), the *Dezernat* was not only highly specialized but committed to the frugality characteristic of much Prussian public building.[10] Established shortly after the founding of the imperial polity in 1871, this office was responsible for the planning and oversight of all new construction of juridical buildings across Prussian territories.[11] The lack of preexisting spatial forms, as well as practical necessities that remained consistent across projects, encouraged formal repetition within the *Dezernat*'s practice.[12] The staircase's ornate and impractical spatial form thus seems ideologically at odds both with its bureaucratic genesis and with frugality as a general principle of state.

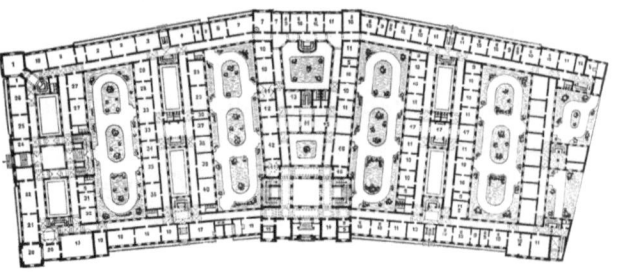

[46]

[46]
Ground floor plan of the initial „Entwurfskizze" of the *Land-* and *Amtsgericht Mitte* attributed to Paul Thoemer.

[47]
Façade projection of the initial „Entwurfskizze" of the *Land-* and *Amtsgericht Mitte* attributed to Paul Thoemer.

This deviation seems all the more unlikely when we consider the several rounds of review new construction underwent at the hands of fiscal, political, and architectural actors. juridical buildings across Prussian territory were commonly first drafted by the *Dezernat*'s long-time director, *Baurat* Paul Thoemer.[13] Possibly Germany's most prolific architect of judicial buildings at this time, Thoemer has often been considered the sole arbiter of these inherently dynamic planning processes. Thoemer came into office just as the spatial necessity of courts expanded exponentially due to the rapid growth of German urban centers at the turn of the century. While he arguably spearheaded the development of the basic shape of the *Justizpalast* in its Prussian iteration, his decisions were not immune to criticism by his contemporaries. His original designs for the building at Littenstraße are all simple rectilinearity, a quality of both ornament and interior—formally restrained. Functionally staggering the space of the main staircase, Thoemer placed the stairways behind an arcaded courtyard, thereby separating the representative vestibule from the space's transitory function.

12   A concise rundown of the typical planning process can be found in Kästner, "Die Architektur deutscher Landgerichte zwischen 1900 und 1920," 41–46.

13   Dieter Dolgner, "1918: Paul Thoemer (1851–1918) Architekt," in *Mitteldeutsches Jahrbuch für Kultur und Geschichte 2018*, eds. Gerlinde Schlenker and Harro Kieser (Stiftung Mitteldeutscher Kulturrat, 2018), 136–40.

When the plan came under review by the building academy (*Akademie des Bauwesens*), it was rejected on aesthetic grounds.[14] Noting the staircase's size and form as a problem, the review requested alterations to space and volume befitting the structure's station.[15] Such calls for alterations were not uncommon but rather a standard element of the elliptical review process instituted within the state planning apparatus. First drafts of buildings developed in the *Dezernat* with a projected budget exceeding 500,000 marks were subject to an additional round of review by the Ministry of Public Works. Prestigious projects underwent jet a further review of the plan's artistic quality by the *Akademie des Bauwesesens,* whose institutional role forbade it from letting plans pass without comment. For our purposes, it is notable that the *Akademie*'s comments here and elsewhere focus nearly exclusively on the building's main staircases, to the exclusion of functional spaces such as clerk's chambers or prosecutor's offices.

Structurally, both the design and the review process focus on the staircase as the most distinct realm of representation within the spatial arrangement of the juridical complex. In the case of the *Amtsgericht Mitte,* alterations following the *Akademie*'s review were undertaken by the *Dezernat*'s staff architects Rudolf Mönnich and Otto Schmalz, who strove to increase the space's "plastic movement and vivid particularity"[16] (*plastische Bewegtheit und lebendige Eigenart*) through the superior "ability for spatial composition"[17] (*Raumgestaltungsfähigkeit*) of baroque form. As was to be expected, their efforts focused almost exclusively on the building's main staircases.

14   Friedrich Raschdorff, "Entwurfskizzen zum Neubau eines Geschäftsgebäudes für die Civilabtheilungen des Landgerichts I und Amtsgerichts I in Berlin," *Centralblatt der Bauverwaltung* 16, no. 24 (1896): 261–64.

15   "Diese [the staircases] im praktischen wie künstlerischen Sinne besonders hervorragenden Bautheile, bedürfen noch weiterer Durcharbeitung und sind ihrer Bedeutung entsprechend offener und weiträumiger umzugestalten und durchzubilden," Raschdorff, "Entwurfskizzen," 261.

16   Schmalz, "Das neue Land- und Amtsgericht," 276.

17   Schmalz, "Das neue Land- und Amtsgericht," 269.

Thinking Space

Mönnich and Schmalz's focus on lively movement dovetails with a shift in architectural discourse exemplified in the writings of the German art historian August Schmarsow. One of the preeminent theorists of architectural space of his day, Schmarsow's writing must be situated within the broad scientification of art history from 1880 onward. In the process of defining and codifying the discipline's purview and scope, particular attention was paid to excavating its methodological core as the foundation of a new discursive regime. A common *topos* of this effort was the definition of so-called 'elemental terms' (*Grundbegriffe*), an effort now closely associated with the work of Heinrich Wölfflin.[18]

Schmarsow first presented his model of architecture as essentially characterized by physical, spatial experience in his 1893 inaugural lecture at the University of Leipzig. This lecture, entitled *Das Wesen der architektonischen Schöpfung*, attempted to link the "natural relation" of "internal man" to his spatial enclosure through architecture.[19] This relationship is described through a structural model that aims to deduce the three dimensions of geometric space from man's bodily and mental constitution.[20] The first dimension, height, is derived from the vertical orientation of the body, from man's upright posture.[21] The source of the second dimension, width, is

18 Indeed, much of Schmarsow's thinking was very explicitly developed in opposition to Wölfflin's formulation of *Grundbegriffe* in his habilitation. Andrea Pinotti, "Body-Building: August Schmarsow's Kunstwissenschaft Between Psychophysiology and Phenomenology," in *German Art History and Scientific Thought: Beyond Formalism*, eds. Mitchell B. Frank and Dan Adler (Routledge, 2012), 13–31. The understanding of baroque style Mönnich and Schmalz engage with above is broadly in line with Schmarsow's reading of the era, a counter to Wölfflin's famous paradigm. See also Ute Engel, *Stil und Nation: Barockforschung und Deutsche Kunstgeschichte* (Wilhelm Fink, 2018), 328–31.

19 August Schmarsow, *Das Wesen der architektonischen Schöpfung: Antrittsvorlesung, gehalten in der Aula der K. Universität Leipzig am 8. November 1893* (Hiersemann, 1894), 3.

20 It is this focus on physiology that makes Schmarsow's thinking here so different from Wölfflin's. See Engel, *Stil und Nation*, 330–33.

21 Schmarsow, *Das Wesen der architektonischen Schöpfung*, 15.

22
Schmarsow,
*Das Wesen der
architektonischen
Schöpfung*, 17–19.

23
The original German
reads: "die wichtigste
Ausdehnung für das
eigentliche Raum-
gebilde vielmehr die
Richtung unserer
freien Bewegung,
also nach vorwärts,"
Schmarsow,
*Das Wesen der
architektonischen
Schöpfung*, 16.

the span of the arms outstretched from the body, demarcating its space of dexterity (*Tastraum*).[22] The third dimension, depth, is the "direction of our free movement—forwards."[23] This is anthropologically expressed in man's stride and gaze, which extend past the *Tastraum* into the *Gesichtsraum* (space of vision).

Though this model of the body is later rephrased in explicitly kinesthetic terms, the early model already builds on a physio-psychological aesthetics of empathy (*Einfühlungsästhetik*), in which perception does not passively register but is rather par of a subconscious, somatic process of comprehension.[24] While Schmarsow does acknowledge that spatial perception varies across historical periods and regions, finding and identifying general rules of human behavior and perception advances and upholds a fixed anthropological notion of man as a species-being.

From Space to Subject

Reading the *Amtsgericht* with Schmarsow elucidates the contradiction noted at the outset. Planners labored under the expectation that they would create spaces that could integrate an unknowing public into the still novel mundane, and largely administrative legal praxis that required the citizen to appear in legal spaces and in person.[25] The structure of the review process not only focused on staircases as sites for this presentation to occur, it also encouraged planners to demonstrate a virtuoso command of space. This parallel reading should not suggest that Schmarsow's conception is the definitive experience of these spaces. Instead, I wish to elucidate the larger *dispositif* or situatedness of planning at this time—not because theory fully explicates the actual architecture, but because it explores how a metaphysics of space shapes and directs what stakeholders of political power considered to be communicable in the medium.

24   Schmarsow draws on and explicitly references
      Theodor Lipps as an influence on his work here.
      Schmarsow, *Das Wesen der architektonischen Schöpfung*, 3.
      Additionally, see Rainer Schützeichel, "Architecture as
      Bodily and Spatial Art: The Idea of Einfühlung in Early
      Theoretical Contributions by Heinrich Wölfflin and August
      Schmarsow," *Architectural Theory Review* 18, no. 3 (2013):
      293–309.

If we approach the *Amtsgericht* through Schmarsow's understanding of architecture, the freestanding tabernacle thus acts as a counterpart to man's uprightness. As an articulation of the dimension of height, it marks upward extension and emphasizes the spatial excerpt through its internal cavity. At the same time, the sculpture moves the viewer into the vestibule's central axis, marked in the diamond floor pattern. This axis is pivotal to Schmarsow's understanding of a subject projected by architecture's enclosure, and he explicitly posits the possibility of the legal subject appearing at this node.

> At higher levels of supposition, art creates emanations of an ideal entity; the legal person, the corporation, the municipality, or even an abstract idea derived from state, social or religious communities—a factor of existing civilization, of prevailing cultural work—takes the place of the originally human subject, for example in the courthouse, the Christian place of worship, or the *universitas literarum*.[26]

25 This (shattered) expectation is made explicit in Rudolf Mönnich's statements on the failure of the *Justizpalast* developing as a type, which Mönnich draws from the prevalence of the court's administrative function, see Rudolf Mönnich, "Neue Gerichtsbauten in Berlin und Umgegend: Nach Einem Vortrage des Herrn Reg.-u. Brt. Moennich, Gehalten im Architekten-Verein zu Berlin," *Deutsche Bauzeitung* 41, no. 93 (November 20, 1907): 656: "Es liege das daran, daß unsere Gerichte noch ebenso viel Verwaltungsstätten wie Orte der Rechtsprechung seien, also in unserem heutigen Gerichtsverfahren selbst. Offenbar mache sich aber in diesem z. Zt. ein Zug geltend, der nach breitester Öffentlichkeit, weitestgehender Heranziehung des Laien-Elements strebe. Werde unsere Rechtspflege in diesem Sinne weiter aus- und umgestaltet, dann trete das Geschäftshaus hinter den großen Verhandlungssälen immer mehr zurück, wir würden uns wieder mehr der alten Grundform der Basilika nähern."

26 Schmarsow, *Das Wesen der architektonischen Schöpfung*, 16: "Ja, auf höheren Stufen der Supposition schafft die Kunst Ausstralungen [sic] einer idealen Einheit; die juristische Person, die Körperschaft, die Gemeinde, oder gar eine abstrakte, aus der staatlichen, sozialen, religiösen Gemeinschaft abgeordnete Idee, ein Faktor der vorhandenen Civilisation, der herrschenden Kulturarbeit vertritt die Stelle des ursprünglich menschlichen Subjekts wie z.B. im Justizpalast, im christlichen Gotteshaus, in der *Universitas literarum*."

[48]   View of the stairway and tabernacle.

Blurring the boundaries of the virtuality of the ideal type and the distinct body, Schmarsow sees both emerging at the same spatial point. This coalescence of the universal macrocosm and the microcosm of the human sensory body will become particularly problematic in Schmarsow's conception of the planner's body.[27]

27   This is not to say that a productive coalescence is impossible here. As Timothy Hide points out: "Between the two extents of actual individuals and generic humanity, many other modes of embodiment exist, instrumental and readily discoverable in the workings of a variety of disciplines. Among these, architectural history might find direction in another discipline with an equally fundamental recognition of duration: the law. And more specifically, in the manifestations of legal subjectivities, embodiments or legal persons, which attain qualities of duration while retaining models of intention, motive, and desire," Timothy Hyde, "Notes on Architectural Persons," *Aggregate* 1 (2013): 3.

From this location, width, ordered by symmetry and loosely associated with the plane of painting, extends bilaterally from the viewer; it is made palpable in the simultaneous presence of other bodies in space alongside one another, their *Nebeneinander*. In terms of spatial feeling, our static subject in the central axis of the *Amtsgericht* is thus bisected by a lateral plane. Extending left and right of the viewer, this stratum is punctured by and shared with the staircases, particularly the heavy ventilation boilers nestled at the base of the runs. Iconographically, the other bodies appear in the frieze of knights which winds around the ground floor pillars' perimeter.[28]

The kinetic reorganization of the model is achieved by recontextualizing the third dimension, depth, as the inherent dimension of architecture, governed by the principle of rhythm. This vitalist turn invigorates both Schmarsow's model viewer and the praxis of architecture as a whole. A temporal figure, rhythm itself is resonant in bodily cadences such as breath, heartbeat and the ambulatory nature of walking. But this sense of movement is partly owed to the inherent dynamism of depth within Schmarsow's system. In its transgression of the *Tastraum,* depth shifts the *Nebeneinander* into a *Hintereinander,* moving the mode of perception from calm simultaneity to dynamic succession.[29]

28   On width see Schmarsow, *Das Wesen der architektonischen Schöpfung,* 17–19. See also Andrea Pinotti, "Rhythmologie in der Kunstwissenschaft zwischen dem 19. und 20. Jahrhundert: Der Fall August Schmarsow," in *Mythos Rhythmus: Wissenschaft, Kunst und Literatur um 1900,* eds. Massimo Salgaro and Michele Vangi (Franz Steiner Verlag, 2016), 41–53.

29   For the passages on rhythm, see August Schmarsow, "Über den Werth der Dimensionen im menschlichen Raumgebilde," in *Berichte über die Verhandlungen der Königlich-Sächsischen Gesellschaft der Wissenschaften zu Leipzig,* ed. Königlich-Sächsische Gesellschaft der Wissenschaften (Teubner, 1896), 55–59; for an elucidating overview, see Björn Spiekermann, "Laokoons Schatten: Bewegung, Sukzession und Rhythmus in der Kunsttheorie August Schmarsows," in *Denkfigur Rhythmus: Probleme und Potenziale des Rhythmusbegriffs in den Künsten,* ed. Boris Roman Gibhardt (Wehrhahn Verlag, 2020), 165–90.

30   Schmarsow, *Das Wesen der architektonischen Schöpfung,* 10–15.

31
Schmarsow,
"Über den Werth
der Dimensionen,"
55–59.

This premier quality of space can be experienced only by traversing it. Schmarsow's architect shapes this experience, derived from the experience of his own embodiment, through the arrangement of the systole and diastole of successive spaces.[30] Because of this focus on waxing and waning, transitory spaces as areas of high contrast take on an important role in the designed space. Within Schmarsow's understanding of perception, the subject's movement along the depth dimension produces irregular mental planar images (*Flächenbilder*), which are synthesized into a memory image (*Erinnerungsbild*).[31] This virtual image, encompassing the totality of a given spatial experience, can be reflected upon as a whole, after the fact, not unlike a piece of music or theatre. It is of this spatial composition and its perception, not the built form itself, that rhythm is a quality.

[49]   View from the parapet onto the stairs.

Rhythm as Order

Entering the staircase of the *Amtsgericht Mitte,* the civilian is led from the chaos of unshaped outdoor space through irregular antechambers into the high central air space as seen from below. But the elements most suited to the experience of the depth dimension are the stairways themselves, where the dimension of depth layers itself onto that of height. The run's winding shape repeatedly moves the viewer from confused darkness into interaction with the central airspace and delivers them into a state of clarity in the luminous top gallery enclosed by the vaulted ceiling.

The stairs' eclectic and nonrational shape may be read through Schmarsow's framework as exemplary of man's dimensional constitution, which makes up his immediate relation to the world. In thematizing our own mental organization, architecture is able to transport a certainty of being through its communion with the primal source of the real.[32] Architecture as the shaper-of-space (*Raumgestalterin*) as described by Schmarsow, becomes the ultimate pedagogical tool to communicate transcendent truth because it addresses the inherent organization of the body directly.[33] Since architecture is the art most directly geared toward inherent bodily order, it is capable of heightening and addressing this essence from which perception arises. Indeed, this attitude is mirrored in the *Amtsgericht*'s original ceiling inscription, stylized as a continuous ribbon of golden letters, which read:

> Everywhere above the universe you see the world's governing laws standing in calm grandeur. They enclose the fleeting moment of your being as well as the dead stones of this house. The world of God above you shows itself to you in the harmony of the spheres, in time and space, in the fullness of life and death, the stream of which glides through the sacred hands of the Norns; the world of men beside you in the forms of states and law; your own world within yourself in your conscience and sense of art, beauty, morality. Their work is order; their observance mutual advancement, development, union to the greater whole; their violation carries in itself the penalty of impossibility, of ill-birth, of being outcasts, of annihilation; O man realize this, never forget it, and live by it![34]

32
Schmarsow, "Über den Werth der Dimensionen," 45–58.

33
In the original German, Schmarsow states: "Die architektonische Schöpfung ist von Anfang an keine Nachahmung des menschlichen Körpers … sondern sie ist ein Correlat des Menschen und zwar seines ganzen Wesens." This may be translated as: "Architectural creation is, from the very beginning, not an imitation of the human body … but rather a counterpart to the human in its very essence," Schmarsow, "Über den Werth der Dimensionen," 47.

Both Schmarsow and the inscription on the staircase's ceiling work with a common understanding of rhythm at the center of much of European avant-garde thinking at the turn of the century. Broadly conceived of as a transcendent organizing force, rhythm (or ur-rhythm) was a supratemporal drive that permeated both individual interiority and the terrain of the social and natural worlds. As such, it constituted the germ of a total experience. A central tenet of this thinking was that the structuring potential of rhythm had been partially or completely lost in modernity.[35] Confronted by this phenomenal lack, its proponents strove beyond rhythm's mere reinstatement, aiming instead to revive and heighten a supposedly pristine, primal 'ur-rhythm.' This narrative of reintroduction gives these projects an inherently pedagogical bent: rhythm paradoxically was a natural constant of human life that nonetheless had to be revived, taught, and communicated. Here, rhythm serves to naturalize both the model of perception and its apparent source in the experience of transcendent order through spatial perception. Before examining the effects of this narrative on the citizen's relationship to the institution, we turn to the question of what exactly this aesthetic moment is doing structurally for the judicial institution it was embedded in and why a rationalized and normative legal order required such flamboyant forms in its most mundane sites.

34   Otto Schmalz, "Das neue Land- und Amtsgericht Berlin-Mitte," *Zeitschrift für Bauwesen* LVI, no. VII-IX (1906): 410: "Überall über dem All siehst du der Welt waltende Gesetze in ruhiger Größe stehen. Sie umschließen den flüchtigen Augenblick deines Seins so gut wie die toten Steine dieses Hauses. Die Welt Gottes über dir zeigt sich dir in der Harmonie der Sphären, in Zeit und Raum, in der Fülle des Lebens und Sterbens, deren Strom durch der Nornen heilige Hände gleitet; die Welt der Menschen neben dir in den Formen der Staaten und des Rechts; die eigene Welt in dir in dem Gewissen und dem Gefühl für Kunst, Schönheit, Sittlichkeit. Ihr Werk ist Ordnung; ihre Befolgung gegenseitige Förderung, Entwicklung, Zusammenschluß zum größeren Ganzen; ihre Verletzung trägt in sich die Strafe der Unmöglichkeit, der Mißgeburt, des Ausgestoßenseins, der Vernichtung; O Mensch erkenne das, vergiß es nie und lebe danach [my translation]!"

35   Gabriele Brandstetter, "Rhythmus als Lebensanschauung: zum Bewegungsdiskurs um 1900," in *Aus dem Takt: Rhythmus in Kunst, Kultur und Natur*, ed. Christa Brüstle (transcript, 2005), 33–43.

[50]   The stairway's landing at the top floor gallery.

Seeing the Law

As the aside on the review process has shown, the main staircase of the *Amtsgericht Mitte* was explicitly shaped for representation. Far from being a mere aspect of finesse or impe-
rious ostentation, I would like to consider its representative
function in the *Amtsgericht* as a constitutive necessity for
institutional legitimacy. Given the legal code's relative novelty, expressing legal order and the individual's role within
it was of utmost importance. In this context, the type of the
Amtsgericht functions as an organizing form, that is, the specific formal association of groups of persons towards the ful-
filment of a task or goal.[36] In this function, however, it is only
one outgrowth of an institutional form; the greater symbolic
order underpinned by certain principles.[37] Thus the discrete
unit of the *Amtsgericht Mitte* is undergirded by the all-encompassing order of the novel, equalizing legal code.

177

This distinction is taken from the sociologist Karl-Siegbert Rehberg, whose work on institutional stabilization emphasizes depiction and appearance as constitutive necessities of institutional functioning.[38] An institution's mechanisms for symbolizing foundational norms and principles serve to stabilize patterns of order, allowing it to guide actions and enact sanctions. Within this paradigm, institutions—such as marriage or the family, which function without rigid delineation—do not necessarily require a prescriptive organizational form. An organization, on the other hand, must necessarily have institutional forms that represent its goals and constitution because this depiction of principles and claims to legitimacy stabilizes it outwardly.[39] This externalizing of principles makes the institution legible to the public while at the same time implicating our citizen-viewer-subject in its structures and co-constituting them in the process.

Beyond this necessity to make the institution legible for an outside public, formulating central ideas acts as an intra-organizational synthesizing process, bundling divergent possible orientations into a fictional unity. It is toward the organizational spirit codified in this process that both the members of the institution and the public feel obligated, so that it serves as an orienting fiction.[40] The *Amtsgericht Mitte*, as one of the organizational components of the institution of the law, renders legible its central ideas, i.e., the equal and autonomous agency of all citizens under the law and the law's ability

36 I take the terminology in this section from Karl-Siegbert Rehberg's writing on the topic. The term 'organizing form' is my translation of Rehberg's *Organisationsform*, see Karl-Siegbert Rehberg, "Die stabilisierende 'Fiktionalität' von Präsenz und Dauer: Institutionelle Analyse und Historische Forschung," in *Institutionen und Ereignis: Über Historische Praktiken und Vorstellungen Gesellschaftlichen Ordnens*, eds. Reinhard Blänkner and Bernhard Jussen (Vandenhoeck & Ruprecht, 1998), 390.

37 Karl-Siegbert Rehberg, "Institutionen als symbolische Ordnungen: Leitfragen und Grundkategorien zur Theorie und Analyse institutioneller Mechanismen," in *Symbolische Ordnungen: Beiträge zu einer soziologischen Theorie der Institutionen*, ed. Hans Vorländer (Nomos, 2014), 66–68.

38 Rehberg, "Institutionen als symbolische Ordnungen," 43–45.

39 Rehberg, "Institutionen als symbolische Ordnungen," 55.

to institute beneficial social order. However, these ideas are not simply expressed by an analogous signifier but re-presented, making institutional order imminently present.[41]

In reading the *Amtsgericht* with Schmarsow, we can see the *Raumkomposition* of the staircase as the central idea of autonomous, sovereign pursuit of self-interest with the structure of the law made present in the immediacy of heightened spatial perception. Following this reading, the role of the temporality of experience within an institutional logic of generating legitimacy can be glimpsed; it symbolizes the presence of institutional time on the temporal plane of primal rhythm.[42] Extending through the spatial arrangement of the staircase, it is the prerequisite of experience as conceived by Schmarsow, undergirding the co-constitution of man and space.

In the plans for the *Amtsgericht,* the order of the law is not represented but made imminently perceptible and therefore plausible in the experience of order both within and without. The theoretical benefit of this projection lies not only in its strong truth claim and self-evidence (*Evidenz*) but also in its pre-reflexive communication of order. The immanence of aesthetic experience is here taken to affect all subjects in the same way, while Schmarsow's dimensional model claims to bring this realm of experience under unchanging, rational rules.[43] Not reliant on an educated subject capable of identifying iconographies, the *Einfühlungsästhetik* engaged here equally refuses to simply obliterate the viewer through opulent spectacle. Instead, planning references a mode of

40 This process of codifying and synthesizing divergent potential definitions of the institution draws heavily on the concept of "guiding differences" (*Leitdifferenzen*), for which Rehberg in turn draws heavily on Saussure and Luhmann. Rehberg, "Institutionen als symbolische Ordnungen," 66–68; Rehberg, "Die stabilisierende 'Fiktionalität' von Präsenz und Dauer," 389–99.

41 Rehberg takes this notion of presence directly from Hans Ulrich Gumbrecht, with whom he was in close contact, see Rehberg, "Institutionen als symbolische Ordnungen," 197, and Hans Ulrich Gumbrecht, "Zehn kurze Überlegungen zu Institutionen und Re/Präsentation," in *Präsenz*, Hans Ulrich Gumbrecht (Suhrkamp, 2012), 213–22.

42 See Rehberg, "Die stabilisierende 'Fiktionalität' von Präsenz und Dauer," 399–400, and Rehberg, "Institutionen als symbolische Ordnungen," 56–57.

aesthetic perception meant to heighten an inner sense of self. The offer of individuation presented by the experience of the *Amtsgericht* thus engenders the possibility of the private legal subject as they are found at the basis of liberal civil law.

Order and Orientation

What this examination has shown is not only how virtuality was an important plane on which the broader *dispositif* of planning saw representation occurring, but also the stabilizing role this plane of immanence could serve in an institutional context. In its more fantastical flourishes, the staircase serves to orient the viewer toward a distinct mode of self-perception with an imbricate organizational mode. This virtual space is engendered in the built environment, but as we have seen in the ceiling's inscription, these are presumed by planners to be not merely contiguous but identical. Conceptions of the planning phase are presumed to materialize unchanged into physical space, which in turn can be perceived *in toto* by the building's real-world users. This conception of planning correlates to Schmarsow's conception of the planners' sensory body, which becomes his tool for imagining 'correct' enclosure through architecture, in turn serving as the base of his practice.[44] Importantly, Schmarsow takes this act of enclosure to function unchanged for both real and ideal subjects.[45]

Schmarsow's architectural model presupposes a leap from the physical into a charged virtual space, as we have seen in the transcendent moment of *Einsicht*. If we follow the immanent relationship between built world and

[43] The role of historical and local variability of perception in Schmarsow is astutely described in Johanna Gullberg, "Voids and Bodies: August Schmarsow, Bruno Zevi and Space as a Historiographical Theme," ed. Branko Mitrovic, *Journal of Art Historiography* 14, no. 1 (2016): 1–20.

[44] This is the statement at the core of Schmarsow's famous dictum of architecture as space creator: "Raumgefühl und Raumphantasie drängen zur Raumgestaltung und suchen ihre Befriedigung in einer Kunst; wir nennen sie Architektur und können sie deutsch kurzweg als Raumgestalterin bezeichnen," Schmarsow, *Das Wesen der architektonischen Schöpfung*, 11.

[45] In the original German he speaks of "unserm Princip, der Raumumschließung eines wirklichen oder idealen Subjekts." Schmarsow, *Das Wesen der architektonischen Schöpfung*, 30.

physio-psychic experience as envisaged by Schmarsow, we can see how this reciprocity is split here to accommodate the legal order grafted upon it. In the ceiling inscription's interlocking realms, the subject of architecture and the subject of law become permutations of each other. This transposition shifts the imagined relation between space and man into a situation where man is not simply made aware of his own organization but is produced in his ideal relation to the law. Our attention here returns to the novelty of the legal space of the *Amtsgericht* at this historical moment. The territorial expansion of the legal code, the ideological role played by legal equality within the project of imperial unity, and the means by which representation addresses an imminent, sensory human capacity lead us to ask what the political implications of this orienting subjectivity are and whether they are conducive to political action. In short, we turn to the experience of this space and inquire about its political implications in both its virtual and actual articulations.

Despite the virtuality of Schmarsow's orienting schema, we want to inquire after its meaning and how its experience by actual users shapes a notion of the citizen's role in the *Rechtsstaat*. The attempt at making the legal code's revisions, aimed at creating comparability among diverse citizens, palpably precipitates in the relation of citizen-viewer to the legal order set by the space of the staircase. The figure of the law that emerges here characterizes the citizen-viewer through their sameness before it. This is formally mirrored in aesthetic experience, as posited by Schmarsow, which emphasizes sameness based on bodily givenness and metabolism. The sensory experience of architecture is thus an anthropological constant, the "common fate of all men [which] arises out of the human condition."[46] If we inquire after the political potential of this rush of sameness, we must see that:

> From the viewpoint of the world and the public realm, life and death and everything attesting to sameness are non-worldly, antipolitical, truly transcendent experiences.[47]

Although the *Amtsgericht* thus fulfilled the demand that new court buildings be public spaces, this relation did not materialize the implicit democratic arrangement we may associate

46
Hannah Arendt,
The Human Condition,
(University of Chicago
Press, 2010), 215.

47
Arendt,
Human Condition,
215.

48
Arendt,
Human Condition,
178.

49
Arendt,
Human Condition,
198.

50
"Thus action not only
has the most inti-
mate relationship to
the public part of
the world common to
us all, but is the one
activity which
constitutes it,"
Arendt,
Human Condition,
198.

with the category today. This arrangement towards transcendence over plurality reveals the planning *dispositif*'s reactionary core. In striving for unity, Schmarsow's anthropological
model reduces the plurality of society to the supposed bodily
sameness of its members. Within this paradigm, architecture's
ability to make meaning arises from and is reflexive of this
sameness, which it strives to ennoble. But Arendt's mus-
ings on transcendence here return us to the political reality of
other people, since she sees the experience of transcendence
as oppositional to that of plurality. This core reality of political life, whose emergence must be guaranteed for politics
to occur, describes the condition of "living as a distinct and
unique being among equals."[48] Within this reality, *men qua
men* actualize in speech and action, where "I appear to others as they appear to me."[49] Arendt refers to this appearing
as spatial, because the extension of plural selves generates a
relational in-between.[50]

The virtual space antecedent to legality generates
fungible subjects, without producing equal but distinct individuals in the mode of democratic politics. Despite the ten-
uous nature of this virtuality the space does carry political
implications in its actual form.[51] Entering the staircase system, we have already noted its tendency toward confusion,
without wanting to overextend this as a romantic metaphor,
we merely note that our observation has left us as a singular
being, thrown back on ourselves, navigating the built world.
This incidental quality is indicative of the nature of power in
the space. The subcutaneous communication of this meaning—the tactility Benjamin notes as architecture's characteristic—becomes explicit where the orienting fiction of transcendent space is gleaned, most clearly in the inscription.[52]
Eliciting attentive engagement in an altogether different mode
of reception, open to contemplation, the appearance (*das Auf-
scheinen*) of the ideal doesn't produce a place or subject to
serve as its counterpart.[53] This is true even in the ostensibly communal spaces of the waiting halls. Where reception
changes from diffused (*zerstreut*) to attentive, the stairway's
orientation opens an endless expanse toward a celestial horizon which remains categorically elusive.

It is into this space that the viewer's alienation arises. The transcendent relation—as we have seen in Arendt and as the staircase shows us—is monodirectional; the viewer strives toward it. Transcendence serves as a horizon and the orientation toward it is laden with a spatiality itself, even where it only blinks into existence.[54] Unlike the Arendtian *in-between*, the infinite *toward* of the transcendent, which the extension of the staircase's space already implies (albeit imperfectly), still marks a power relation. If we think transcendence from the subject position, the void of its categorical remoteness describes a fixed place apart from power, which it can yearn for but never inhabit.

51 Arendt sees the enclosure of the law and built structures as important stabilizers, though not guarantors, of the speech and action which characterize and take place in the public realm: "It is as though the wall of the polis and the boundaries of the law were drawn around an already existing public space which, however, without such stabilizing protection could not endure, could not survive the moment of action and speech itself," Arendt, *Human Condition*, 198.

52 Walter Benjamin, *Das Kunstwerk im Zeitalter seiner technischen Reproduzierbarkeit* (Suhrkamp, 2020), 69–73.

53 It is important to caveat the reading I advance here with the latent possibility of political action, which cannot fully be prohibited by the built world itself. As Jan-Werner Müller points out: "spaces do not determine human conduct (even if behavior can recodify the meaning of spaces); but how spaces enable (and disable) movement, and how they create particular flows, is usually intentional and carries political meaning," Jan-Werner Müller, "Just How is Architecture Ideological?," *Journal of Political Ideologies* 28, no. 3 (2023): 418.

54 As the choice of terminology already implies here, this relationship is structured this way in part because meaning is made from a tertiary position external to the relation. The intentional object here is the citizen-viewer who appears against the horizon of transcendent order. To attempt to inhabit this position in the actual situation of the staircase requires the citizen viewer to view himself from afar.

A Moment in Time?
Arendt, Moten, and the Futures of Black Action in Little Rock
Noah Grossmann

On the morning of September 4, 1957, 15-year-old Black[01] student Elizabeth Eckford attempted to enter Little Rock Central High School in Arkansas. After decades of struggle, school segregation had been deemed unconstitutional, and nine African American students had been registered to attend the previously whites-only school. However, the governor of Arkansas defied the Supreme Court Decision *Brown v. Board of Education* as well as the federal government and made it clear on TV that no Black child would enter the school. Accordingly, Governor Orval Faubus ordered the National Guard to line up all around the school on the morning of September 4.[02] Still, the Little Rock school superintendent persuaded the parents and NAACP activists to send the selected nine children to the school, trusting they would be protected.[03] Later that night, the NAACP changed plans but was unable to reach the Eckfords in time.[04] As a result, on the morning of September 4, Elizabeth approached the school alone,[05] where she was already expected by a white mob shouting things like "Lynch her!"[06] The scene was closely followed by several photographers—among them Ira Wilmer Counts Jr., who captured a striking image for the *Arkansas Democrat-Gazette*, later featured in *LIFE* magazine.

01 Throughout the article I capitalize the terms 'Black' and 'anti-Black' and keep 'white' in lowercase to disrupt the convention of either capitalizing or lowercasing both terms. I use 'Black' rather than 'African American' because it is a more inclusive term. See Kathryn T. Gines, *Hannah Arendt and the N***o Question* (Indiana University Press, 2014), 13.

02 See Daisy Bates, *The Long Shadow of Little Rock: A Memoir* (David McKay Company, 1962), 61.

03 Bates, *Long Shadow*, 63.

04 The National Association for the Advancement of Colored People.

Another photo of the situation—paralleling Eckford's experience with that of Dorothy Count's—was featured on the front page of *The New York Times* on September 5.[07]

[51]

Soldiers and Jeering Whites Greet Negro Students

LITTLE ROCK, ARK.: As a white student walks through the National Guard barrier at the left, 15-year-old Elizabeth Eckford is barred from entering Central High School.

Associated Press Wirephotos

CHARLOTTE, N. C.: A crowd of students follows Dorothy Counts as she is escorted to Harding High School by Dr. Edwin Tompkins. She became first Negro to attend school.

[52]

185

These pictures of Elizabeth Eckford and Dorothy Counts had a profound impact on the civil rights movement and the American political landscape.[08] In the images, the faces of Counts and Eckford are positioned more or less at the center. To observers, the hate-filled face of Hazel Bryan, 15 at the time, uttering an insult and the faces and gestures of white boys jeering immediately stand out. The contrast between the aggressive expressiveness of the white mob and the composed, deadpan faces of the Black teenage girls is striking. Elizabeth and Dorothy walk toward the camera, their eyes fixed on something we cannot see.

Among those moved by these pictures was Hannah Arendt, who most likely saw them on the front page of the *New York Times*.[09] She was particularly drawn to the faces of the teenagers and moved in such a way that she wrote an article arguing against school desegregation.[10] Seventy years later, Fred Moten was similarly moved by a photo of Elizabeth Eckford's face, her gaze hidden behind sunglasses. In 2018, he turned to the iconic photo in his search for radical potentials in Black history.

The point of departure for this contribution is two theorists who look at two Black teenagers' faces—and who develop differing interpretations of the photographs. Especially in Arendt's case, many scholars have already extensively contextualized her perspective on Little Rock, focusing also on the photographs and their relevance. These analyses typically

05 They did not reach the Eckfords because they did not have a telephone, see Gines, *Hannah Arendt and the N***o Question*, 16.

06 Bates, *Long Shadow*, 70.

07 The particularities of the photos are described in Ulrich Baer, "Die Zukunft in einem Bild aus der Vergangenheit erblicken: Hannah Arendt, Garry Winogrand und das Fotografieren der Welt," in *Hannah Arendt zwischen den Disziplinen*, eds. Ulrich Baer and Amir Eshel (Wallstein Verlag, 2014).

08 See Martin A. Berger, *Seeing Through Race: A Reinterpretation of Civil Rights Photography* (University of California Press, 2011).

09 This view is shared in the secondary literature but cannot be definitively proved. See Gines, *Hannah Arendt and the N***o Question*, 16; Baer, "Zukunft in einem Bild," 217–18; Danielle Allen, *Talking to Strangers: Anxieties of Citizenship since Brown v. Board of Education* (University of Chicago Press, 2004), 197.

either criticize or defend Arendt's "Reflections on Little Rock" as an examination of a particular socio-historical moment.[11] However, what I aim to bring into focus is that both Arendt and Moten think about possible futures lying ahead of a racist moment captured in a photo. They do not merely see these images as capturing a critique-worthy moment in time but instead engage with the photographs as holding that very moment open for different figurations of the future.[12] Thus, I want to show that Arendt and Moten take up their theoretical work precisely because it is unclear what will become of this captured moment. Accordingly, the focus of my analysis is to explore how each looks at the teenagers' faces and projects different futures onto them.

My interest in the intersection between photography's captured moment and theory's speculation about futures is helpful in two ways. First, it highlights that both theorists constantly risk failing to do justice to the particular lives of those photographed. Second, it enables a reassessment of Arendt's and Moten's texts in a new light—structured by different visions of the future, ranging from progress and integration to impasse and revolution.

Accordingly, I do not attempt to provide an all-encompassing reconstruction of Arendt's or Moten's texts on Little Rock. Nor do I seek to examine the historical figures themselves (others have focused on Eckford's and Count's experiences).[13] Instead, this article aims to analyze Arendt and Moten as theorists who interrogate possible futures beyond a moment of racism, examining their differences while also identifying points of similarity. I read their texts as speculations about futures—attempts to move beyond a particular historical moment captured by photographs. Ultimately, I seek to reveal Arendt's and Moten's writings as dynamic force fields of conflicting temporalities in which they struggle to situate the moment.

10
The "essay was written in 1957 at the request of the editors of *Commentary*, but did not appear until 1959 when it was published *by Dissent*," Seyla Benhabib, *The Reluctant Modernism of Hannah Arendt* (Rowman & Littlefield, 2003), 146.

11
For an overview of the strands of criticism and defense see Maike Weißpflug, *Hannah Arendt: Die Kunst, politisch zu denken* (Matthes & Seitz, 2019), 64.

12
See Baer, "Zukunft in einem Bild," 229.

13
For the particularities of Count's case, see Gines, *Hannah Arendt and the N***o Question*, 16–17.

Climbing up the Social Ladder, Pseudo-Politics, and Progress

14
For instance all the texts referenced in footnote 9 above.

15
Hannah Arendt, "A Reply to Critics," *Dissent* 6, no. 2 (1959): 179.

16
For her perspective on teenagers see Sana M. Nakata, "Elizabeth Eckford's Appearance at Little Rock: The Possibility of Children's Political Agency," *Politics* 28, no.1 (2012): 19-25.

17
Hannah Arendt, "Reflections on Little Rock," *Dissent* 6, no. 1, (1959): 50.

Arendt starts her "Reflections" with an observation about the expression on Elizabeth Eckford's face. In fact, the secondary literature widely agrees that Arendt most likely mistakes Dorothy Count's face for Elizabeth's or merges both.[14] Nevertheless, Arendt refers only to Eckford's case, noting that "her face bore eloquent witness to the obvious fact that she was not precisely happy."[15] Arendt misinterprets the two teenagers as lacking political agency, reading their facial expressions as merely displaying suffering.[16] However, she does not only look at the suffering in the moment it was captured, but suspects that the teenager's suffering has a (pre-) history and is directed toward a particular future: "The girl, obviously, was asked to be a hero—that is something neither her absent father nor the equally absent representatives of the NAACP felt called upon to be."[17] In making this claim, Arendt insinuates that Black civil rights activists and Elizabeth Eckford's father are engaged in a kind of action that leads to the suffering of teenagers, perhaps even deliberately causing it in order to achieve particular goals in the future.[18]

She implies that the future envisioned by Black parents and the NAACP is one in which a teenage girl's suffering is an accepted cost, as they are "involved in an affair of social climbing."[19] According to Arendt, both the parents

18   Two things should be noted here. First, the background facts contradict Arendt's thesis that Eckford's parents expected Elizabeth to be facing the white crowd alone. Their latest information came from a meeting the evening before in which people from the school and the NAACP persuaded the parents to not accompany their children but trust a minimum of safety measures that would accompany the nine students. From this perspective it is still appropriate to say that the Eckfords, like Black parents all over the country, sent their children into such situations not knowing what would happen to them. Secondly, it should be noted that the trope of the absent Black father entails certain assumptions about Black men and is part of racist discourses in the USA, see Omarr K. Rambert, "The Absent Black Father: Race, The Welfare-Child Support System, and the Cyclical Nature of Fatherlessness," *UCLA Law Review* 324, no. 68 (2021). Additionally, Arendt only looks at the male parent to take up public action, not considering the mother.

19   Arendt uses this phrase in a statement that followed up on her "Reflections," see Arendt, "Reply to Critics," 179.

and the civil rights activists belong to an oppressed minority and as such "were never the best judges on the order of priorities in such matters and there are many instances when they preferred to fight for social opportunity rather than for basic human or political rights." The parents, in her view, accept their daughter's sorrow as a necessary sacrifice for social mobility. The NAACP pursues the same goal, being "almost exclusively concerned with discrimination in employment, housing and education."[20]

Arendt—moved by suffering that demands change—conceives of the future of this moment in binary terms. On the one hand, she argues that a promising future will only become possible when Black people fight against discriminatory, racist laws, such as restrictions on interracial marriage and electoral rights.[21] On the other hand, she attempts to distinguish these legitimate struggles for equality from what she views as misguided efforts by Black people to gain access to white social spaces.[22] She defends the "social custom of segregation" with reference to the constitutional right to free association.[23] Arendt states that "discrimination is as indispensable a social right as equality is a political right."[24] To support this claim, she defends Jewish people's right to restrict "vacation resorts ... according to ethnic origin." In the same vein, she argues, white parents should be allowed to decide who their children go to school with.[25] For

20
Arendt, "Reflections," 46.

21   It has been argued that a reason for this is that Arendt takes up elements of the integrationist and opportunist-parvenu figure from her historical analysis of modern totalitarianism (see Benhabib, *Reluctant Modernism*, 149) and leaves out the elements of the pariah, "rebels who defend Jews as a group, and justice, by public actions to make exclusion from citizenship a political issue," George Shulman, "Fred Moten's Refusals and Consents: The Politics of Fugitivity," *Political Theory* 49, no. 2 (2021): 293.

22   In fact, Arendt perceives buses and restaurants as not being part of the social. They are part of the public infrastructure; hence segregation should be even more vehemently fought, Arendt, "Reflections," 52.

23   Arendt, "Reflections," 49.

24   Arendt, "Reflections," 51. Discrimination in this case should be understood as the "right and freedom of like-minded individuals to associate, to communicate, and to create a space in common without making this accessible to all," Benhabib, *Reluctant Modernism*, 150.

Arendt, schools are analogous to those vacation resorts for Jews only, since white parents and Jewish people alike make use of their right to free association. Consequently, she treats schools as a matter of free association and fails to acknowledge how unequal education leads to unequal participation in political processes.[26]

My reading elucidates the temporal dichotomy that structures this theorization of the photographs. On one hand, Arendt charts a clear path for a better future for Black people: "The right to marry whoever one wishes" should be fought for, as should "political rights, like the right to vote" for Black people. Arendt envisions a temporality of steady progress through an expansion of rights. However, such advancement necessitates the active presence of Black parents and activists in front of Little Rock Central High School and within the political arena. On the other hand, Arendt observes that parents and NAACP members appear in the photograph only by virtue of their absence. To her, they seem to shy away from their civic responsibility for the "world into which they have borne their children," a world that it is their task "to change or improve."[27]

With regard to the parents, this second future can be elaborated as follows: they remain stuck in their stories of non-progress and mere opportunism.[28] With regard to the representatives of the NAACP, Arendt suspects that while they do try to act in the political field, they do so by pursuing a mistaken strategy—one that indeed existed[29]— that relied heavily on a symbolic politics and the deliberate creation of images intended to arouse pity and sympathy. Thus, Arendt seems to perceive the staging of affect-producing images as a pseudo-political action that fails to contribute to a future of competition among equals through argument. From Arendt's viewpoint, the activists seem incapable

25   Arendt, "Reflections," 52–55.

26   For the relation between segregation, racism, and education see Gines, *Hannah Arendt and the N***o Question*, 26–27.

27   "Reflections," 49–50.

28   Or as Arendt puts it, in their "fight for social opportunity," Arendt, "Reflections," 46.

29   See Maurice Berger, *For All the World to See: Visual Culture and the Struggle for Civil Rights* (Yale University Press, 2010).

of a "public-political struggle [that] must transform narrow self-interest into a more broadly shared public or common interest."[30] According to Arendt, both the Black parents of Little Rock and the NAACP activists, by demanding mere integration, were acting opportunistically rather than creating possibilities for a post-racist future. Only the struggle for marriage rights and voting rights, or more broadly full legal rights together with Black participation in politics, are portrayed as capable of bringing equality to the Black population.

However, Arendt's gaze not only wanders to the promised land of law and politics. The lonely teenagers surrounded by racist violence also bring up a dark memory and lead her to project a totally different future onto Eckford's face.

Stuck in an Impasse or Moving Towards Disaster

In "Reflections," there are moments where Arendt's gaze is averted from the possible future of steady progress. A few pages into the text, Arendt cautions that the increasing integration of Black people into society may inadvertently exacerbate their racialized status:

> The more equal people have become in every respect, and the more equality permeates the whole texture of society, the more will differences be resented, the more conspicuous will those become who are visibly and by nature unlike the others.[31]

In the parts of "Reflections" mentioned previously, Arendt projects a progressive future onto measures that extend equality in the realm of the "public domain," be it public transport or politics and individual rights. The quoted passage, however, puts those measures aiming for equality in a totally different light and inserts them into another model of the future. Now, political[32] and individual rights are no longer trusted to eradicate racial differences—indeed, quite the contrary. Arendt's sudden shift to this pessimistic view of the future corrects her idealizing views regarding the achievement of certain procedures for achieving political equality. She now seems to consider racism as something resisting change: "the principle of equality, even in its American form, is not omnipotent; it cannot equalize natural, physical

30
Benhabib, *Reluctant Modernism*, 201.

31
Arendt, "Reflections," 48.

characteristics." This breaks down the opposition between opportunistic integration and political progress shown at work earlier. Instead, Arendt now encourages us to reassess American equality as Janus-faced: on the one hand, she describes it as having the "enormous power to equalize what by nature and origin is different." But Arendt also suggests that, on the other hand, Black people simultaneously keep being different and that the racialization of Black people is constant in its mere existence but changes its concrete form. Thus, she appears to hold the "natural, physical characteristics" of racialization as insurmountable through the "principle of equality, even in its American form." Arendt insists that racial otherness does not diminish in times of seeming integration but only shifts its appearance because it is absolutely necessary to American society: the racial otherness of Black people is needed because only then are the "differences by which people belong to certain groups" kept alive.[33]

I want to suggest that her defense of the free right to association, which is also the right to exclusion and discrimination in the social sphere, shows that the group identity of whiteness is bound to the right to discriminate against Black people. Arendt laments the fact that a group's identity "demands that they discriminate against other groups," but she diagnoses that the American way of life, the "pursuit of happiness," is only possible if discrimination is held as an "indispensable ... social right."[34] According to this diagnosis, the equal opportunities and freedoms of the US need to be seen as inseparably interwoven with the right to discrimination, which can be described as a racist common sense that makes Black people appear to be different by nature. This

32 Arendt implicitly wonders what "qualities" for a new beginning a Black candidate can showcase when these criteria are set by the 79% of people sharing a deeply racist common sense. In a democratic election even the most radical "qualities" in "judgment and opinion" still "depend upon the qualities of the electorate," Arendt, "Reflections," 50–51. Thus she questions how a singular Black perspective aiming at a post-racist order could ever gain general value for the foundation of a political community which is built on devaluing Black life and at the same time change its way of togetherness.

33 Arendt, "Reflections," 48–51.

34 Arendt, "Reflections," 51.

perspective allows one to view white supremacist layers of racism—not only anti-Black racism[35]—as a *conditio sine qua non* of American society. Arendt works on this perspective in other parts of her oeuvre as well and warns that Black people are and might keep being excluded from the "tacit *consensus universalis* of the nation."[36] In the vein of this diagnosis, it is naïve to believe in a USA without racism and thus not to recognize how profoundly racial common sense shapes whiteness as a people's identity. Thus, Arendt sees two coexisting, interrelated futures ahead of Elizabeth Eckford's walk to school: first, the process that might realize comprehensive equality for all, and second, beneath this potential success story, a shape-shifting racialization that consists of perceiving Black people as others and being able to treat them differently. In the course of such an integration that keeps racism intact the "difference" of race may come to be "resented" even more.[37] For this threatening scenario, Arendt refers to a "danger point well known to students of history."[38] By following this reference to the escalation of antisemitic violence in the Europe of the 1930s and 40s, we can better understand how Arendt fundamentally revises her previous model of a progressive future. In *The Origins of Totalitarianism,* Arendt parts with the historical trajectory of a steadily secured and improved position of racialized Jewish people through an expansion of equality. Instead, she shows that the acceptance

---

35   It should be noted that the events of Little Rock encompass not only anti-Black racism but also antisemitism: Dr. Benjamin Fine, education editor of the *New York Times* at the time, who consoled Elizabeth Eckford on the bench of the Bus stop, reports the following: "A girl I had seen ustling [sic] in one of the local bars screamed 'A dirty New York Jew! Get him!' A man asked me, 'Are you a Jew?' I said, 'Yes.' He then said to the mob, 'Let him be! We'll take care of him later,'" Bates, *Long Shadow,* 71.

36   "We know that this original crime could not be remedied by the Fourteenth and Fifteenth Amendments; on the contrary, the *tacit* exclusion from the *tacit* consensus was made more conspicuous by the inability or unwillingness of the federal government to enforce its own laws… An explicit constitutional amendment, addressed specifically to the N***o people of America, might have underlined the great change more dramatically for these people who had never been welcome," Hannah Arendt, *Crises of the Republic* (Harcourt Brace & Company, 1972), 90–91.

37   Arendt, "Reflections," 48.

of more and more Jews into social spaces, mostly on legal grounds, was accompanied by "social resentment against Jews" and the development of "ideologically charged antisemitism."[39] Steady inclusion went hand in hand with an equally steady racialization of the group, reinforced by self-contradicting ideological constructs to which mobs reacted with racist violence.

There are two aspects to this conception of a future that combines integration and continuing, even intensifying, racist violence. First, Arendt assumes that the equality granted to racialized people must be seen warily as only temporary. She understands the equality of Jews—and analogously that of Black people—"as an entitlement one secures when one is considered sufficiently normal by one's fellow citizens."[40] This granting of acceptance and "normality" leaves intact, even strengthens, the common sense of racial otherness.[41] Racialized people might be granted certain rights and a status of 'normality,' but they constantly have to prove that they adhere to white standards. This provisionally granted and therefore always endangered position leads to the other aspect of this temporality, the future danger point. Second, the racialized group, even when seemingly integrated, always remains on the brink of being rejected from the realm

38   Arendt, "Reflections," 48. For the relation of Anti-Black racism to antisemitism, see Danielle Allen, "Law's Necessary Forcefulness: Ralph Ellison vs. Hannah Arendt on the Battle of Little Rock," in *Multiculturalism and Political Theory,* eds. Anthony Simon Laden and David Owen (Cambridge University Press, 2007), 327.

39   Ainsley LeSure, "The White Mob, (In) Equality Before the Law, and Racial Common Sense: A Critical Race Reading of the N***o Question in 'Reflections on Little Rock,'" *Political Theory* 49, no. 1 (2021), 12.

40   Le Sure, "White Mob, (In) Equality Before the Law, and Racial Common Sense," 5.

41   "Whenever equality becomes a mundane fact in itself, without any gauge by which it may be measured or explained, then there is one chance in a hundred that it will be recognized simply as a working principle of a political organization in which otherwise unequal people have equal rights; there are ninety-nine chances that it will be mistaken for an innate quality of every individual, who is 'normal' if he is like everybody else and 'abnormal' if he happens to be different," Hannah Arendt, *The Origins of Totalitarianism* (Harcourt Brace & Company, 1964), 54.

of normality for arbitrary reasons. Whenever the ruling class or certain political actors consider it useful, the progressive reduction of racial injustices can be used to incite resistance on the part of the white population, which will defend its racial difference, its freedoms, and its privileges. If these privileges of racialization continue to be dismantled, the basis that made racial differences possible will be depleted and violence will seek other, even worse ways. With this temporal horizon in mind, Arendt is indeed very aware of the white violence captured in the photos but also senses that this could be only a portent of much worse anti-Black violence to come once Black people substantially endanger the realms of white privilege.

This opens up a new future emanating from Eckford's sorrowful face. Projecting the horror of Nazi antisemitism as a warning of a possible future, Arendt calls on Black people to refrain from further actions aiming at more social equality. She urges them to accept a certain amount of inequality and violence and not to fight for their rights because the price might be the breakdown of an order that sustains a minimum degree of protection.[42] Thus we can conclude that Arendt looks at Eckford's troubled face turned away from the white violence and reacts with two contradictory calls. On the one hand, we can hear her yelling at the parents and NAACP activists to "move forward," on the other, we can hear her hushing them, as if to say "don't move at all." In both cases the frame for thinking about possible futures beyond Eckford's suffering is Arendt's commitment to the "survival of the Republic,"[43] be it as the possibility for progress or the guarantee of a minimum degree of safety. We can interpret the coexistence and contradiction of Arendt's claims as central to the stability of American post-slavery society, in which Black people must believe in the ideal of increasing equality and their potential to one day "climb" the social ladder.[44] For American society cannot exist without this story of progress. Mostly because of the inclusion of Black Americans in the sphere of the free market, self-responsibility has proved to be useful and rewarding for employers.[45] But at the same time, the freed slaves and their descendants must stay "Black" people, as American society needs a white identity and its corresponding privileges. Gazing at Elizabeth Eckford's sorrowful

42
See Allen,
"Law's Necessary
Forcefulness," 327.

43
Arendt,
"Reflections," 47.

44
Arendt,
"Reply to Critics," 179.

45
See the historical
analysis in
Saidiya Hartman,
*Scenes of Subjection:
Terror, Slavery,
and Self-Making
in Nineteenth-
Century America*
(Norton, 2022),
201–368.

46
Arendt,
"Reflections," 47.

47
This tension is aptly
described as one of
political movements
and Black activists/
intellectuals in
Hortense Spillers,
"The Crisis of the
N***o Intellectual.
A Post-Date,"
in *A Companion to
African-American
Philosophy*,
eds. Tommy Lee Lott
and John P. Pittman
(Wiley Blackwell,
2003).

48
Fred Moten,
*The Universal
Machine*
(Duke University
Press, 2018), 100.

face with Arendt shows us a simultaneity of possible futures that shape American society: despite the existence of liberal rights, procedures, and narratives of progress, Black individuals continue to navigate a landscape marked by racism, in which not progress but standstill is felt. Progress, stalemate, and an intensification of racism are seen as scenarios lying ahead of Eckford's sorrowful face.

Once Arendt's commitment to the "survival of the Republic"[46] is seen as the tacit precondition to her conceptions of possible futures, we can ask what other futures could be projected onto the moment of the photograph. Eckford's walk and the pictures taken of it are now widely seen as a central and iconic moment in the struggle of Black people for a better life and for a post-racist order. In the history of this struggle, the extent to which the institutions and rights and the "survival of the republic" might be said to help or hinder the achievement of a post-racist *status quo* has always been controversial.[47] Accordingly, there have been diverse attempts to think about possible futures for Black people. In 2018 Fred Moten explored the photograph of Elizabeth Eckford also focusing on her face. He builds on an African-American tradition of thought which had to grapple with the realization that Black participation in politics, and even a Black president, could not make Black lives matter differently in the United States. The 60 years separating Moten from the events at Little Rock and Arendt's article make a difference insofar as certain visions of progress no longer hold any promise for the likes of Moten. Hence, Moten builds on the thesis that the civil rights movement not only demanded more rights for Black people but also sought to completely destroy the everyday life of the Southern states in order to invent a new reality.[48] Accordingly, he looks at Elizabeth Eckford's face in search of a future that radically breaks with Arendt's beloved American Republic.

An Ongoing History of
an Already Existing Alternative

In the essay "Refuge, Refuse, Refrain," published in his book *Universal Machine,* Fred Moten looks at the iconic photo of Elizabeth Eckford and focuses on her eyes, describing them as "obscured by shadow and by sunglasses, which could be mistaken for a blindfold."[49] Moten criticizes the fact that Arendt and the political theorists who succeeded her all see Eckford's walk only as a preliminary stage to the steady path to legal and political equality. As I showed above, this criticism is already latently inherent in Arendt's own text.

Moten draws on historical analyses that show that the Western "political" relies on a concept of the autonomous universal human being endowed with equal rights, which was developed within capitalist nation-states in the same historical period that they were enslaving Black people.[50] This coincidence of the western capitalist nation-state and its procedures of political emancipation with the historical appearance of slavery leads Moten to state that the "ontological categories" of the political subject and the related progress story of its procedures are de facto predicated on grammars of anti-Black antagonism.[51] Hence, Moten can—against his own caricature of Arendt[52]—be read as radicalizing Arendt's questioning of the supposed success story of an expanding equality for the marginalized by means of social inclusion, democratic participation, and legal rights.

In contrast to Arendt, Moten makes it clear from the outset that he is reading something into Elizabeth Eckford's face, that he is theorizing a future based on his act of looking at her face: "Eckford appears to those who want to feel, to place her eyes and thoughts elsewhere." Moten's indeterminate "elsewhere" indicates that Eckford's walk is directed by her "alternative vision" aiming at a post-racist future. For this interpretation, Moten makes use of the photo's arrangement: Eckford's gaze is directed at the camera and, as it were, through and beyond the viewer. He thus states that Eckford's walk is moving towards something that most viewers are unable to see and imagine, a "refusal of time and place." This aims at "another mode of organization altogether,"[53] "something other than transcendental subjectivity," something that can so far only be "called nothing."[54]

49
Moten, *Universal Machine,* 76. Moten does not specify which photo he has in mind, which is why I assume he refers to the well-known photo taken by Counts.

50
Moten, *Universal Machine,* 100.

51
This thesis is developed in Fred Moten, "Blackness and Nothingness (Mysticism in the Flesh)," *The South Atlantic Quarterly* 112, no. 4. (2013), 739–40.

52
He portrays Arendt as the most important theorist of the political sphere of autonomous, isolated political subjects.

53
Moten, *Universal Machine,* 72–76.

54
Moten, "Blackness and Nothingness," 778.

55
Moten,
Universal Machine, 76.

56
Moten,
Universal Machine, 76.

57
Ralph Ellison,
"In Interview,"
in *Who speaks for
the N***o?*,
Robert Penn Warren
(Random House, 1965),
344.

58
Moten,
Universal Machine,
104.

This touches a central question of the discourse of Black Studies, namely the extent to which something positive can be attributed to Black life beyond negation. For present purposes, it is crucial that Moten speaks of Elizabeth Eckford as appearing to him through a photo, walking somewhere, someplace we don't know, and that he describes this appearance as a "nonperformance, which bears the story, the ongoing history, of an already existing alternative."[55]

Moten is not thinking about alternative futures we can read in or out of Eckford's act. Instead, he searches for "ongoing histories" that existed in Little Rock but have so far been neglected. In contrast to Arendt, he draws on further material beyond the photos to describe two "ongoing histories" into which, on his account, Elizabeth Eckford is to be inserted. These histories come as two different answers to the question of where Elizabeth Eckford "came from, and where she slipped to."[56]

In a first answer to this question, Moten inserts Elizabeth Eckford in the history and future of Black social bonds, of which families are seen as only one form. He states that Elizabeth Eckford, and Black people in the American South in general, need to be located on a continuum of physical and psychological terror. Moten takes up an argument that Ralph Ellison brought up in an interview directly responding to Arendt's "Reflections": that Arendt has "absolutely no conception" how the "terrors of social life" structure relations for Black people and their families in particular.[57] Ellison breaks up Arendt's binary between Black opportunism and political progress and makes palpable Arendt's incapability to imagine that Black parents in the South cannot guarantee safety for their children. Moten generalizes Ellison's insight by stating that violence and separation inevitably happen to any kind of Black relationship. With this he situates Eckford's concrete suffering on a continuum of situations in which Black people in the USA are constantly forced to experience what it means to live in a violently racialized Black body. The violence captured in the photo needs to be seen as an "intensification of previously existing conditions."[58] He states that this quasi-*a priori* woundedness of Black people does not mean that their relationships are constantly breaking apart or aim at integration, as Ellison argues. Rather, he asks how relationships and families are built around, answer, and "offer existing alternatives" [59] to this anti-Black violence.

Moten draws on Elizabeth Eckford's own account of the events that highlights how her family prayed with her in the morning and how her mother held her in her arms after the white terror.[60] By drawing on these practices of preparation and care, he suggests that a sociality between Elizabeth and her parents can be seen to "frame[s] what is supposed to be Eckford's abandonment." In Moten's account, the individual violence of the moment in the photograph that captured Arendt's attention dissolves in two conflicting temporalities. He inserts Eckford's shaded eyes into a history of never-ending racist violence that is always already interwoven with a counter-history of resisting sociality. This tipping figure of two dialectically interwoven histories and futures behind and ahead of the photo makes Moten speculate that Elizabeth Eckford's state of mind amidst the terror is drawn towards her parents in the sense that she anticipates, moves towards a different state of being-together he calls "assembly." This is epitomized in the thesis that the "absolute woundedness is also an absolute blessing."[61]

Such a conception of the future that sees in Eckford's woundedness a blessing runs the permanent risk of viewing Eckford's suffering as a necessary precursor to Black sociality. This is problematic because, so construed, Moten can only tell one story of the captured moment of violence, namely that it may and will be cured in sociality. Moten's story is in tension with Elizabeth Eckford's life, in which this very violence has remained haunting and traumatic. In addition, this temporality tends to romanticize the relationship between Elizabeth and her parents as establishing an ideal togetherness of care and love.[62]

But Moten's text does provide an antidote to these dangers and gives another answer to the question of where Elizabeth Eckford "came from, and where she slipped to."[63] He projects another future onto Eckford's shaded eyes by stating that one can perceive Eckford as "a soloist who is not one."[64] Moten doesn't argue that Eckford really performs a solo but uses the temporal logic of the jazz solo to situate Eckford's walk in a particular history: this ongoing history

59
Moten, *Universal Machine*, 76.

60
Moten references Eckford's own perspective in Allen, "Law's Necessary Forcefulness," 323–24, that references Bates, *Long Shadow*, 73–76, in which Eckford is quoted.

61
Moten, *Universal Machine*, 104.

62
Moten uses the paradigm of "love" in this regard but it should be noted that he frames it also as a "destructive revolutionary force," Moten, *Universal Machine*, 86.

63
Moten, *Universal Machine*, 76.

64
Moten, *Universal Machine*, 101.

65
The other paradigm is the religious gesture of blessing and "charismata," Moten, *Universal Machine*, 103–05.

66
Moten is influenced by theorists like Amiri Baraka, who emphasize that the cultural activities historically developed by slaves and their descendants create relations and thereby experiences that enable running away, being fugitive, "making our refuge, on the run," Moten, *Universal Machine*, 243.

is modeled after the way a solo takes up previous musical moments, another solo, or an ensemble playing in the sense that it formulates an expectation or request to be taken up and continued. Moten argues that musical improvisation and other cultural techniques[65] can be situated in a chain of actions in which each part gestures toward a juncture at which someone else is required to further advance the process. To look at Eckford's shaded eyes through the analogy of a jazz artist's temporal milieu means to describe Eckford's walk and her parents' actions as being at once preceded by actions, continuing them, but most of all being fundamentally uncertain and open for a continuation unknown at the moment of action itself. Just like the soloist does not know what comes after her solo has ended, Eckford's gaze is shaded or indeterminable because she cannot know what comes next.[66]

It is debatable whether Eckford's walk is indeed structured by the same radical openness that structures a jazz improvisation. It is certainly a bold poetic claim that Eckford's gaze anticipates and moves toward a continuation that may be wholly different, thereby embodying a belief that someone (or something) else will continue the struggle. To be clear: Moten makes his own gesture of looking at Eckford's face in this way transparent as a gesture of speculation. Nevertheless, he refrains from marking the limits of his technique of analogy. To do so, he would have to describe in detail how Eckford's walk engenders possibilities that differ from the possibilities that are enabled by a jazz solo. He does not spell out the obvious difference between improvising with other people and being attacked on the basis of your racialization. Accordingly, the incomparably greater risk for Elizabeth Eckford's actual body tends to be leveled out through his use of analogy.

The particular temporal logic into which he inserts Eckford is defined not only through the moment of radical openness towards another mode of continuation. His reference towards musical and cultural techniques is not only an analogy but also a claim about specific historical relations. He states that Black forms of struggle are intertwined with other cultural or religious techniques, which together point towards another state of order. Or, in Moten's words, Eckford's "alternative vision" must be understood as a "sight made plain by sound or song."[67] This presupposes the well-established argument that Black forms of resistance unfold through a network of subterranean relations, between practices at different times—and that this network spread temporally and geographically across socio-cultural life in the Black Atlantic, cultivating a mode of believing in another future.[68] Moten does not spell out this thesis of interconnected, separate, and simultaneously connected practices. He only vaguely implies it to suggest that certain forms of practice are necessary preconditions for Elizabeth Eckford's performance. The exact juncture of the history of Black cultural-political practices and the concrete life of Elizabeth Eckford remain open, and Moten simply assumes that she visited Black churches, listened to Black music—or was in another way trained in the "aesthetic sociality" of "black music" and other Black cultural practices.[69]

These explanations are intended to make palpable the risks inherent in Moten's move to insert Eckford into what he calls the "ongoing history of an already existing alternative" in Black aesthetic practices.[70] But there are undoubtedly also benefits: Moten allows us to see through Eckford's walk, through her shaded eyes another version of a future beyond a racist moment. Moten thus can be said to highlight a particular aspect of Eckford's walk: that she engages in a history of Black cultural-political resistances against an anti-Black order and realizes a moment of unfulfilled potential in the cause for a post-racist society. Moten makes it transparent that he looks at the sunglasses and hears a "call," hears Eckford inviting, "out of a brutally imposed languishing,"[71] others to "go to the school we tore down and rebuilt for all of us."[72] This clearly doesn't refer to the High School and town of Little Rock that kept being a place of white supremacism and anti-Black violence.[73] He makes clear that the particular moment didn't reach the goal of a post-racist society and didn't build another form of High School. On the contrary, Eckford's endeavor can be said to share the feature of defeat with many undertakings in the history of Black people in the US. Moten's theory tries to rewire a broken but also interconnected web of cultural practices and forms of resistance aiming for "another mode of organization altogether"[74] that is ongoing and not yet fully realized. By looking beyond

67
Moten,
Universal Machine, 76.

68
See Paul Gilroy,
The Black Atlantic: Modernity and Double Consciousness
(Harvard University Press, 1993).

69
Moten,
Universal Machine, 74.

70
Moten,
Universal Machine, 76.

71
Moten,
Universal Machine, 127.

72
Moten,
Universal Machine, 88.

73
For an account of the white terror in the weeks and years after see Bates, *Long Shadow*, 91–93 and 116–17.

74
Moten,
Universal Machine, 72.

the established narratives about Little Rock and the objective historiography of Black resistance movements, Moten tries to gain something different from the pain and missed chances: a chain of beginnings, fragmented continuities, devoid of closure that keep the door to fundamental change ajar.

Concluding Thoughts

Throughout this article, Arendt's and Moten's theories appeared as continuations and sequels to particular moments in time captured by photographs. Each author employs different temporal registers of progress, stalemate, rupture, and rollback to grasp what lies ahead of the moment of the photographs. By doing so, they develop fertile tensions between conflicting conceptions of the future.

On the one hand, Arendt projects the future of steady progress through participation in democratic procedures onto Eckford's sorrowful face. On the other hand, she outlines a pessimistic vision of the future that sees racism as a necessary corollary, not to be overcome through democratic procedures, of the American Republic. Through this, Arendt's text opens up a simultaneity of futures that shape American society: despite the existence of liberal rights, procedures and narratives of progress, Black individuals continue to navigate a landscape marked by racism. The tension is fruitful because it makes clear that, besides the democratic procedures that aim to transcend or transform the established form of racist sociality, there needs to be a theory that acknowledges the ongoing dynamic of racism despite these reforms.

Moten looks at Eckford's shaded eyes and deepens that tension. He looks at Eckford's face and works through temporal registers that Arendt used as well (progress and stalemate) while urging us to think about a post-racist state beyond the mechanisms of the American Republic. Moten's theory moves toward the lived reality, the ongoing histories of Black people. His text leaves us with a theory of Eckford's walk that is demanding, speculative, problematic, and fascinating because he states that an alternative exists for Eckford. But he is also torn. Do the Eckfords realize a revolutionary and utopian sociality of preparation and care? Should Eckford and her family be placed outside the dialectical temporality of suffering and liberating sociality? In trying to get beyond such a logic Moten suggests looking at the transhistorical continuum of Black cultural techniques and modes of being-together, ranging from the Black family's solidarity after the event to jazz improvisation. His technique of transhistorical collage links separate moments, of which Eckford's is one among many, and his own theory as well. From this perspective, empowerment and resistance cannot be thought of as happening at points in time changing a previous state for the better.

Moreover, he sees a temporal chain of different practices which are all oriented towards an "elsewhere" that no point in time sufficiently captures.[75] In order to do justice to the specificity of this committed theory position and non-Western theoretical languages (and to be able to criticize them), the intersection of theory and media warrants further investigation. Moten works with the same photos as Arendt, but relates himself to them differently, writing from a different position. This position of speculation—or fabulation[76]—is still foreign to dominant theoretical paradigms. Moten and other theorists in the field of Black Studies look at photos (listen to music, view artworks) and theorize ongoing histories which do not fit easily into models of progress through democratic institutions. In doing so, they write themselves into Black history. And they try to shed light on the openness and on future continuations still unthinkable at the moment of Eckford's action.

75
Moten,
Universal Machine, 76.

76
See Saidiya Hartman,
*Wayward Lives:
Beautiful Experiments*
(Serpent's Tail, 2021).

Being and Appearance, Process and Medium
Reinhold Görling

01
Hannah Arendt,
"Thinking and Moral
Considerations,"
Social Research 38,
no. 3 (1971), 419.

02
Hannah Arendt,
The Life of the Mind
(Wallstein Verlag,
2024), 30.

In a lecture that appeared in the journal *Social Research* in 1971 and of which Hannah Arendt also included large parts in the "Introduction" to her unfinished three-volume work *The Life of the Mind,* Arendt speaks of the "discrepancy between words, the medium in which we think, and the world of appearance, the medium in which we live."[01] She goes on to ask whether the discovery of this discrepancy was not the beginning of philosophy and metaphysics, except that in the beginning, for example with Heraclitus and Parmenides, the path to true being was seen in thinking, "be it as *nous* or as *logos*," while over time the emphasis shifted from speech to appearance, "hence to sense perception and the implements with which we can extend and sharpen our bodily senses." However, by speaking of a discrepancy between two media and not of a juxtaposition of two realms of being or two human faculties, she points to a third, in which words and appearances resemble or combine with one another: the term medium, common to both determinations, refers neither to determinable objects that are perceived by our senses nor to truths withdrawn from perception, but to ways of relationality, to paths, procedures, external tools or inner capacities through which we relate to the world and to others. Arendt thus points to a way out of the juxtaposition of thinking and perceiving, as well as out of the differentiation of content and form, which are always already interwoven in the creation of relationships. Accordingly, the alternative between a primacy of thinking and a primacy of perception also dissolves. In *The Life of the Mind,* Arendt will therefore speak of a "primacy of appearance."[02] Living beings exist in a constant relationship and exchange with the world; the senses and cognition, perception and thinking are prerequisites for this exchange. Life cannot therefore precede appearance, it coincides with it: "In this world, into which we appear from a nowhere and from which we disappear into a nowhere, Being and Appearing coincide."[03] With this thesis, further differentiations—such as those between the general and the particular or between semblance and reason—become blurred, even though there may well be poles or weightings in the process of appearance. In her late work, Arendt also programmatically expresses this necessity of rethinking the relationship between the individual and the general, because life is always a singular event that encompasses thinking and perception. I will begin my discussion by turning back to her earlier work, *The Human Condition* (1958), and with the concept of the medium, which has been neglected so far, before discussing the consequences that arise for a political theory of thinking and action in her later work.

The Medium of Appearance

It is well known that the concept of appearance in *The Human Condition* is mainly associated with the notion of the space of appearance. It is not yet used in explicit connection with the term medium. The latter, however, appears in two argumentative contexts. The first concerns the deconstruction of the juxtaposition of passivity and activity in a thinking of processuality: "the actor always moves along and in relation to other acting beings, he is never merely a 'doer' but always and at the same time a 'sufferer.'" Acting and suffering belong together like two sides of the same coin, because the story that begins with an action also includes the consequences of the action. "These consequences are boundless, because action, though it may proceed from nowhere, so to speak, acts into a medium where every reaction becomes a chain reaction and where every process is the cause of new processes."[04] The phrase 'acts into a medium' is as unusual as it is remarkable. It indicates that action is situated both outside and within the medium, that it takes place in a medium, but does not have or must not have its origin in it, instead having its starting point, impulse or intention in, 'so to speak,' a nowhere. It is thus conceived as ultimately groundless or unfounded and, in this respect, is associated with freedom. Here, passivity and activity mean that action is related to a medium as well as within a medium. Activity and passivity thus prove to be

03
Arendt,
Life of the Mind, 27.

04
Hannah Arendt,
The Human Condition
(University of Chicago
Press, 1958), 190.

205

05
Alfred North
Whitehead,
*Process and Reality:
An Essay in Cosmology*
(Free Press, 1978).

06
Arendt,
Human Condition,
296–97.

07
Hannah Arendt,
*Vita activa oder
Vom tätigen Leben*
(Piper, 1999), 236–37.

the difference of a spatial temporality that takes place in the medium itself. While the medium is continuous, thinking and action are discontinuous and event-like. This interrupting dimension of the event is developed most poignantly by Arendt in her concept of natality. With this relationship between the continuity of the medium and the discontinuity of the event of thinking and action, Arendt places both in a process-philosophical framework. The action itself may be highly indeterminate, but it realizes itself as an event that enters into other events without a limitation of this process being determinable. The idea of a chain reaction is not in contrast to the indeterminacy of the action itself. The spatial and temporal infinity is far too complex to define action as determinate; the event is a singular phenomenon, but one that in turn gives rise to new events, new concrescences.[05] Arendt makes the process-philosophical horizon explicit at a later point in *The Human Condition*, when she speaks, with direct reference to Alfred North Whitehead, of the replacement of the concept of being by that of process:

> In the place of the concept of Being we now find the concept of Process. And whereas it is in the nature of Being to appear and thus disclose itself, it is in the nature of Process to remain invisible, to be something whose existence can only be inferred from the presence of certain phenomena.[06]

Being and process are not separate occurrences; appearance is part of the process into which it is incorporated, and yet it is not determined by the process. It points to the medial dimension of the process, in which it is taken up by a new event, a new appearance. In the German edition of the book, which she prepared herself, Arendt then adds to the quoted phrase that every action "acts into a medium" the determination that it will "strike into the medium of the infinite fabric of human affairs."[07] The novel choice of verb reinforces the autonomous, disruptive and singular character of the action, while the additional stipulation that it is the medium of human affairs emphasizes the communicative character. The mediality of the action is the communicative dimension associated with the singular, non-general nature of the action.

The Medium of Promise

The second context in which Arendt uses the concept of the medium in *The Human Condition* is that of the promise. Here, too, she uses the concept to express the peculiar relationship between limitation and boundlessness that is akin to processuality. The "faculty of promising" and, as she adds in the German edition, the ability "to keep" promises,[08] serves "to master this twofold darkness of human affairs" that results from the indeterminability of the consequences of human action and man's "inability to rely upon himself or to have complete faith in himself (which is the same thing)"[09] She calls this "the price human beings pay for freedom" and "for plurality and reality, for the joy of inhabiting together with others a world whose reality is guaranteed for each by the presence of all." Once again, the singularity of the act is at stake in the medium of the promise, although here it is supplemented by the dimension of worldliness, which in turn is plural and thus ultimately always singular. Unlike in societies based on sovereignty, which legitimize their rule through something outside the human sphere, in societies based on agreements and contracts—and thus ultimately on the promise—the only bond is freedom. Freedom thus becomes possible as a "positive mode of action," as Arendt adds in the German edition.[10]

> The danger and the advantage inherent in all bodies politic that rely on contracts and treaties is that they, unlike those that rely on rule and sovereignty, leave the unpredictability of human affairs and the unreliability of men as they are, using them merely as the medium, as it were, into which certain islands of predictability are thrown and in which certain guideposts of reliability are erected.[11]

Precisely because Arendt marks a certain impropriety in the use of the term 'medium' here with the phrase 'as it were,' it is important to understand what exactly she is referring to. As in the context of the relation between continuity and discontinuity in the medium of the infinite fabric of human affairs, the medium of the promise is also about a relationship between limitation and unlimitedness, between determinacy and indeterminacy, between passivity and activity and between singularity and communicability. The promise creates

08
Arendt,
Vita activa, 312.

09
Arendt,
Human Condition,
244.

10
Arendt,
Vita activa, 312.

11
Arendt,
Human Condition,
244.

12
Arendt,
Human Condition, 24.

a new space-time relationship because it introduces a specific and new discontinuity into the flow of the process. It is a discontinuity made possible by memory, which is constitutive of social relationships and their binding force. Unlike in societies in which discontinuity is supported by the dimension of a principle transcending human relationships, for example by a divine or otherwise sovereign institution, this is a dimension of discontinuity that arises through action and lies entirely within the responsibility of the individual.

Promises are acts and events that influence the processual dynamics of continuity and discontinuity. Yet the transformation remains fragile. The relationships it creates are bonds that counter unpredictability only to the extent that they are held and not broken. Their ground is, as it were, their abyss. There is therefore something like a groundless or non-original origin of the social and political, which becomes the basis of coexistence in societies based on contract and not on sovereignty. They utilize social power, a faculty that sovereignty suppresses or at least leaves unused. Uncertainty gives rise not to security but rather to a social obligation that can be disregarded:

> The moment promises lose their character as isolated islands of certainty in an ocean of uncertainty, that is, when this faculty is misused to cover the whole ground of the future and to map out a path secured in all directions, they lose their binding power and the whole enterprise becomes self-defeating.[12]

The medium of the promise creates something new in the space of uncertainty, something that binds or connects, but it only works as long as its own fragility is recognized and respected: it is a capacity to create islands of another temporality in the flow of time without damming the flow of time itself, as well as a capacity to create places and paths without negating the infinity of space.

Medium and Space of Appearance and Concealment

While Arendt speaks of a medium of appearance in *The Life of the Mind*, she does not take up this term in her discussion of the concept of appearance in *The Human Condition*, where she instead uses the term space(s) of appearance. However, although this term may be self-explanatory, it tends to draw too much attention to the spatial dimensions of appearance at the expense of temporal dimensions, which are so central to Arendt's thinking on processuality. It can be assumed that Arendt became aware of this problem at the latest through the reception of her book. To this day, her concept of spaces of appearance is often associated with the distinction between the private and the public. However, Arendt emphasizes in the first chapters of *The Human Condition* that this distinction is no longer valid in modern times. Arendt relates "the distinction between a private and a public sphere of life" to "the rise of the ancient city-state," but explicitly describes "the emergence of the social realm, which is neither private nor public" as a "relatively new phenomenon whose origin coincides with the emergence of the modern age."[13] The "decisive division between the public and private realms, between the polis and the sphere of household and family, and, finally, between activities related to a common world and those related to the maintenance of life ... is entirely blurred." As it appears in *The Life of the Mind*, the concept of the private is not opposed to a space of the public but to inner sensations and dreams.[14] An apparently topographical distinction has been replaced by a distinction of relationality, one that is no longer about the separation between the domestic and the political but about the connection between the self-related and the social or worldly.

Like processuality, relationality is not visible; it has no objective form. The processuality that is constitutive for the realm of the social is a dimension of social relatedness or the intersubjective, which does not present itself through categories or determinations of value but is inherent to the appearance and singular in its eventfulness. Formulated from a process-philosophical perspective, the singularity of the event and the generality of the social do not stand opposed to one another, because the event of action or the appearance

13
Arendt,
Human Condition, 28.

14
Arendt,
Life of the Mind,
53, 55, 107.

15
Arendt,
Life of the Mind, 107.

is understood as a singular way of taking up, actualizing and crystalizing the unlimited eventfulness in the medium of human relationships, an actualization of the past and of anticipated effectivity. This actualization can also be grasped as judgment. We will see that Arendt is looking for exactly this when she turns to the question of the capacity of judgment, as analyzed by Kant in his *Critique of the Power of Judgment* in the last part of her *The Life of the Mind*.

But this question runs through this work from the very beginning. In its first volume, Arendt writes that aesthetic judgment, "as Kant knew so well," draws "its metaphorical language from the sense of taste ... the most intimate, the most private and most idiosyncratic of senses, somehow the opposite of sight and its 'noble' distance."[15] The judgment, however, claims "general agreement." The generality is potential, but as such it is never fully actualized. I will return to Arendt's explicit reflections on the faculty of judgment. The question, then, is what relationality is effective in judgment itself, or, formulated in the context of process-philosophical figures of thought, how the actualization of the social dimension enters into something that is so closely connected with the intimate dimensions of sensuality, with the inner senses, as an aesthetic judgment.

This can no longer be thought about in terms of the concept of space because judgment, even if it is interruption and thus has spatial quality, has a fundamentally temporal dimension: it is at the same time memory and an appeal to what is to come. (This is why the current boom in talk of so-called memory spaces also easily distracts from the actual problem of the actualizing temporality of judgment). Let us, however, dwell on the question of appearance, which cannot be separated from judgment, even if it presupposes it in the logical sense. The precondition for judgment is the spatialization of the social, the appearance of an interruption in the flow of continuity. I assume that it was precisely this element that motivated Arendt to speak of spaces of appearance.

Nevertheless, a closer reading of *The Human Condition* reveals that already here the space of appearances is not linked to any specific topographical or technical conditions, but rather, like the medium of the promise, creates islands in the flow of the medium of the network of human affairs, refers to a potentiality that "comes into being wherever men are to-gether in the manner of speech and action."[16] 'To come into being' does not mean that potentiality is transformed into a factuality, which could be said of a possibility that is realized; potentiality remains potentiality even then—because it remains inherent in speech and action, because it is something that is carried along and that does not itself appear in speech and action. And yet it remains bound to the appearance.

The space of appearance "predates and precedes all forms of constitution of the public realm and the various forms of government, that is, the various forms in which the public realm can be organized." Like the medium of appearance, the space of appearance is a condition of the constitution of the public realm, but it is not something that is realized in the latter, because the quality of potentiality is inherent in speech and action.

> Its particularity is that, unlike the spaces which are the work of our hands, it does not survive the actuality of the movement which brought it into being … but disappears … with the disappearance or arrest of the activities themselves. Wherever people gather together, it is potentially there, but only potentially, not necessarily and forever.[17]

In the space of appearance, no object appears, but rather an event appears that, because it is a social event, is always connected to intersubjectivity.

The fact that public space can precisely have the effect of preventing appearance, of suppressing the social dimension of experience, makes it abundantly clear how problematic it is to equate public space with the space of appearance. Appearance is associated with seeing, thinking and judging, not with the public. This is undoubtedly one of the conclusions Arendt draws from the experience of political and social development in Germany, which she understands as a collapse of thinking—not of the public sphere, which National Socialism knew how to use to great effect. The necessity of expanding the theory of appearance, as developed in *The Human Condition,* into a theory of the life of the mind is clearly stated by Arendt herself in the preparatory work and also in the introduction to *The Life of the Mind.*

16
Arendt,
Human Condition,
199.

17
Arendt,
Human Condition,
199.

18
Arendt,
"Thinking and Moral
Considerations,"
418–19.

19
Hannah Arendt,
*Responsibility
and Judgment*
(Schocken, 2003), 59.

20
Arendt,
*Responsibility
and Judgment*, 252.

21
Arendt,
*Responsibility
and Judgment*, 54.

Referring to her 1963 book *Eichmann in Jerusalem: A Report on the Banality of Evil,* she writes that she associated the phrase "the banality of evil" with "no theory or doctrine but something quite factual," describing the phenomenon that misdeeds of gigantic proportions were carried out by someone whose only special characteristic was something completely negative: "it was not stupidity but a curious, quite authentic inability to think." Thus, the question arose:

> Could this activity of thinking as such, the habit of examining and reflecting upon whatever happens to come to pass, regardless of specific content and quite independent of results, could this activity be of such a nature that it 'conditions' men against evil-doing? (The very word con-science, at any rate, points in this direction insofar as it means 'to know with and by myself', a kind of knowledge that is actualized in every thinking process).[18]

The "sadists and perverts" who "stood in the limelight in the publicity of these trials, in our context they are of less interest."[19] In "Auschwitz on Trial," her essay on the Frankfurt trials of 1963–1965, she writes: "The clinical normality of the defendants notwithstanding, the chief human factor in Auschwitz was sadism, and sadism is basically sexual."[20] However, "the true moral issue did not arise with the behavior of the Nazis but of those who 'coordinated' themselves [*sich gleichschalteten*] and did not act out of conviction."[21] Arendt uses the verb *gleichschalten* in the active voice, no doubt in deliberate contrast to the passive use in the formula of '*Gleichschaltung durch den nationalsozialistischen Machtapparat*' (coordination through the National-Socialist apparatus of power) used by so many historians. The question of evil does not arise as a psychological problem of individuals or groups, but results from the observation of a breakdown of judgment affecting large parts of society, an "almost universal breakdown, not of personal responsibility, but of personal *judgment* in the early stages of the Nazi regime," arising "with the phenomenon of 'coordination', that is, not with fear-inspired hypocrisy, but with this very early eagerness not to miss the train of History."

In brief, what disturbed us was the behavior not of our enemies but of our friends, who had nothing to bring this situation about. They were not responsible for the Nazis, they were only impressed by the Nazi success and unable to pit their own judgment against the verdict of History, as they read it. ... I think the early moral disintegration in German society, hardly perceptible to the outsider, was like a kind of dress rehearsal for its total breakdown, which was to occur during the war years.[22]

22
Arendt,
*Responsibility
and Judgment*, 24–25.

If social relationality comes into effect in the event of appearance, then what Arendt describes here for the initial period of the National Socialist government in Germany is the extensive suppression of appearance by acts performed in the public space. Arendt describes this moral disintegration as a dress rehearsal, an unusual metaphor chosen, no doubt, with some care: Arendt does not speak of a prelude or even of a rehearsal, both of which would be terms in which the action lay with those she calls enemies. By contrast, those who take part in a dress rehearsal don a new habit themselves, rehearse a new role, occupy it at least provisionally. They are not spectators, the 'coordination' goes hand in hand with an inability to bring their own and singular judgment into play against what they saw as the judgment of history—an apparently general judgment.

Finally, this extraordinary metaphor of the dress rehearsal points to the exemplary nature of theatrical thinking for the space of appearance. If it is true that, in the space of appearance, one not only communicates something through acting and speaking, but "in all this also always oneself at the same time," what does it mean for the idea of the space of appearance if adaptation to the 'moral' order is tantamount to a dress rehearsal? It is about social concealment of oneself to oneself, not the concealment of sadism, the exhibition of which was one of the central techniques of National Socialism. The concept of the space of appearance requires a supplement or extension in which the social and political are linked with the individual capacity for thought and judgment.

This is the project that Arendt pursues in *The Life of the Mind*. Its third and concluding part, which unfortunately remains largely fragmentary, is dedicated to judgment.

23
Arendt,
Life of the Mind, 199.

24
Arendt,
Human Condition,
199.

25
Arendt,
Human Condition,
181–83.

Since Kant sees judging in line with the faculty of pure reason and practical understanding as a faculty of its own, "we shall have to ascribe to it its own modus operandi, its own way of proceeding."[23] This is based on the collaboration of two individual faculties, that of the imagination and that of the *sensus communis*.

Mimēsis, Imagination and the Original Split

The space of appearance is related to the social realm, not to the public space. It is "the space where I appear to others as others appear to me, where men exist not merely like other living or inanimate things but make their appearance explicitly."[24] This social realm is made possible not by the existence of a collective but by the relationship of one singular individual to another. "The manifestation of who the speaker and doer unexchangeably is, though it is plainly visible, retains a curious intangibility that confounds all efforts toward unequivocal verbal expression." Even if "most words and deeds are about some worldly objective reality," there is always something more,

> a disclosure of the acting and speaking agent. Since this disclosure of the subject is an integral part of all, even the most 'objective' intercourse, the physical, worldly in-between … is overlaid and, as it were, overgrown with an altogether different in-between which consists of deeds and words and owes its origin exclusively to men's acting and speaking directly *to* one another.[25]

The theme of imagination is not explicitly developed in *The Human Condition*, but it is inherent in the process of thinking intersubjectively. As relationality, intersubjectivity is a constitutive part of appearance and worldliness. The clearest passage in which Arendt develops this idea in her earlier writing is in her thoughts on *mimēsis*, which basically anticipates the question of imagination. Since "the specific revelatory quality of action and speech, the implicit manifestation of the agent and speaker, is so indissolubly tied to the living flux of acting and speaking," it cannot be directly evaluated, it "can be represented and 'reified' only through a kind of repetition, the imitation or *mimēsis*." Arendt thus sees the significance and necessity of *mimēsis* in its ability to transfigure something barely perceptible in the flow of time into a metastable scene or image. According to Aristotle, *mimēsis* "prevails in all arts but is actually appropriate only to the drama ... Only the actors and speakers who re-enact the story's plot can convey the full meaning, not so much of the story itself, but of the 'heroes' who reveal themselves in it." In this, the doubling in the imitative play of the actors on the one hand and the chorus on the other is constitutive for the Greek tragedy. While the identities of the agents of the story remain intangible, the universal meaning of the tragedy "is revealed by the chorus, which does not imitate and whose comments are pure poetry ... This is why the theater is the political art par excellence; only there is the political sphere of human life transposed into art."[26]

Worldliness presupposes intersubjectivity. But intersubjectivity is tied to an inner dissociation that is closely connected to the imagination. Intersubjectivity is a reference to the other, which presupposes a reference to oneself. Neither the self nor the other is immediate; both are inconceivable without imagination. This applies to all thinking: *"Every mental act rests on the mind's faculty to have present to itself what is absent from the senses."*[27] The subject is never fully present to itself because consciousness is connected with imagination and thus with a fundamental split. When the ego says "I am I," it carries a difference within itself, an "original split." "As long as I am conscious, that is, conscious of myself, I am identical with myself only for others to whom I appear as one and the same. For myself, articulating this being-conscious-of-myself, I am inevitably two-in-one." A search for identity that hopes to overcome this split would result in a loss of consciousness and thus also of the relationship to the other:

> Human consciousness suggests that difference and otherness, which are such outstanding characteristics of the world of appearances as it is given to man as his habitat among a plurality of things, are the very conditions for the existence of man's ego as well. For this ego, the I-am-I, experiences difference in identity precisely when it is not related to the things that appear but only to itself.[28]

26
Arendt,
Human Condition,
187–88.

27
Arendt,
Life of the Mind, 75.

28
Arendt,
"Thinking and Moral
Considerations," 442.

215

29
Arendt,
"Thinking and Moral
Considerations," 442.

30
Arendt,
Life of the Mind, 48.

31
Arendt,
Life of the Mind, 45.

32
Arendt,
Life of the Mind, 38.

33
Arendt,
Life of the Mind, 41.

Arendt points out that Plato's definition of thinking as a "soundless dialogue with oneself" and Socrates' ideal of inner harmony presuppose a dissociation. Consciousness is not the same as thinking, "but without it thinking would be impossible. What thinking actualizes in its process is the difference given in consciousness."[29] If difference and alterity are the outstanding features of the world of appearances, then the same is true for the human self. When the self refers to itself, it experiences a difference in identity. But this, too, requires imagination, because the thinking ego "does not appear to others and unlike the self in self-awareness, it does not appear to itself, and yet it is not nothing."[30]

The inner sensations take place in a relentless succession, which "prevents each of them from assuming a lasting, identifiable shape." Arendt approvingly quotes from Maurice Merleau-Ponty's *The Visible and the Invisible:* "The 'psychism' is opaque to itself." Therefore, "inner sensations" and emotions can only be "unworldly."[31] When we talk about psychic experiences, Arendt argues, we never talk about the experiences themselves, but always about what "we think about it when we reflect upon it."[32]

Negation and Disavowal

In *The Life of the Mind,* Arendt states that psychoanalysis is a science that deals with the affections of the soul, with "the ever-changing moods, the ups and downs of our psychic life,"[33] but not with thinking and judging. This is partly understandable when viewed against the background of certain lines of tradition in psychoanalysis. In particular, the post-World War II North American discussion, dominated by ego-psychology, disregarded the fundamental distinction in Sigmund Freud's theory between primary and secondary processes, between the pleasure principle and the reality principle. However, this difference corresponds in many ways to Arendt's distinction between inner sensations and consciousness, soul and thinking. This also goes for the distinction between appearance and concealment, which is contained in the dynamics that follow the psychoanalytic distinction between the conscious and the unconscious. The problem or weakness of Arendt's argument is not the separation of feeling and thinking itself, but the omission of reflection on the dynamics of this separation. However, these dynamics can be particularly significant when it comes to the question of judgment and the intersubjective relationship that is effective in it. What we think about inner sensations is, as Arendt herself says, strongly determined by the imagination with which we relate to ourselves. And this, in turn, is also related to how we want to reveal ourselves to the other.

Indeed, the dimensions of this dynamic become particularly clear in the light of Freud's theory of judgment, as he outlines it in the 1925 text "Negation" in particular. Here, Freud distinguishes between a judgment function that follows the pleasure principle and an intellectual one. He understands the former as a judgment of taste in the sense of "the oldest—the oral—instinctual impulses ...: 'I should like to eat this,' or 'I should like to spit it out.' That is to say: 'It shall be inside me' or 'it shall be outside me.'"[34] In other words, the "original pleasure-ego" makes pure subjective decisions, it "wants to introject into the self everything that is good and eject from itself everything that is bad. What is bad, what is alien to the ego and what is external are, to begin with, identical." The "function of intellectual judgment [*der intellektuellen Urteilsfunktion*]" is distinguished from this "affective process" in that it no longer passes judgment on the basis of direct sensory perception but on the basis of an idea, that is, a product of the imagination. Freud reminds us that all representations that originate from perceptions are repetitions. "Thus originally the mere existence of a presentation [*Vorstellung*] was a guarantee of the reality of what was presented." Freud uses the German word '*Vorstellung,*' which can be translated as presentation in the sense of (theatrical) performance as well as in the more philosophical sense of imagination. But following Freud's understanding of the mental processes, it is obvious that he means the latter. Imagination is different from sensory perception; it arises only through a thought process that refers, figuratively and by remembering, to something that is not itself present but is formed only through the imagination. "The first and immediate aim, therefore, of reality testing is, not to *find* an object in real perception which corresponds to the one presented [*dem Vorgestellten*], but to *refind* such an object, to convince oneself that it is still there."[35]

34
Sigmund Freud, "Negation," in *Standard Edition of the Complete Psychological Works of Freud: Volume 19* (Hogarth Press, [1925] 1961): 237.

35
Freud, "Negation," 237–38.

36
Freud,
"Negation," 237–38
[translation amended].

37
Freud,
"Negation," 239.

38
Sigmund Freud,
"Fetishism,"
in *Standard Edition
of the Complete
Psychological Works
of Freud: Volume 21*
(Hogarth Press,
[1927] 1961), 156.

39
Immanuel Kant,
*Critique of the
Power of Judgment*
(Cambridge
University Press,
2001), 174 [B 159].

The intellectual function of judgment thus occurs at the level of imagination (*Vorstellung*). But it not only serves to judge the presence or absence of the imagined in reality; it also serves the judgment of taste because it arises from "the interplay of the primary drives [*Triebregungen*]"[36] and, to a certain extent, draws on this play. "Judging is a continuation, along lines of expediency, of the original process by which the ego took things into itself or expelled them from itself, according to the pleasure principle." What Freud calls negation now arises from this dual function, which the faculty of judgment first acquires as thinking, that is, in the secondary process. Now, the intellectual function of judgment separates reality testing and taste in negation. In the examples that Freud cites from his therapeutic practice, this happens when something that the ego does not want to assimilate, although it has taken note of something repressed in the imagination, denies reality. It can thus expel it again. This is a process of thinking, as Freud emphasizes again at the end of his essay, because his analytical experience has taught him that "we never discover a 'no' in the unconscious."[37]

Freud's most extensive reflections on the process of denial or disavowal can be found in the text "Fetishism," written two years after "Negation." They implicitly presuppose Freud's remarks on negation, except that here the point is to cling to an object that one finds pleasing in one's imagination while at the same time acknowledging that it no longer exists or has been lost. The imagination thus splits the object in such a way that the subject can both take "full account" of the intellectual judgment of its loss and of the desire to possess and assimilate it.[38] This process of thinking thus undermines one of the three "maxims of common sense" that Kant postulates as prerequisites for the ability to judge at all: "Always to think in accord with oneself."[39] What is denied must have been perceived, so the disavowal is also a process of thinking and not of the unconscious or the primary process. In his late work *Outline of Psycho-Analysis,* published from his posthumous papers, Freud also writes that in the process of disavowal, in which the "rejection" of reality is "always supplemented by an acknowledgment; two contrary and independent attitudes arise and result in the situation of there being a splitting of the ego." Negation and disavowal are both processes of thinking: processes of a failure to think, to realize the soundless dialogue with oneself. But while negation manages to deny a notion of reality to such an extent that it can be preserved in the unconscious, in denial two contradicting notions coexist in thinking or in the ego. "The difference between this case and the other ... is essentially a topical or structural one, and it is not always easy to decide in an individual instance with which of the two possibilities one is dealing." Both are "efforts of defense," efforts to conceal from the ego and the other something that belongs to the realm of appearance in speech and action.[40]

Freud's models of psychic structures or the topics are functional models that are intended to help describe the dynamics of the conflicting demands with which the subject must learn to deal. The relationship to the other person, on whose help the person is dependent from the first day on, the relationship to the other person as an object of desire, the relationship to the self as self-preservation, the relationship to the self as an ego ideal acquired in interaction and as a memory of experience, the relationship to the self as an acquired superego through identification, and finally the regulation of affects and drives form a complex structure, whose interplay is precarious and can often only be maintained in an illusory way through negation and dissociation in the form of repression or disavowal. Both interrupt the communication between these demands, undermining the subject's inner dialogue and thus also their inner harmony.

Negation and disavowal are not pathological processes per se, just as dissociations are everyday phenomena. The two are banal. The capacity for aesthetic judgment, on the other hand, is a highly complex mental process of synthesis of imagination and reference to the other, of self-reference and alterity. While Arendt is no less interested in mental processes than Freud, she focuses on the processes directed towards the other rather than the internal processes between 'I and I.' These are complementary perspectives, they enrich each other. If they are seen in a binocular way, it becomes clear that the scandal of psychoanalysis and the scandal of Arendt's thinking about judgment arise at the same stumbling block: in both cases, the lack of judgment concerns the problem that othering very often includes the scheme of the

40
Sigmund Freud, "An Outline of Psycho-Analysis," in *Standard Edition of the Complete Psychological Works of Freud: Volume 23* (Hogarth Press, [1940] 1964), 204.

41
Arendt,
Life of the Mind,
32–33.

42
Whitehead,
Process and Reality,
237.

pathological into which it is so easy to settle vis-à-vis the other. The core of othering consists of a judgment that proceeds in a subsuming manner. The distinction between norm and deviation is the prime example of this procedure. But how might a way of thinking that avoids this proceed? What is aesthetic judgment when it becomes effective outside the narrower field of art? One crucial way of addressing this is exemplary or paradigmatic thinking. Its theory is also the vanishing point that we will find in Arendt's discussion of Kant's theory of judgment.

Sensus Communis

In a process-philosophical sense, every appearance is characterized by a relation to the other as well as to oneself. Even if one disregards the specific problem of negation and disavowal, every appearance is also a concealment, because an appearance is connected with a decision: "[A]ppearances never only reveal, they also conceal ... they do not only expose, they also protect from exposure, and, as far as their ground is concerned, this protection may even be their most important function."[41] Whitehead's philosophy of process also takes this into account. He speaks of a negative prehension, which excludes data from the synthesis that leads to an event.[42] This corresponds to Arendt's statement that in every action and the judgment on which it is based, a limitation is necessarily set to the infinity of the fabric of relationships, however unpredictable its consequences may prove to be. The relation to the other is necessarily part of this decision, to the extent that appearing itself can take on the function of concealing. So how can we think of a judgment that does not produce the relation to the other primarily negatively, primarily in a concealing or denying way, but rather enables a surplus of social relationship, a surplus of worldly relationality in the first place? That is the question that arises for a political theory of judgment.

Arendt sees this as the question that drives Kant's reflection on judgment, which is why she understands Kant's *Critique of the Power of Judgment* as his actual, albeit unwritten, theory of the political and also gives her lectures on Kant's work the title *Lectures on Kant's Political Philosophy*. The difficulty that arises here is that Kant's understanding of judgment is initially framed, in his *Critique of Pure Reason*, as the establishment of a relationship between the particular and the general, but a dynamic of judgment that relates to something new and to the realm of the socially expansive cannot proceed from a general that has revealed itself as an established value or established knowledge. Kant therefore introduces a new faculty in his *Critique of the Power of Judgment*, that of aesthetic judgment.

Kant essentially distinguishes three faculties of judgment. The first is 'the faculty of thinking the particular as contained under the general.' Of this, Kant says that it "subsumes the particular under it" and proceeds "determining."[43] A second faculty proceeds reflexively. It is active when we are dealing with the "manifold of forms in nature," for which we "cannot borrow" a universal from experience because "as empirical, they may seem to be contingent in accordance with the insight of our understanding," so that we must nevertheless, in accordance with the requirement of the concept of nature, regard them "as necessary on a principle of the unity of the manifold, even if this principle is unknown to us." This reflective faculty of judgment "can only give itself such a transcendental principle a law." The third faculty of judgment, which Kant calls the aesthetic faculty, can certainly refer to the "real of an empirical concept" and be objective in this respect, but since it cannot refer to general concepts or laws, norms or regulations, it is based solely on "the relation to the feeling of pleasure and displeasure, by means of which nothing at all in the object is designated, but in which the subject feels itself as it is affected by the representation."[44] Kant thus links aesthetic judgment not directly with sensory perception, but with the capability of the imagination and self-reflection. "For we can generally say, whether it is the beauty of nature or of art that is at issue: that is beautiful which pleases in the mere judging (neither in sensation nor through a concept)."[45] Quoting this sentence, Arendt continues: "It is not important whether or not it pleases in perception; what pleases merely in perception is gratifying but not beautiful. It pleases in representation, for now the imagination has prepared it so that I can reflect on it. This is 'the operation of reflection.'" Taste is an inner, non-objective sense, but there is a "nonsubjective element in the nonobjective senses" which is

43
Kant,
Judgment, 67
[B XXVII].

44
Kant,
Judgment, 89 [B 3].

45
Kant,
Judgment, 185 [B 180].

46
Hannah Arendt,
*Lectures on Kant's
Political Philosophy*
(University of
Chicago Press, 1992),
67.

47
Arendt, *Lectures*, 82.

48
Kant,
Judgment, 101 [B 26].

49
Kant,
Judgment, 121 [B 63].

50
Kant,
Judgment, 101 [B 26].

intersubjectivity. (You must be alone in order to think; you need company to enjoy a meal.) Judgment, and especially judgments of taste, always reflect upon others and their taste, take their possible judgments into account. This is necessary because I am human and cannot live outside the company of men.[46]

Aesthetic judgment, whose specific capacity Arendt extends to the political, is as distinct from the subsumption of a singular phenomenon under a general concept as it is from reflective judgment, which inquires into the laws of phenomena. It is both singular and social, perception and thought;[47] it is connected not only with the imagination but also with what Kant calls *sensus communis*. This is not the application of general rules, but something that holds itself between the singular and the general, establishing a connection between the singular phenomenon and a manifold of social and wordly relations. Judgment in this sense follows the manner of the judgment of taste. The beautiful is a sensation and a quality belonging to the object only insofar as it can evoke this sensation in us. As a sensation, however, it cannot be subsumed under a general concept, which is why we cannot argue about a judgment of taste.

Kant claims "that in the judgment of taste nothing is postulated except such a universal voice [*allgemeine Stimme*]," which "lays claim to the consent of everyone."[48] But what is a universal voice? It is not a law, not a rule, not a single sound. A general voice, it could be said, can only exist as a chord, as a resonance of many voices. It is the result not of an accumulation of individual sounds, but of an interference, a tuning of many voices, which in their sound, like the strings of a polyphonic instrument, also absorb the vibrations of other voices. Such tuning in the sense of resonating with the other and at the same time with oneself is also subject to Kant's idea of tuning in and tuning out: "The judgment of taste ascribes assent to everyone [*sinnet jedermann Einstimmung an*]."[49] Or, also: the judgment of taste "only ascribes this agreement to everyone [*sinnet nur jedermann diese Einstimmung an*], as a case of the rule with regard to which it expects confirmation not from concepts but only from the consent of others."[50] The judgment of taste is therefore something genuinely social, based not on a given generality, but itself expressing a capacity for communication, a sense of intersubjectivity, and even more: a claim, a request. The verb *'ansinnen'* was as rarely used in Kant's time as in ours; the word *'sinnen'* addresses both the movement in one direction and the connection between perception and contemplation, the question of the meaning of events. As a noun, an *'Ansinnen'* also means something like a request addressed to another. When Arendt points out that the common sense was understood by Thomas Aquinas as the sense of the attunement of the five senses, as "a kind of 'sixth sense'"[51] it takes on the meaning of the intersubjective as the sense of the desire, which can be understood as an implicit claim to the inclusion of the other in one's own judgment, precisely as attunement. In the aesthetic faculty, therefore, something is at work that can never be fully realized or actualized, something that 'senses' (*sinnet*) as potentiality but never arrives.

Insofar as it concerns art, this potentiality of intersubjectivity can be seen in the process of production as well as in the process of reception. What characterizes art is that it does not show something known, does not represent concepts, but suggests a mental process. How can this be part of the political sphere?

If "the universal communicability of a feeling presupposes a common sense [*gemeinschaftlichen Sinn*]," Kant writes further, then this "must be able to be assumed with good reason ... as the necessary condition of the general communicability of our cognition."[52] The necessary condition of the universal communicability is a medium or something that is inherent to all mediality as potentiality. This "idea of a communal sense [*gemeinschaftlichen Sinnes*]" implies, according to Kant, that "this happens by one holding his judgment up not so much to the actual as to the merely possible judgment of others, and putting himself into the position of everyone else." This "faculty for judging a priori the communicability of the feelings that are combined with a given representation (without the mediation of a concept)" is "combined with something else in order to be able to connect with satisfaction on an object a further pleasure in its existence (as that in which interest consists)." The fact that the judgment of taste is without "noticeable interest" means that "the idea of its universal communicability almost infinitely increases its value."[53]

51
Arendt,
Life of the Mind, 54.

52
Kant,
Judgment, 123 [B 157].

53
Kant,
Judgment, 174–77
[B 157–64].

54
Arendt, *Lectures*,
67 and 123–24.

The 'pleasure in the existence of an object,' of which Kant speaks, connects the object of judgment with communicability in a way that also includes the object itself. A pleasure in the existence of an object that is 'without perceptible interest' cannot refer to possession or utility but includes both a pleasure in the intersubjective communicability of a feeling and a cognition as well as a pleasure in the phenomenality of the world or its objecthood. When Kant writes that the idea of general communicability increases its value 'almost infinitely,' he exactly highlights the potentiality as that which will never be fulfilled as such.

In this, the *sensus communis* is the furthest removed from a common sense related to values, norms and propriety, because it is linked to the pleasure in the difference of the other and the unknown, to curiosity. The world of appearance is a world permeated by the *sensus communis,* a world that we actively share through our imagination but never possess. In Arendt's concept of worldliness, there is a clear echo of this figure of thought.

The Exemplary Nature of Appearance

Arendt links her reading of *Critique of the Power of Judgment* with another of Kant's works, in which she sees a judgment expressed by him about the world of appearances that follows the faculty of aesthetic judgment but is to be understood as a political one: Kant's remarks on the French Revolution.[54] Arendt refers to a passage from Kant's *The Controversy of the Faculties* from 1798, in which he sees in the French Revolution an 'anticipatory sign' of a better, republican form of government that makes it possible

> to predict to the human race—even without prophetic insight—according to the aspects and omens [*Vorzeichen*] of our day, the attainment of this goal. That is, I predict its progress toward the better which, from now on, turns out to be no longer completely retrogressive. For such a phenomenon in human history will *not be forgotten,* because it has revealed a tendency and faculty in human nature for improvement such that no politician, affecting wisdom, might have conjured out

of the course of things hitherto existing… But so far as time is concerned, it can promise this only indefinitely and as a contingent occurrence.[55]

Kant makes this judgment explicitly as a spectator—and not an isolated one, but one who finds himself connected, finds "in the hearts [*Gemütern*] of all spectators (who are not engaged in this game themselves) a wishful participation that borders closely on enthusiasm."[56] This applies to the "experiment" of the revolution, which "may succeed or miscarry." Kant calls the French Revolution phenomenon, experiment, game and anticipatory sign. The ancient Greek *phainómenon* initially means nothing other than something that shows itself, something that appears. But how does a historical event or a series of historical events become a manifestation, a phenomenon? Two operations of the imagination are at work here. The phenomenon is to a certain extent doubled, without it being possible to separate what is doubled, because the phenomenon arises from interference. One operation of the imagination is the transformation of a series of events into a relationality of singular events, a figure in the unlimited field of human relations that does not result from their chronological sequence, but potentially even runs against it, because what appears is independent of the success of the 'experiment.' The second operation is that this net of relations 'uncovers' something, i.e., also makes it appear, which itself has no other form than this event itself. It is something that exemplifies the event and thus turns the 'game' into an experiment. Kant calls this the "tendency and faculty in human nature for improvement."[57] A faculty can only manifest itself in an event or in actions and words. It is not a law or a rule, it is a potency and therefore cannot be separated from the singular phenomenon itself. It has no universality as something realized, but it has the potency to enter into other events as an increased richness of relations. Other events may be similar to the French Revolution in that this faculty also appears in them, but this similarity is not established through a rule because the faculty itself cannot manifest itself beyond an event as a singular constellation, cannot exist beyond a singular network of actions and words.

55
Immanuel Kant, "The Conflict of the Faculties (1798)," in *Religion and Rational Theory*, Immanuel Kant (Cambridge University Press, 2001), 304.

56
Kant, *Conflict of the Faculties*, 302.

57
Kant, *Conflict of the Faculties*, 304.

225

58
Arendt,
*Responsibility
and Judgment*,
141–42.

59
Arendt,
*Responsibility
and Judgment*,
139–40.

60
Arendt,
*Responsibility
and Judgment*, 138.

What do Arendt's considerations have to do with this? Let's take another step back and take a closer look at how Arendt understands the *sensus communis*. Social relations have no objective character, but something becomes imaginable in the medium of appearance that is not only subjective. Something non-subjective is effective within it, something that appears without appearing and in this sense is a potentiality through which we may become 'members of a community': "If common sense, the sense through which we are members of a community, is the mother of judgment, then not even a painting or a poem, let alone a moral issue, can be judged without invoking and weighing silently the judgments of others, to which I refer just as I refer to the schema of the bridge to recognize other bridges."[58]

In her lecture, Arendt had previously introduced a differentiation that distinguishes between the singular appearance of an object and the schema with which we determine an object. In the representation or the imagination at work in it, two different images interfere: the image that the perception of the singular bridge recalls, and the image that can be understood as the schema of a bridge. "This second schematic bridge never appears before my bodily eyes; the moment I put it down on paper it becomes a particular bridge, it is no longer a mere schema." This capacity of representation is fundamental to knowledge that is shared with others. First of all, Arendt concludes from this that "the schemata that appear in knowledge become examples in judgement."[59]

When she transfers aesthetic judgment to the field of morality, she presupposes the assumption "that the field of human intercourse and conduct and the phenomena we confront in it are somehow of the same nature."[60] But how can abstract schemata be found in them that are comparable in their function to the schema of a bridge? What can take the place of schemata that allows a transfer without sacrificing the singularity of the phenomenon? What is it that could enable an intersubjectively shared perception such as that of an object as a bridge for the network of relationships of human affairs or the space of appearance? Let us go back to what we were able to experience with Arendt as the central moment of Greek tragedy, the capacity of *mimēsis*. *Mimēsis* differs from empathy in that it does not so much claim to take the place of another as that it applies to a constellation. However, a constellation never appears as such; it can only be perceived in a singular situation. The singular action is always part of a situation, and it is only from here that the perception of the singular event broadens itself to the wider field of the net of human affairs.

Arendt becomes aware of this problem in the course of her discussion of Kant's text on the power of judgment, as we find it in the notes to her lectures and seminars from 1966–68. In the course of her discussion, she expands the two images of representation to include a third: this time using the example of the table, Arendt differentiates between a schematic table, which has all the necessary properties of a table, an abstract table, which takes into account the "minimum qualities common to all of them," and "an example of how tables should be constructed and how they should look."[61] With this third image, she introduces the aesthetic dimension and thus also the *sensus communis* into the idea of the example—without, however, further developing this 'should' and the ethical quality of aesthetic judgment addressed by it. If no general law, no independently existing value motivates this 'should,' it must be effective as a special and proper power of the singular appearance or the singular event. This force does not proceed from a general rule embodied by the example, nor from an abstract schema, but from a scenic constellation, the figuration of a tension that emerges in the mesh of relations without being visible as either an object or a rule, but as a communication of the elements that are part of the figuration.

Such an example is not limited to art. As Arendt explains, many concepts developed by historiography and political science have this exemplary character: "Achilles for courage, Solon for insight (wisdom), etc. Or take the instances of Caesarism or Bonapartism."[62] Last but not least, literary figures such as Macbeth, Henri IV or King Lear also have an exemplary character. What Arendt says about the science of history and politics also applies to psychoanalysis, which can easily be shown by the significance that such figures as Oedipus or Electra, Michelangelo or individual case histories had and still have in Freudian theory.

61
Arendt, *Responsibility and Judgment*, 144.

62
Arendt, *Responsibility and Judgment*, 144.

63
Arendt,
Human Condition,
194.

64
Giorgio Agamben,
*On the Signature of
All Things: On Method*
(Zone Books, 2009), 37.

When we understand a story as exemplary, we associate it not only with a particular person in his or her singular identity, but rather with a complex structure of actions and suffering, of activity and passivity that concretizes in the appearance of a figure in an infinite network of conditions. Arendt had already referred to the figure of Achilles in *The Human Condition*. Achilles may be an exemplary figure for his courage, but this has little to do with a subjectivity that we empathize with. Not even that which "for the individual may be the utmost effort beyond which there can be no further" makes him an exemplary figure: "What gives the story of Achilles its paradigmatic significance is that it shows in a nutshell that *eudaimonia* can be bought only at the price of life."[63] Even in Achilles, the exemplary is connected not only with his action, but with a singularity that does more than create a new pattern that could be imitated, but reports "in a uniquely concrete way" of something that itself has no objectivity, consisting rather in a notion of *eudaimonia*, a correspondence between the acting self and the self, the deed and its history, perception of the self and its perception by the other. Homer's narrative is imitation not in that it identifies or strives to live like Achilles, but in that it creates a figure, an image or a thought for a highly complex constellation that can be thought. As readers of Homer, we share a mental space. In it, judgment is added to an apparition just as little as the apparition has an illustrative character. There may be other examples of the idea of *eudaimonia*, but it is itself something that can only be thought and communicated as a singular example.

Arendt ascribes 'paradigmatic significance' to this story of Homer. Giorgio Agamben, who is very familiar with Arendt's writings, defines the paradigm as something that appears "when an element suspends and simultaneously exhibits its belonging to an ensemble, with the result that it is impossible to distinguish between the character of the example and that of the particularity within it."[64] A constellation that takes on a figure in the example, that can be remembered, has no generality that can be understood as the difference between being and appearance or between law and illustration. Rather like a promise, it is an island in the flow of time, one that is always newly and differently constellated and yet shows similarities to other constellations.

Appearance is a medium because it combines singularity and communication or communicability. That which appears, which is perceptible by our inner and outer senses, can only be something singular and yet at the same time it must be more in order to become shareable, in order to enter into communication with the other, the self and the intersubjective other. The paradigm is itself a paradigm of appearance. It does not take its path via a universal, it only goes from appearance to appearance, even if it is more than what appears, because it carries a meaningful constellation with it: a constellation cannot be fixed in a concept because it is complex, not fixed in its limitations, like islands in time that float and change their edges. We feel and think with these constellations, but always differently. We can look at certain works of art over and over again, read certain poems or novels over and over again, listen to certain pieces of music over and over again. We recognize them, but each encounter is new. It is the same with people; in this sense they are apparitions as soon as we have begun to perceive them in their singularity. Political events have the quality of appearance, too. They may be past, but never entirely. And ultimately, the same is true of thinking itself, the life of the mind. It is a process, an intertwining of continuity and event: "The need to think can be satisfied only through thinking, and the thoughts which I had yesterday will be satisfying this need today only to the extent that I can think them anew."[65]

65
Arendt,
Thinking and Moral Considerations, 422.

Active Objects
Helena W. Crusius

> Cézanne's difficulties are those of the first word. He considered himself powerless because he was not omnipotent, because he was not God and wanted nevertheless to portray the world, to change it completely into spectacle, to make *visible* how the world *touches* us. A new theory of physics can be proven because calculations connect the idea or meaning of it with standards of measurement already common to all men. It is not enough for a painter like Cézanne, an artist, or a philosopher, to create and express an idea; they must also awaken the experiences which will make their idea take root in the consciousness of others. A successful work has the strange power to teach its own lesson.[01]

What can objects *do?* For what might they be responsible?

The 'Appears'

For Hannah Arendt, Plato accomplished the supersession of the *dokei moi*, "it-appears-to-me,"[02] by the *phainesthai*, "'to appear' and 'shine forth.'"[03]

These are both ancient Greek verb phrases.[04] *Dokei moi* is an impersonal third-person present verb in the active voice and a pronoun in the dative case. The (active, present) infinitive form of *dokei* is *dokein*. The impersonal *dokei moi* is something of an idiom and may obscure *dokein*'s rather singular use of the dative—the first two words of Plato's *Symposium,*

01 Maurice Merleau-Ponty, "Cézanne's Doubt," in *Sense and Non-Sense,* Maurice Merleau-Ponty (Northwestern University Press, 1964), 19.

02 Hannah Arendt, "Philosophy and Politics," *Social Research* 57, no. 1 (1990): 81.

03 Hannah Arendt, *The Human Condition* (University of Chicago Press, 1958), 226.

for instance, are *doko moi*. While *doko* is the first-person to *dokei*'s third, the dative *moi* appears here in a "reflexive" use "virtually confined to [*dokein*]." K. J. Dover suggests that we take this *doko moi* as "I think that I...," something (perhaps) subtly different than 'I appear to me.'[05] Per the LSJ, senses of "seeming" are delimited to "objects" ("c. dat. pers. et inf. pres.").[06] The word 'appear' does not appear.

Phainesthai is a present-tense infinitive.[07] We have a Sappho fragment (31) nicknamed *phainetai moi* (third-person verb and dative pronoun) after its opening words, usually taken in translation as "he seems to me." In the third stanza, the speaker seems to herself, "φαίνομ᾽ ἔμ᾽ αὖτ[α]" (16), to be close to death in passion for her beloved where the "he" of "he seems," sitting next to her beloved, seemed equal to the gods, "ἴσος θέοισιν" (1).[08] But translations of seeming (shared with *dokein*) elide a phenomenal specificity to which Arendt rightly orients us wherever she invokes this lemma: *phainesthai,* particularly in the middle-passive form she always uses, is the *glowing* verb, "freq. of fire [shining brightly]," "freq. of the *rising* of heavenly bodies," "of the first gleam of daybreak [original emphasis]."[09] The man sitting next to the speaker's beloved *shines* to her equal to the gods; she *gleams* to herself "dead—or almost."[10]

04   For explicit references to *dokei* moi and *dokein,* see Arendt, "Philosophy and Politics," 80–85; Hannah Arendt, "Thinking," in *The Life of the Mind,* Hannah Arendt (Mariner Books Classics, 1981), 21, 25, 38, 77, 94; Hannah Arendt, *Lectures on Kant's Political Philosophy,* ed. Ronald Beiner (University of Chicago Press, 1992), 55–56; Hannah Arendt, *Denktagebuch: 1950–1973,* eds. Ursula Ludz and Ingeborg Nordmann (Piper, 2022), 391, 399, 402, 406, 420, 784, 796–97. For explicit references to phainesthai and the related adjective phanos (morphology and alpha privative notwithstanding), see Arendt, *The Human Condition,* 143, 225–26; Hannah Arendt, "What Is Authority?," in *Between Past and Future: Eight Exercises in Political Thought,* Hannah Arendt (Viking, 1961), 112; Arendt, *Denktagebuch,* 391, 457, 459, 531; Arendt, "Thinking," 131, 143, 165, 170. See also Arendt, "Philosophy and Politics," 77. This list is probably incomplete.

05   Plato, *Plato: Symposium,* ed. K. J. Dover (Cambridge University Press, 2009), 77.

06   Henry George Liddell and Robert Scott, "δοκέω," in *A Greek-English Lexicon,* ed. Henry Stuart Jones (Clarendon Press, 1996).

In Arendt's idiom, Heideggerian influence/quarrel notwith-standing, these phrases stand for two distinct (if entangled) experiences of appearance.[11] *Dokei moi,* it-appears-to-me, is shorthand for the reality-giving *perspectivity* necessary to the world and the space of appearance, for the characteristic da-tive-ness of appearance *to* particular and non-overlapping witnesses.[12] For Arendt, every perspective *must* be distinct if appearances are to have any real significance—appearance as such and the public space of appearances (glossed as "people who see and hear" in *The Life of the Mind*) are conditioned on infinitely distinct spectators in the plural number.[13]

By contrast, the *phainesthai*-style 'appears' names both the experience of philosophical wonder and the distor-tion of a *polis* measured by ideas in the political philosophy of a perfidious Plato. For the philosopher, knowledge is the direct experience of the shining what-*is,* that is, *not* the dull seeming-detritus of the world that can only be subject to opinion. From a plural but shadowed and false cave of mere appearance, the philosopher turns to the "clear sky, a land-scape without things or men."[14] His solitude is the real stick-ing point: without a plurality of spectators, the Being of the

07   See Linda M. G. Zerilli, "Wittgenstein, Arendt, and the Problem of Democratic Persuasion," in *Wittgenstein and Democratic Politics,* eds. Lotar Rasiński et al. (Routledge, 2024), 212–13.

08   Sappho and Alcaeus, *Greek Lyric, Volume I: Sappho and Alcaeus,* ed. and trans. David A. Campbell (Harvard University Press, 1982), 79; Sappho, *If Not, Winter: Fragments of Sappho,* trans. Anne Carson (Random House, 2002), 63; Sappho, *Sappho: A New Translation of the Complete Works,* trans. Diane J. Rayor and André Lardinois (Cambridge University Press, 2014), 44.

09   Henry George Liddell and Robert Scott, "φαίνω," in *A Greek-English Lexicon,* ed. Henry Stuart Jones (Clarendon Press, 1996).

10   Sappho, *If Not, Winter,* 63.

11   On the issue of Arendt's disagreement with Heidegger in terms of the dokei moi, see Jacques Taminiaux, *The Thracian Maid and the Professional Thinker: Arendt and Heidegger* (SUNY Press, 1997), 127–128.

12   Arendt, *Denktagebuch,* 428.

13   Arendt, "Thinking," 94, 72; see also Arendt, *Human Condition,* 57, 199.

14   Arendt, "Philosophy and Politics," 95.

phainesthai is apprehended by its beholder—the "invisible eye of the soul"—in speechless contemplation.[15] Indeed, this appearer could not shine to anything but a perspectiveless subject: plural spectators can only apprehend that which appears in its *aspects* and finite sides.[16] To appear to many is incompatible with the shining totality of the absolute.

Socrates' death at the hands of the Athenian people drives Plato to find in this *phainesthai* a tool for the remediation of the primacy of opinion in the public realm. *Dialegesthai,* the form of *doxa*-finding conversation to which Socrates dedicated his life, had failed to secure for him the immortality in remembrance that the *polis* form was meant to afford.[17] Against persuasion, shadows, and seemings, Plato attempts to find a force without bare violence in "his tyranny of truth, in which it is not what is temporally good, of which men can be persuaded, but eternal truth, of which men cannot be persuaded, that is to rule the city."[18] Returning to the cave in order to translate the shining-forth ideas of the *phainesthai,* the philosopher-king has gained "absolute standards" according to which he can judge the people of the city and with which to substitute the predictability of fabrication for the ineffable stuff of politics.[19] Arendt marks this tyrannical measure as "the first catastrophe of Western philosophy."[20] People should not be made like tables.[21] Even the shiniest

15
Arendt, "Thinking," 7; see also Arendt, "Philosophy and Politics," 96–103.

16
Zerilli, "Wittgenstein, Arendt, and the Problem of Democratic Persuasion," 212–14.

17
Arendt, "Philosophy and Politics," 75, 78; Arendt, "What Is Authority?," 93.

18
Arendt, "Philosophy and Politics," 78.

19 Arendt, "Philosophy and Politics," 75.

20 Arendt, *Denktagebuch,* 132; cited in Hannah Arendt, *The Promise of Politics* (Schocken Books, 2005), 3.

21 Though it is not our concern here, I think Arendt is wrong about Plato and too quick to reach conclusions on the use of the verb *phainesthai* in Plato's thought. See, e.g., a recent schematization of the possible senses of one single *phainetai* at *Phaedo* 74b: "It has been plausibly argued that three senses of *phainetai* are possible here: (i) 'turns out'; (ii) 'shows itself (to someone)' or 'is found (by someone)'; (iii) 'seems (to someone).' This threefold distinction will be adopted in what follows. *Phainetai* with senses (i) and (ii) usually (but not always) is completed with a participle and has veridical force, whereas *phainetai* with sense (iii) usually (but not always) is completed with an infinitive and carries no implication of truth. In view of this difference, senses (i) and (ii) taken together are often called 'veridical', and sense (iii) is called 'non-veridical'…

measurement will translate to violence in a realm for whose reality "no common measurement or denominator can ever be devised."[22]

But something's missing from this picture. Shiningness belongs to solitude and speechless wonder, yes, but the world and its things—that is, reality, appearance with datives—are shining-forth constantly. Glory *"shine[s]* through the centuries" in Herodotus' *Histories.*[23] "In private life one is hidden and can neither appear nor *shine.*"[24] "[In the permanence of art, a premonition of immortality] has become tangibly present, *to shine* and to be seen, to sound and to be heard, to speak and to be read."[25] "[A]lthough the durability of ordinary things is but a feeble reflection of the permanence of which the most worldly of all things, works of art, are capable, something of this quality ... is inherent in every thing as a thing, and it is precisely this quality or the lack of it that *shines forth* in its shape and makes it beautiful or ugly."[26] Shining brightness *"obviously* [emphasis added]" inheres to beauty,[27] which in its uselessness "had much more right to become the idea of ideas" than the good but which was snubbed so that ideas could become good *for* something under the rule of the philosopher-king.[28]

In the heroes-and-villains version of the story, the *dokei moi* (as opposed to the *phainesthai*) "is the mode, perhaps the only possible one, in which an appearing world is acknowledged and perceived."[29] Our unique standpoint among

---

A second distinction, which crosscuts the veridical/non-veridical contrast, is that *phainetai* with sense (ii) or (iii) is a cognitive verb that governs an explicit or understood personal dative, whereas *phainetai* with sense (i) is not and merely denotes what proves to be the case," Ryan Bitetti Putzer, "Mere Appearance or More? A Crux at *Phaedo* 74b–c Revisited," *Méthexis* 36, no. 1 (2024): 99.

22 Arendt, *Human Condition,* 57.

23 Hannah Arendt, "The Concept of History: Ancient and Modern," in *Between Past and Future: Eight Exercises in Political Thought,* Hannah Arendt (Viking, 1961), 41.

24 Arendt, "Philosophy and Politics," 81.

25 Arendt, *Human Condition,* 168.

26 Arendt, *Human Condition,* 172.

27 Arendt, *Human Condition,* 225–26.

28 Arendt, "Philosophy and Politics," 77.

other unique standpoints is the condition of the reality of the world and the possibility of our existence. The *phainesthai* is implicated in the attempted projection of fabrication onto politics and the elision of the intersubjectivities that endow public life with significance; the *vita activa* is that which we practice in the "dark cave of human affairs" and the shining illumination of the realm of ideas obliviates this space of appearance.[30]

Alternatively, that beauty *obviously* belongs to the *phanotaton* and *ekphanotaton,* superlatives of the shining-forth adjective *phanos,* might give us particular pause. Arendt assigns the quality of the beautiful to the superlative, worldliest strata of worldly objects: "Without the beauty, that is, the radiant glory in which potential immortality is made manifest in the human world, all human life would be futile and no greatness could endure. The common element connecting art and politics is that *they both are phenomena of the public world* [emphasis added]."[31] In other words, the thingiest, most fit-for-reality thing is the thing that, removed from the deterioration of use, marks the durability of the world that dually precedes and proceeds every living creature's appearance in it.[32] Here, beauty coalesces around what Arendt has above construed as polar and conflictual nodes: the general, Absolute, shining ideas beheld outside the cave in singular, speechless, contemplative wonder and the inextricably particular things appearing to and between plural, quarrelling spectators in dark and necessary partiality, that is, in terms of their aspects and not of their wholes.

There are good reasons that this should be so. Maybe beauty goes wherever appearance goes, falls to whatever in any field of appearance is the most useless and permanent.[33] Maybe Kant, for whom the free play of the imagination was the movement of cognition between the particular and the general (as opposed to more rectilinear subsumption under general concepts or application of general concepts to particulars), offers us a compelling frame with which to insist that beauty must reside in precisely these two kinds of appearance. What's mutually exclusive about the *dokei moi* in the *phainesthai* is not the experience of seeing but the solitude of the philosopher vs. the plurality of the public

29
Arendt, "Thinking," 21.

30
Arendt, *Human Condition,* 226.

31
Hannah Arendt, "The Crisis in Culture: Its Social and Its Political Significance," in *Between Past and Future,* Arendt, 118.

32
Arendt, *Human Condition,* 172.

33
Arendt, "Philosophy and Politics," 77.

34
Arendt,
"The Crisis in Culture,"
210.

35
Arendt, "Thinking," 19.

36
Arendt,
"The Crisis in Culture,"
210.

37
Arendt, "Thinking," 29.

realm—beauty shares in both the disembodied universality of cognition and the internal sensation to which we give the metaphor 'taste.'[34] Let it belong to reality and to truth.

This reconciliation is all the more palatable because beauty, for Arendt, is not a quality that paradigmatically belongs to people, or, as she rather expansively puts it, "sentient beings." The *phainesthai* can interfere here without danger to plurality itself. This living-creature category of appearances requires an explicit *inclusion* in the space of appearance qua appearance, that is, qua not-exclusively-transcendental-subject. Even so, what is beautiful—what shines forth—is not "men and animals" but their reputations and glories, inextricable from the work of fabrication that installs their *doxa* in worldly reality.[35] Conversely, beautiful appearances are elided into objects: "The proper criterion by which to judge appearances is beauty; if we wanted to judge objects, even ordinary use-objects, by their use-value alone and not also by their appearance—that is, by whether they are beautiful or ugly or something in between—we would have to pluck out our eyes."[36] Things suffer precisely the fate of the *polis* under the rule of the philosopher-king:

> In contrast to the inorganic thereness of lifeless matter, living beings are not *mere* appearances. To be alive means to be possessed by an urge toward self-display which answers the fact of one's own appearingness. Living things *make their appearance* like actors on a stage set for them. The stage is common to all who are alive, but it *seems* different to each species, different also to each individual specimen… [J]ust as the actor to make his entry depends upon stage, fellow-actors, and spectators, every living thing depends upon a world in appearance as the location for its own appearance, on fellow-creatures to play with, and on spectators to acknowledge and recognize its existence [emphasis added].[37]

In other words, subjects are allowed to take on the objectivity of objects, but objects are barred from the subjectivity of subjects, the actor's act, the "urge to self-display." They perform an extraordinary function—they relate and separate us—but their shapes are effects of fabrication, not agents of appearance properly speaking. Appearing-as-acting is a capacity left to living creatures around whom living and deliberate form relentlessly gravitates whereas the criterion of shining brightness marks objects as lowercase-b beings. The world is a stage, actors walk upon it, but even the performance-object of the drama only *reifies*.[38] The durable stuff beneath Hamlet's feet is a field for his superimposed intervention. It itself does not and could not *affect*.

Phainesthai, you'll recall, is a middle-passive conjugation of *phaino*. In ancient Greek, the middle and passive look the same in some tenses and different in others—in the present tense (*phainesthai, phainomenon*), they look identical.[39] Were Arendt's *phainesthai* to be read in the middle voice, we would have to understand the appearance of the object not as "caused by some other agent nor as an effect produced in an observer."[40] But if Heidegger was specifically attached to the middleness of the *phainomenon*, Arendt cannot, I think, be read the same way.[41] Her *phainesthai* is an appearance in the passive voice, however much the spectators are plural in an ostensibly active *dokei moi* to which durable objects lend a frame. As *mere* appearance, lifeless matter can be judged and used but cannot *make* its appearance. Things have no urges and therefore no urges to self-display. Subjects share in the objectivity of stone and bridge but stone and bridge qua things do not and cannot, in their existence ever-plotted on an axis of eternity and distance, *change* anything.

What if they could?

---

38   Arendt, *Human Condition*, 187–88.

39   See Jill Frank, *Poetic Justice: Rereading Plato's Republic* (University of Chicago Press, 2018), 123. Philologically, it may be hazardous to delineate sharply between senses of middle and senses of passive in morphologies which themselves do not delineate between them; this is an issue I will not attempt to decide in a footnote.

40   Gary Shapiro, *Archaeologies of Vision: Foucault and Nietzsche on Seeing and Saying* (University of Chicago Press, 2003), 97.

41   Martin Heidegger, *Being and Time,* ed. Dennis J. Schmidt, trans. Joan Stambaugh (State University of New York Press, 2010), 27.

Forth-Shining

Consider, if you will, two stations of Rembrandt's *Passion of Christ* (figures 53 and 54):[42]

[53]

42   On the order of this series and the *Entombment*'s and
     Resurrection's place in it, see Simon McNamara,
     Rembrandt's Passion Series (Cambridge Scholars
     Publishing, 2015), 32–35.

[54]

43
Ernst Bloch,
*The Principle
of Hope: Volume 2*
(MIT Press, 1995),
801–02.

[The] first triumph [of the complicated technique of dark grounding and over-painting which Rembrandt followed throughout his entire work] … is significantly in a picture of the Passion, in the Munich Entombment of Christ. People and even things stand in solitude in the expanse of dark space, the colours come solely from a mysterious reflection of inner light in the world and behind the world, from a paradox of final light. Thus it stems neither from the sun nor from an artificial source of light, nor is the existing world, together with any supernatural world which is believed to exist, at all capable of dispensing this not earthly, not unearthly light… [E]ven the darkness of this background is streaked with golden brown, the group of figures stands in a sfumato perspective of both black and gold, the light works into the darkness, chromatizes even here, penetrates from a strangely existing Nowhere. Thus Rembrandt's paradoxical light is not to be found anywhere in the world, nor has it emanated, despite its continuous reflection, from any ancient metaphysics of heavenly light: it is *perspective light of hope,* deeply led down into nearness and desolation, answered. The open cosmic perspective is obliterated by dark space, but the light which both contrasts with it and mysteriously breaks through from loneliness and blackness *paints the truth of hope or of the brilliance which is not there at all, in the dark-groundings of the existing world…* And this alone is ultimately the source, in the depths, of light not as an element of the world nor of the supernatural world but as a mystical expression of Being of the figures accompanying it. This is most quietly the case in the Munich picture of the Resurrection, with Christ right down at the bottom edge, palely shining, and also escaped from and superior to the mythological heavenly light which breaks down behind the descending angel: an *Ex oriente lux* which itself is only beginning to rise and is reflected from this corpse in extreme remoteness. All Rembrandt's pictures, even the secular ones, are composed from out of the background, and his colours—of night, incense, myrrh, gold—paint the perspective: *hollow space with sparks* [emphasis added].[43]

The perspective and long horizon of these pieces are not located in any literal openness we might identify—e.g., the skyline of Jerusalem lit by the suggestion of a setting sun in the *Entombment* or the sweep of cloud, star and sky upon which the angel descends in the *Resurrection*—but in the light from Nowhere. The utopian bent of the spark-in-the-hollow is that the spark *cannot* arise from and can have *no source* in the darkness that dominates so much of each composition, but there it is anyway. From where? is the wrong question, or at least a question without a determinate answer: it is the truth, not of the Absolute or Eternal itself but of hope, the experience of utopian latency in the smoky that-which-is. As in the *Republic*, there's a fire in the cave—but it's not behind us.

We might be forgiven for maintaining that, even if all this were true, these paintings still fail to *do* anything, i.e., their material is responsible for nothing save sheer perpetuation (like stone, bridge, so on and so forth). We would be in good company. The only comment we have from Rembrandt on any of his work comes as an advertisement for these two paintings in a 1639 letter—"in these two pictures the deepest and most lifelike emotion has been observed [and rendered]"—but this hardly rises to worldly action of appearance-among-appearance.[44] One reader, identifying self-images of Rembrandt in the *Descent from the Cross,* the *Raising of the Cross,* and the *Entombment,* finds in this bereted figure an imploration to "the viewer to again ask themselves ... What am I doing for Christ? What ought I to do for Christ?"[45] But it is the artist, not the figure, who is responsible for these questions, and it is the painter, not the pigment, who *made* the appearance; if the man in the beret were not an artist and/or were not Rembrandt, there would, one suspects, be no exhortation to either heed or ignore.

Why, then, does Ernst Bloch care? The self-purported aim of the text from which this excerpt is taken is to fill the everything-sized hole in extant philosophy that belongs to "venturing beyond." Not until Marx, he says, did we begin to apply ourselves to understanding the problem of hope nor the utopian slant to all human desiderata and since Marx not much progress has been made. "Forward dreaming," "expectation and what is expected," "the huge occurrence of utopia in the world," and "the future tense" stand in apposition

44
For both the letter and the lengthy history of debate on this turn of phrase, see Walter L. Strauss et al., *The Rembrandt Documents* (Abaris Books, 1979), 161–62.

45
McNamara, *Rembrandt's Passion Series,* 127. These are questions from St. Ignatius of Loyola's *Spiritual Exercises.*

46
Ernst Bloch,
*The Principle
of Hope: Volume 1*
(MIT Press, 1995), 5–6.

47
Bloch,
*The Principle of Hope:
Vol. 1*, 7.

48
Bloch,
*The Principle of Hope:
Vol. 1*, 216–21.

49
Bloch,
*The Principle of Hope:
Vol. 2*, 584.

50
Fredric Jameson,
*Marxism and Form:
Twentieth-Century
Dialectical Theories
of Literature*
(Princeton University
Press, 1974), 133.

51
Bloch,
*The Principle
of Hope: Vol. 1*,
214–15.

to the Not-Yet-Conscious, to intending, and to innumerable Becomings.[46] To apprehend not only human beings, not only history, but "the basic determination of objective reality as a whole," it is *this* element we must grasp: the tendency of all things toward utopia captured in affect by the experience of hope and the latency of the longed-for otherwise.[47] He offers this unfinishedness to us, in part, in the enumeration of all things by which utopia makes itself known in *Vor-Schein*, translated by Plaice, Plaice, and Knight as "pre-appearance" (but denoting also pre/before-seeing, pre/before-shining, etc.). This *Vor-Schein* is particularly bright in "great art," i.e., works of genius that penetrate Becoming itself, but is visible in anything at all.[48] Even in instantiations of deceit "as dished up by capitalist democracy and later by fascism,"[49] everything shines, anticipation is everywhere, and "every negative [serves] as a means of access to that positive which it conceals."[50] The task of Bloch's text is, in part, to demonstrate this worldly shining as exhaustively as possible.

For Bloch, these paintings are something other than stages for actors, backgrounds upon or occasions at which people or creatures might appear, nor, as in Arendt, are objects qua objects innocent of their own significance: Light and color are the subjects *making* that which appears (at least grammatically speaking): "the light works into the darkness, chromatizes ... penetrates," "the light ... *paints the truth of hope*," the light is "a mystical expression of Being of the figures accompanying it," "the mythological heavenly light ... breaks down behind the descending angel," Rembrandt's "colours ... paint the perspective: *hollow space with sparks*." Rembrandt is not the *actor*, though his hand and genius are never far from view—it's the lead white doing the work of constituting the truth and perspective "*in aesthetically immanent terms*."[51] It is *this* light, *this* Jesus, *this* "night, incense, myrrh, gold," that show us "the brilliance which is not there at all."

Arendt's art object is also a particular *this*, but the thisness of Arendt's art object and the *dokei moi* it expresses/enables chafes against the thisness of Bloch's light: the *Entombment* and *Resurrection* obviate not only the capacity but the possibility of judgment and perspectivity in our aesthetic engagement. They are both tyrannies: in painting the perspective, the colors of the *Entombment* and the

Resurrection show you something you could neither deny nor be persuaded of. There *is* light. It has no source, but it's there—illuminating Jesus's shroud, sun-rising the Angel at the resurrection—and there is no rhetoric that might change it. This fact is indifferent to Christ's divinity (whatever it may be) and wholly responsive to the *thing* in front of us. Whether we take on board that this indicates a radically open future is a different question—we might, following Fredric Jameson, distinguish between Bloch's hermeneutics and Bloch's philosophy—but, on Bloch's account, there is no living creature interceding to *make* this appearance, however much a living creature may be required to behold it.[52] Our judgment, sight, or *dokei moi* does not determine the significance of either painting. Its shape, *idea*, form, the particular and specific way it and nothing else appears, is Truth qua a particular image and arrangement of material.

At the risk of hijacking *phainesthai* completely, we might say of Bloch's object that it conjugates the appearance of truth from *phainetai*, 'shines,' to the appearance of the attainable pre-appearance in *phainei*, which, in the active voice, signifies something like '*brings* to light.' Where the intransitive middle-passive *phainetai* takes no direct object, *phainei*, like chromatizes, penetrates, and paints, takes a direct object. Where dativeness rules the activity appropriate to Arendt's space of appearance, an accusative that relates to sight rules the experience of Bloch's shining totality. On this paradigm, perspective is flattened (or clarified) to our place in time and sight is hammered against an anvil by the form of that which it sees. The active-transitive-accusative constellation is, like the fabrication to which the *polis* is subjected in Plato, violent. What you see and your judgment of that appearance—its significance for you and for every other spectator—is compacted into the shape and particularity of the thing in question. You can close your eyes or you can lie, but the truth is a blunt instrument.

52
Jameson,
Marxism and Form,
125.

53
Arendt,
Denktagebuch,
428; cited in
Patchen Markell,
"Politics and the
Case of Poetry:
Arendt on Brecht,"
*Modern Intellectual
History* 15, no. 2
(2018): 503;
see also Arendt,
Denktagebuch, 246.

54
Bloch,
*The Principle of Hope:
Vol. 2,* 809.

Conclusion

What, then, can objects *do?* For what might they be responsible? Or: to what voice do we assign the shininess of objects?

Whether objects shine is a different and prior question to which the answer may be no. Even if the answer is yes, grammatical analogies may fail us. The appearance of sentient beings or objects or both may turn out to be irreducible to voices, cases, transitivities. Even if grammatical analogies do *not* fail us, there are voices yet to be plumbed. What about the middle? Might this be the register of what Arendt calls, as opposed to the accusative of violence and the dative of the in-between, the "accusative of the singing poem" in which lies "salvation?"[53] Or, perhaps, the deponent verb, active in meaning but middle-passive in appearance, will be the cipher?

As plausible as these scenarios may be, the dative and accusative modes in Arendt and Bloch's thinking nevertheless lend themselves to useful (if perhaps ultimately specious) archetypes of the impotence or power of things. Whereas the dative may be a more familiar and more intuitively democratic case by which to imagine the meaning of lifeless matter for political life—a case by which persuasion and opinion condition all human living-together—an accusative must, in the absence of a *phanei* that does not *make* visible but mediates visibility elsewise, undergird any attribution of power to objects. If, for example, we want to assign power and possibility to what Bloch calls the "aesthetically portrayed," we need to have answers to the following questions: how can appearances without urges, without decision, and without freedom, properly speaking, show us anything without thereby *forcing* us to see it?[54] What redeems an active object from the malediction of tyranny? If, by contrast, we hold that the condition of human reality is that significance arises from human judgment and intersubjective negotiation without recourse to eternal truths, do we therefore accept that what we see cannot be *made* differently by the appearance of things quite independently of their authors, of other spectators, or of living creatures altogether? That is: does that which appears bring-to-light or seem-to-me?

Why is tyranny, in this instance, objectionable? The word is certainly ugly. But the tyranny of the accusative is not *precisely* Plato's tyranny—there is no philosopher-king measuring twice and cutting once, as the saying goes—but the more abstracted tyranny of causation. Kant remarks that

> if we were to assume that the distinction between things as objects of experience and the very same things as things in themselves, which our critique has made necessary, were not made at all, then the principle of causality, and hence the mechanism of nature in determining causality, would be valid of all things in general as efficient causes. I would not be able to say of one and the same thing, e.g., the human soul, that its will is free and yet that it is simultaneously subject to natural necessity, i.e., that it is not free, without falling into an obvious contradiction; because in both propositions I would have taken the soul in just the same meaning, namely as a thing in general (as a thing in itself) and without prior critique, I could not have taken it otherwise.[55]

Whatever of the *phainesthai* threatens the *dokei moi* threatens it along the lines of such an "obvious contradiction." Lifeless matter should not appear according to the accusative because lifeless matter should not act as an efficient cause on "sentient beings" (cf. Kant's "rational being").[56] The obvious contradiction operates so long as seeing is fundamentally tied up with living sentience, i.e., so long as when, in referring to living creatures, we do so without distinguishing the aspect that belongs to efficient causes and that which does not.

Perhaps a reconciliation for Arendt lies in making such a differentiation—the accusative object upon which the appearance acts belongs to our bodies as matter and not to whatever stores up our faculties of judgment. (She is, after all, willing enough to bifurcate the eyes of the body and the eyes of the mind.) If we are unwilling to divvy up our eyes, we are left, perhaps, with things of two kinds: the paradigmatically passive and the despotically active which threatens, always, to fabricate anew.

55
Immanuel Kant, *Critique of Pure Reason* (Cambridge University Press, 2009), 115.

56
Arendt, "Thinking," 19; Kant, *Critique of Pure Reason*, 678–81.

245

The 'How' of Knowledge
With a Postscript/Preview on Planetary Perception

Susan Buck-Morss

A person's past is marked by digressions into unexpected situations that motivate work. They keep us going.

The work appears consistent not because of lived continuity, but because (we can't help ourselves) there are questions and perceptions that haunt our experiences.

They reappear, they transform themselves. But they don't go away.

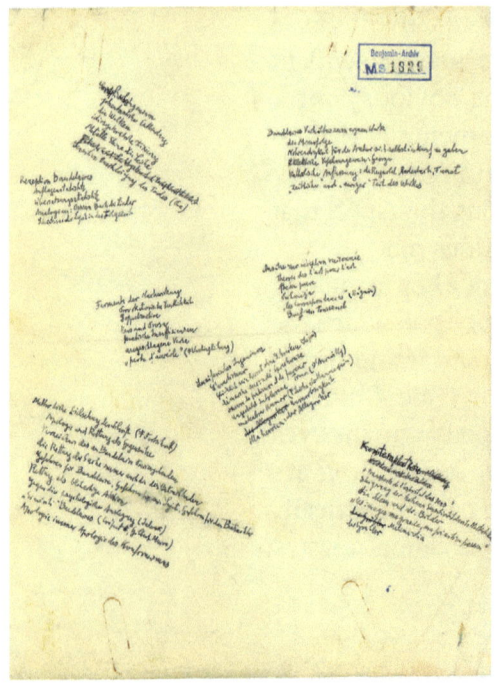

Construction

Fragments. Snippets. Clippings.
Folders of notes. Boxes of images.
Pieces of text that appear as images.
Text blocks as snapshots of reality.
Footprints, traces of the material world.

Walter Benjamin's Arcade Project:
Why it never became a book, why a linear format could not contain his perceptual organizations.

What if you never did write in a linear form? What kind of logic could you claim? Why would you enter a profession of scholarly production? How could you purport to write academic books, research projects, grant proposals, tenure dossiers?

Thought by association.
Juxtaposition of fragments.

Dialectics in open air, not as a line but a leap, landing you in a different space, as thought's reorientation.

[55]

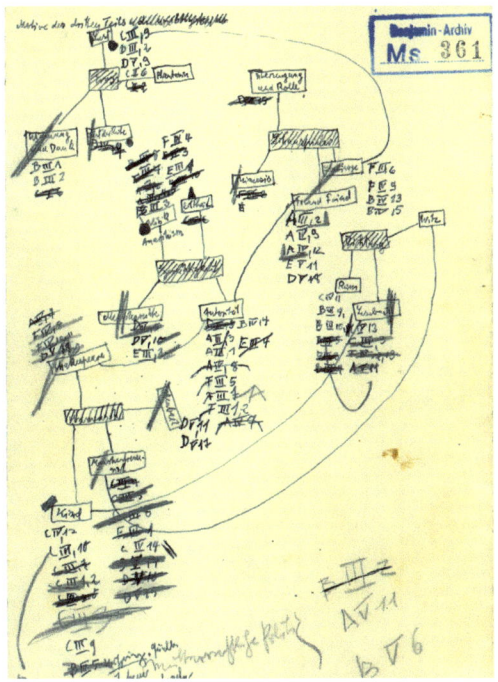

[56]

Benjamin's writing materials:
fragments of a collective past.
Temporary arrangements as experimental designs, marshalled together to fit the task: a literary review, a philosophical constellation.

Visual Organization:
If we think about a book as an apparatus, it becomes interesting to think its elements of construction as modules of thought. Movable parts. Changeable function. Like constructivist furniture.

Rodchenko called socialist commodities 'comrades' because they worked with you, conforming to the changing needs of daily life.

Folding chairs. Folding beds. Multipurpose tables. Personal use values.

Pieces of text that transform themselves. Rooms of thought arranged as sets for action.

247

[57]

Pedagogic function: to teach by seeing. "I have nothing to say, only to show."
—Walter Benjamin[01]

"If they don't give you a seat at the table, bring a folding chair."
—Shirley Chisholm[02]

01   Walter Benjamin, "Das Passagen-Werk," in *Gesammelte Schriften: Vol. 5,* ed. Rolf Tiedemann (Suhrkamp, 1982), 574.

02   This quote is attributed to Shirley Chisholm by fellow activist Donna Brazile. See for instance Eric Andersson, "See Regina King as Trailblazing Black Congresswoman Shirley Chisholm in *Shirley* First Look Photos," *People Magazine,* January 9, 2024, https://people.com/see-regina-king-first-black-congresswoman-shirley-chisholm-shirley-8424082.

Early Cinema as Inspiration

Eisenstein controlled the meaning of montage for purposes of political education. But Vertov played with it. The effect was cognitive liberation. He showed us the apparatus.

[58]

Images convey ideas without the abstraction of words. Reality talks.

[59]

Images are the storehouse of memory.

[60]

Vertov's film editor Elizaveta Svilova is working at the editing, then seen sorting shots into specific positions on the labelled shelves.

[61]

[62]

The shelves where Svilova stores the film are labelled:

- *City Scenes*
- *Factory*
- *Machines* (cars)
- *Bazaar* (marketplace)
- *Fokusnik* (man with movie camera)

[63]

"Any person today can lay claim to being filmed."
—Walter Benjamin

[64]

"What, I wondered, would an art of memory look like today..."
—Robert Edgar[03]

"For every image of the past that is not recognized by the present as one of its own concerns threatens to disappear irretrievably."
—Walter Benjamin[04]

03 Ben Davis, "Memory Theater One: Robert Edgar,"
    The Atlanta Art Papers, 1985,
    https://www.mit.edu/~bhdavis/Edgar.html.

04 Walter Benjamin, "Theses on the Philosophy of History,"
    in *Illuminations*, ed. Hannah Arendt (Schocken Books 1968),
    255.

251

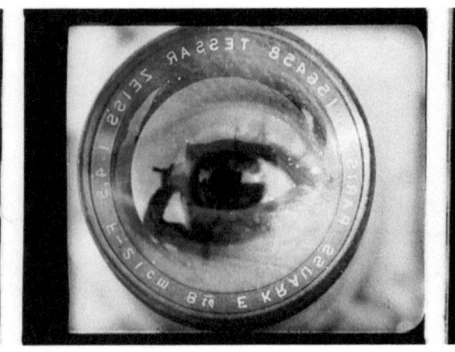

[65]

The camera: "I am an eye. A mechanical eye. Freed from the boundaries of time and space, I co-ordinate any and all points of the universe, wherever I want them to be. My way leads towards the creation of a fresh perception of the world. Thus I explain in a new way the world unknown to you."

—Dziga Vertov, cited by John Berger in *Ways of Seeing*.[05]

John Berger's television series *Ways of Seeing* (1972) cut through the mystification of traditional art history by paying attention to the social realities visible in the paintings, as well as the social implications of where and how they were viewed.

Berger asked "what happens when a painting is shown on a television screen. The painting enters each viewer's house. There it is surrounded by his wallpaper, his furniture, his mementoes. It enters the atmosphere of his family. It becomes their talking point. It lends its meaning to their meaning. At the same time it enters a million other houses and, in each of them, is seen in a different context. Because of the camera, the painting now travels to the spectator rather than the spectator to the painting. In its travels, its meaning is diversified."[06]

Berger's television series became a book, rather than the other way around.

05   Dziga Vertov (1923), as cited in John Berger, *Ways of Seeing* (Penguin, 1972), 17. The quote can be found in a different translation in Dziga Vertov, "The Council of Three," in *Kino-Eye: The Writings of Dziga Vertov*, eds. Annette Michelson and Kevin O'Brien (University of California Press, 1984), 17.

06   Berger, *Ways of Seeing*, 19–20.

Encyclopedia Project

1976: My dissertation on Theodor Adorno was written in the company of students on strike in two countries. Its completion led to a job at the Institute for Policy Studies (IPS), a leftist think tank in Washington, D.C. I was to work on an 'Encyclopedia of Knowledge for Social Reconstruction.' Brainchild of IPS founder Marc Raskin, it aspired for the twentieth century what the French *Encyclopédie* had accomplished for the eighteenth—new knowledge for a new social order.

I would relocate to the affiliated Transnational Institute (TNI) in Amsterdam. I would meet with intellectuals to bring them into the project, the wide-flung friends of IPS and fellows of TNI: John Berger (Switzerland), Susan Sontag (New York), Ivan Illich (Mexico), Paul Feyerabend (Austria), Paulo Freire and Marcos Arruda (Brazil), Eqbal Ahmad (Pakistan), Basker Vashee (Zimbabwe), and Susan George (France).

All were critics of the hegemonic order; some were followed by the CIA.

[66]   Handwritten note by John Berger in *Le Monde des livres* (May 16, 1977). Berger writes this note to Raskin who sends it to Buck-Morss.

TNI's new director, and my future boss in Amsterdam, was Orlando Letelier, ambassador to the US under Salvador Allende, the elected Socialist president of Chile who died in the presidential palace, a victim of the coup of Augusto Pinochet (backed by Kissinger) on September 11, 1973.

What was the New Knowledge? A series of books? Collaborative writing? A global conversation? If Enlightenment's reason was no longer the claim for universality, was left politics a sufficient bond for collaboration?

How could funding be secured— funding that gave life support to worthy intellectuals in their writings critical of the established order?

On September 21, 1976, during preparations to relocate, Orlando Letelier was assassinated by a car bomb on the streets of Washington. Our co-worker Ronni Moffit died with him. Her husband Michael survived the explosion. I wasn't there; I heard later. The rain, the police response held me up in traffic. We met together at IPS wordless.

 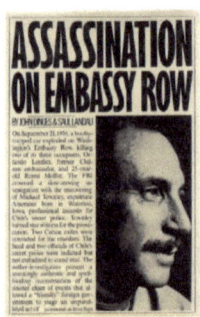

[67]–[68]

A student radical with a new PhD knows nothing of the world. She experiences now a political crime of the highest magnitude, the violent deaths of two vibrant people, caused not by accident but by design. It happens in the center of the US capital while government officials turn a blind eye. She finds herself days later in the midst of a massive demonstration by the staffs of embassies of developing nations and others in protest against this assassination as well as so many US actions— in Chile, Brazil, Nicaragua, Cuba, Rhodesia (now Zimbabwe)—US support of coups against social revolutions, US support of dictators against popular movements, US support of racist regimes of white minority rule. The streets filled with men and women of every nationality, in solidarity with those assassinated in the September rain.

What is the lesson? A student rebellion is not a revolution. Solidarity is not personal friendship but a global commitment. Political positioning is a stance toward life. And death.

She commits herself that day to the intellectual tradition of thinkers, wherever they reside, whose lives those in power find expendable.

History as repair. Not restoring wholeness, but saving fragments. A radical rescue of tradition. An ethical mandate for work.

Meeting John Berger

Among the collaborating fellows of TNI was the exemplary thinker in images, John Berger. He invited me to visit soon after my arrival in Amsterdam.

[69]

At lunch, with pad and pen, John proposed this idea of an encyclopedia of knowledge for our time: we should focus on lived experience in its corporeal manifestations—aesthetics in the literal meaning of the term, as sensory perception, where hand and eye, thought and physical practice were not separated in knowledge production and knowledge sharing.

Encyclopedia entries might focus on the use value of things (roads) in their contemporary form (highways) as encountered in daily life.

We sat over lunch and drew lists.

John suggested these words for entries: necessity; leisure; mobility; shelter; tool; age; theft; nudity; war; mirror; food; dust; pain; trust; solidarity; dreams; security/danger/crisis. And places: museum, factory, housing, shops, park, cemetery, bank, asylum office, restaurant, prison, zoos. The point of these would be to make materially visible the lived modernity that needed to be reflected upon, critically.

A pilot volume was imagined from A (anger) to Z (zoos). L is for locks (the only security of possession is not a lock technology, but social acceptance of the legitimacy of the private property regime...

Reading reality like a book.

Thinking a book as reality.

The centrality of visual perception to philosophy in our time.

255

John drew a sketch during lunchtime (I complained it looked like a man. Adjustments were made.)

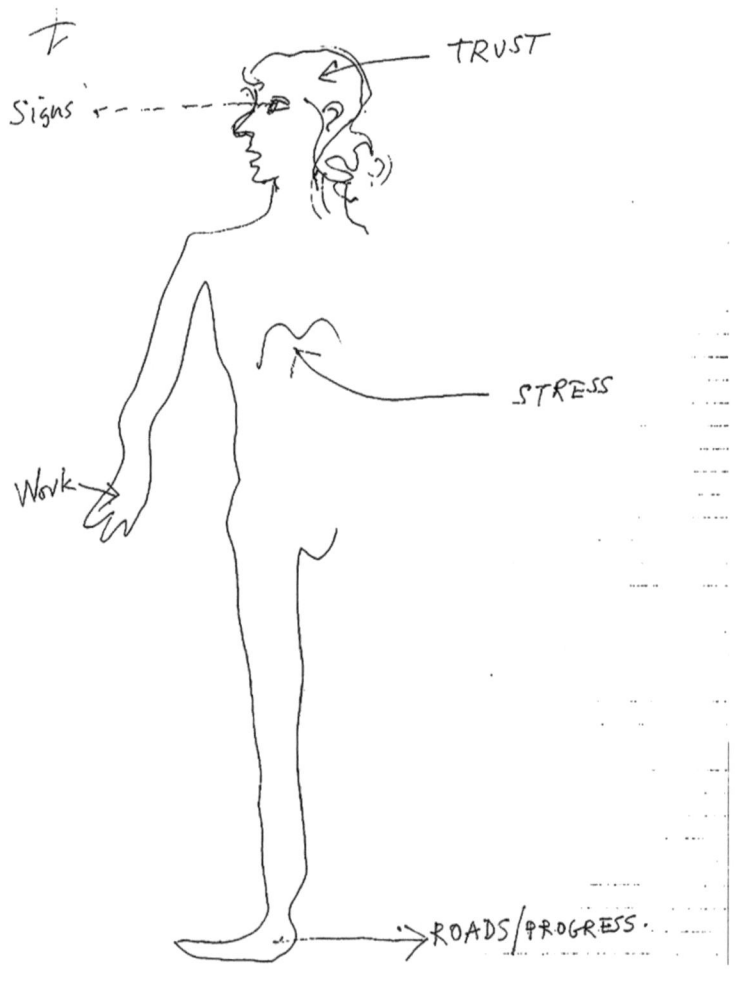

[70]

An Experiment:
Image as Philosophy/
Philosophy as Image

1978: Mirtos, the south shore of Crete. I sat for months in the crossroads cafés where tourists' romantic dream-worlds and villagers' existential precarity overlapped. In images passing by, with no understanding of the language, I learned to see what was going on. (One foot in the boat, adrift, one on the secure shore of academia...)

[72]

What has happened within him is not distinct from what happens within millions of others who are not migrant workers. It is simply more extreme. He experiences suddenly as an individual, as a man who believes he is choosing his own life, what the industrial consumer societies have experienced gradually through generations without the effort of choosing. He lives the content of our institutions: they transform him violently. They do not need to transform us. We are already within them.

[71]

My task was to teach political theory in the Department of Government where habits of instruction were visually impaired. I wanted to change that. I wrote a proposal for doing philosophy in image form: dialectical negation, capitalist deceptions, class differences, in Vertovian/Eisensteinian fashion. I was told, if I wanted to stay at Cornell, I should drop this project of philosophizing through images.

This village experiment was disrupted by being offered a position at Cornell.[07] I said yes. Despite such extraordinary colleagues as Benedict Anderson and Martin Bernal, I was uneasy.

07 Susan Buck-Morss, "Semiotic Boundaries and the Politics of Meaning: Modernity on Tour—A Village in Transition," in *New Ways of Knowing: The Sciences, Society, and Reconstructive Knowledge*, eds. Marcus G. Raskin and Herbert J. Bernstein (Rowman & Littlefield Publishers, 1987).

Officially, I gave up on the project. But its way of working was smuggled into a book on Walter Benjamin and the Arcades Project.[08] No one knew where to shelve my book on Benjamin: Philosophy? History? Literature? Political theory? Cultural studies? Critical theory?[09]

Benjamin was brilliant in creating 'dialectical images' as thought-montages of past and present, visible within the text itself:

"Bomber planes make us remember what Leonardo Da Vinci expected of the flight of man; he was to have raised himself into the air 'in order to look for snow on the mountain summits, and then return to scatter it over the city streets shimmering with the heat of summer.'"

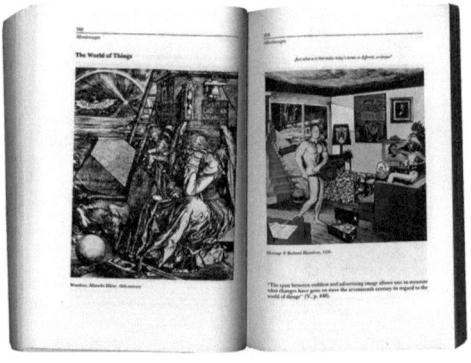

[73]

—Walter Benjamin[10]

08 Susan Buck-Morss, *The Dialectics of Seeing: Walter Benjamin and the Arcades Project* (MIT Press, 1989).

09 Richard Bernstein, "Putting Together the Pieces of an Unfinished Book," New York Times, July 16, 1990.

10 Walter Benjamin, "Das Passagen-Werk," 609.

Lesson one: Dialectics:

[74]

Lesson two: Inequality: Golf Course/Slums:

[75]

Lesson three: Commodity Form:

[76]

An unexpected meeting in Moscow, 1987, with Soviet philosophers just discovering Adorno and Benjamin, led to a sustained collaboration. Valery Podoroga, who wrote on Eisenstein's cinema and Soviet dreamworlds, led a seminar on visual anthropology.[11] He read literature through the sensory traces the texts contained. For five years, as the Cold War order crumbled around us, we conversed and collaborated with and about images.[12]

At Cornell, I began teaching Visual Culture and Social Theory, first with Hal Foster, and later as Director of Visual Studies, a nonexistent interdisciplinary department, housed in a virtual building designed by Patrick Foran who planted a socialist avantgarde construction in the center of the Cornell arts quad.

When slide transparency technology became obsolete, I dropped the large lecture course, shelving my four hundred transparencies and double-mounted slide carousels. The images migrated to a personal website created by the design studio Project Projects, founded by Adam Michaels and Prem Krishnamurthy in lower Manhattan.[13]

In academic publishing, 'figures' and 'texts' are too often treated as different species of thought. Images go to art departments and copy stays with the editor, rather than seeing text blocks as images and images as text. Articles on the website allowed another relationship to grow between them.

[77]

[78]

11   Valery Podoroga, *Mimesis: The Analytic Anthropology of Literature* (Verso Books, 2022).

12   Susan Buck-Morss, "A Global Public Sphere?," Radical Philosophy, no. 111 (2002) 2–10.

13   See it here: https://www.susanbuckmorss.info.

At the CUNY Graduate Center in 2022, I began a new course, "Politics of the Image." Available materials have multiplied. The issues are crucial to political life.

Students today are at home with the task of constructing ideas with images.

Benjamin's thinking remains central.

The antidote to aestheticizing politics is perhaps less to politicize art than to politicize perception itself—aesthesis in the original meaning of the word. Any image counts as evidence. Books are not superseded. No technology is. In film, on television, with computers, in books, the ways of seeing transform us. Wikipedia took on the task of knowledge for the twenty-first century. But questions of method, the 'how' of knowledge, remain.

"Remember the Romanian uprising in 1989, when protesters invaded TV studios to make history? At that moment, images changed their function. Broadcasts from occupied TV studios became active catalysts of events—not records or documents. Since then it has become clear that images are ... nodes of energy and matter that migrate across different supports, shaping and affecting people, landscapes, politics, and social systems. They acquired an uncanny ability to proliferate, transform, and activate."
—Hito Steyerl[14]

[79]

14   Hito Steyerl, "Too Much World: Is the Internet Dead?,"
      e-flux Journal 49 (2013).

261

Postscript/Preview on Planetary Perception

Critical Theory has missed the opportunity to respond to the ecological crises of our time. Nature too has agency, within a scale of time and space that dwarfs the (Kantian) anthropocentric world. Hence a return to post-Hegelian (Marx–Adorno) approaches to history/nature (Marx's *1844 Manuscripts,* Horkheimer & Adorno's *Dialectic of Enlightenment*) is not enough.

I am proposing something more radical: a rejection of the Kantian doctrine (prominent in Habermas' work) that knowledge divides into three forms, characterized by distinct and different critical methods of analysis: Reason (1st critique), Morals (2nd critique) and Aesthetics (3rd critique). As a philosophical positioning, none of them speaks to the holistic transformation of consciousness that is required as a political response the ecological crises: Reason leads to instrumental/transactional politics and (perhaps) the rationalization of revolutionary violence; Moral purity (Hegel's 'beautiful soul') may send individuals to heaven but they leave a sullied earth behind; Aesthetics, understood today in the diminished sense of 'art,' enacts political protest as 'autonomy' that cannot escape the financial interests of the artworld.

Seeing is an aesthetic form of cognition. Images matter. Perception shifts our sight from the era of the 'posts' (post-modernism, post-Marxism, post-colonialism) and acknowledges our situation as pre-planetary.

We need a transformation in vision.

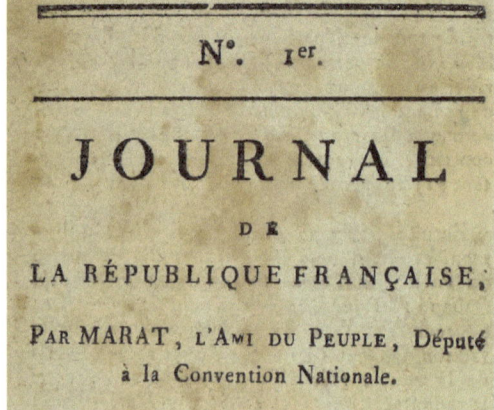

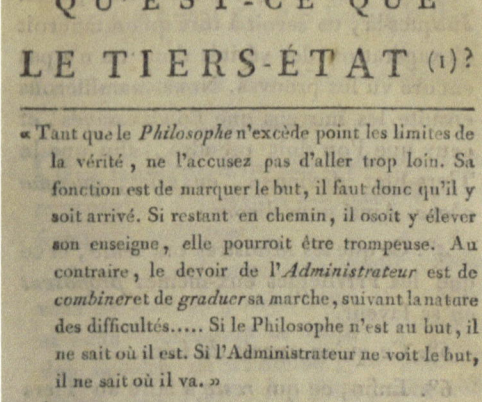

[80]–[81]

GAZETTE NATIONALE, ou LE MONITEUR UNIVERSEI

Nº. 21.   DU 20 AU 21 JUILLET 1789.

De Paris.

Suite des détails des circonstances qui ont amené la prise de la Bastille, et relation de cet événement.

Les citoyens de tout rang, de tout ordre, de tout âge, tous les Français qui se trouvent dans la capitale se font inscrire sur la liste des soldats de la Patrie, et se décorent de la cocarde verte. Il est statué que chaque districts formera des patrouilles pour garder la ville, qu'on s'incorporera avec les brigands, afin de les désarmer sans effort, et que le prévôt des marchands avisera aux moyens de fournir promptement des fusils et des munitions de guerre (1).

Après cet arrêté, les drapeaux de la ville furent déployés, on fit des décharges de canons, pour tenir les citoyens en alerte, on établit des tranchées, des barricades dans les fauxbourgs et dans quelques rues du centre, on posta par-tout des corps-de-garde; et, en moins de trente-six heures, Paris présenta l'image d'une ville de guerre, et vit dans son enceinte au moins cent mille hommes qui se divisèrent par compagnies, nommèrent des commandans, et veillèrent à la tranquillité publique.

Les intrépides Gardes-Françaises viennent aussi, au nombre d'environ trois mille, se ranger sous les étendards de la Patrie, pour partager les périls et diriger les efforts de ses défenseurs. Leurs chefs avaient depuis quelque tems pénétré les sentimens qui les animaient, et cherché les moyens de rendre

leur patriotisme inutile à la capitale, et peut-ê funeste à ceux qui l'éprouvaient. On prétexte d'ab l'ordre de les réunir au camp de Saint-Denis, et leur ordonne d'y aller sans armes. C'était les c voyer à la boucherie; ils refusent de marcher. l'hôpital du Gros-Caillou, on fait entendre à le canonniers qu'il est important qu'ils aillent gar l'hôtel de Richelieu, considéré en ce moment com quartier-général; et dès qu'ils sont partis, on ch eux, restés à l'hôpital, s'apperçoivent de la man vre, et vont avertir leurs camarades : ils quitt aussitôt l'hôtel de Richelieu. Le sixième batail abandonne ses casernes, tous courent à l'hôpit d'où ils transportent leurs canons dans leur poste la rue Verte.

[82]

In the French Revolution, news of the public assemblies spread through the European presses, which made journalism central to modern political life. Literacy was not universal, but this was a specifically bourgeois revolution.

Mediation through the word—then as now—softened the violence of revolutionary acts, so that even as restrained a man as Kant could, at the end of his life, have 'enthusiasm' for the revolutionaries.

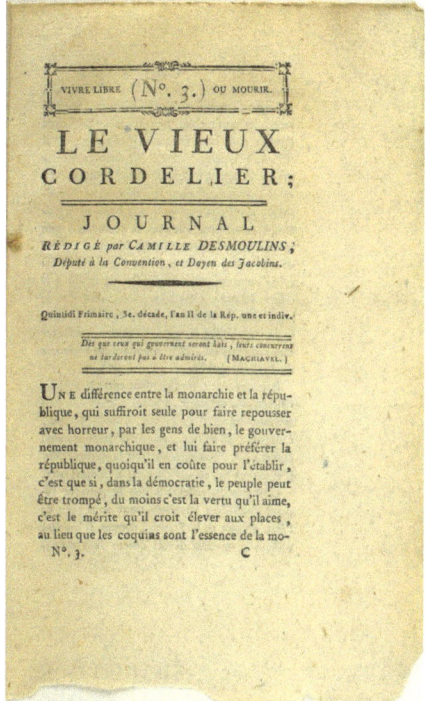

[83]

[84]

bodily harm inflicted on persons who speak to us of their pain. Instead of attempting to 'scale up' politics (world government), the technological reproducibility of sensory experience meets us at home.

The old ways of interpreting the world ring false when they repeat the conceptual mappings of the past. Under conditions of the technological transformation of experience—we can call this 'mediated immediacy'—the act of perception itself has changed. We *see* a world before we comprehend it, before we can articulate its meaning. Under conditions of mediated immediacy, spaces of appearance overflow national boundaries.

What Habermas recently called the 'fragmentation of the public sphere' on the national level can lead to the assemblage of a different order. My point is that spaces of appearance cannot—can no longer be—(merely) national. Our challenge is to develop a political understanding commensurate with a Planetary Public Sphere.

The task is not to 'think' the world differently but to see it differently—no longer as a globe (1492 to the present), but as a planet (in images sent back to us from space), which Heidegger disparaged as "a mass of matter deposited somewhere," and Arendt feared marked the end of politics.[15]

On the planet seen from space, there are no political divisions into nations. Technology shows us a different topology, alienated from human 'common sense.' The question is whether the mediated experience that it provides, in wounding human institutions can heal them again. The anaesthetic effects of distant war-killings are reversed when cell phones (close to our bodies) show us, daily, the devastating

15   Martin Heidegger, "The Origin of the Work of Art," in *Poetry, Language, Thought,* ed. Albert Hofstadter (Haper Collins, 2009), 41; Hannah Arendt, *The Human Condition* (University of Chicago Press, 1998), 1–2.

[85]–[87]

The truly revolutionary aspect of the 2011 events that unfolded with the Arab Spring was the creation of a new trans-local archipelago of democratic events on every continent, that was visible to a planetary population.[16]

We experienced their unfolding viscerally, as affects, in perceptions that, once seen could not be made *un*-seen. These affects echoed in 2024, when 'the people' acted democratically to occupy public space in Bangladesh, South Korea, Georgia, and, in the early days following the fall of Assad, in Syria as well. This challenged, once again, the presumption of the unseeability of the non-Western world. (Once seen, these images cannot be un-seen).

The planetary is already here, visible in the mediated immediacy of the world we share. As political actors we find ourselves within it. Reflection/action is required.

List of Illustrations and Image Credits

Martha Crowe
We Need to Talk: A Museum's Response
to Political Polarization in Post-Unification Germany

[01]   Eva-Maria Stange, *Kleine Anfrage der Abgeordneten Karin Wilke, AfD-Fraktion: Drs.-Nr.: 6/10834: Thema: Abhängen von DDR-Kunst in der Galerie Neue Meister Dresden,* October 18, 2017, scan, State Ministry for Science and the Arts Saxony, https://www.s3.kleine-anfragen.de/ka-prod/sn/6/10834.pdf.

[02]–[05]   David Pinzer, *Gesprächsrunde in der Veranstaltungsreihe "Wir müssen reden. 'Bilderstreit' mit Blickkontakt"* on November 6, 2017, in the Lichthof of the Albertinum Dresden, 2017, photograph. © SKD/© David Pinzer.

Martin Renz/Julius Schwarzwälder
Revolutions of the Senses

[06]   Andrew Davidson, [*Toblerone*], 2022, digital logo. © Mondelez International.

[07]   Modified image detail of Andrew Davidson, [*Toblerone*], 2022, digital logo. © Mondelez International.

[08]   [*What Has Been Seen... Cannot Be Un-seen*], 2007, digital image, Genmay, https://www.genmay.com/post-you-pics-t763689-s2600.html#p21940715.

[09]   [*Welche Thiere gleichen einander am meisten? Kaninchen und Ente*], 1892, drawing, *Fliegende Blätter*, 147, Braun & Schneider, October 23, 1892, https://www.commons.wikimedia.org/wiki/File:Duck-Rabbit.png

[10]   Fibonacci, *Café Wall*, 2007, digital image, Wikimedia Commons, https://www.commons.wikimedia.org/wiki/File:Caf%C3%A9_wall.svg.

[11]–[12]   John Berger, [*Paintings are often reproduced with words around them...*], 1972, book scan, in *Ways of Seeing*, John Berger, Penguin, 1972, 27–28.

[13]   Image detail of Louis Brion de La Tour, *Geógraphie moderne, historique et politique: système ptoléméique*, 1786, map, in *Atlas Général et Élémentaire pour l'étude de la Géographie et de l'Histoire moderne*, Polona Biblioteka Narodowa, Warsaw, object no. ZZK 0.858, https://www.polona.pl/ item-view/59745614-3987-4bae-a645-a505f5cd7d00?page=17.

[14]   Christophe Guérin and Jean-Michel Morceau, *Prise de la Bastille: le 14 Juillet 1789.* 1792–1799, engraving, eau-forte, chisel, 9.5 × 5.5 cm, BnF Gallica, Paris, object no. ark:/12148/btv1b6942828d, https://www.gallica.bnf.fr/ark:/12148/btv1b6942828d. © gallica.bnf.fr/BnF.

[15]   Jean-Louis Prieur, Pierre-Gabriel Berthault and Jean Duplessi-Bertaux, *Prise de la Bastille: le 14 Juillet 1789*, 1802, engraving, eau-forte, chisel, 24 × 29 cm, BnF Gallica, Paris, object no. ark:/12148/btv1b6942791t, https://www.gallica.bnf.fr/ark:/12148/btv1b6942791t. © gallica.bnf.fr/BnF.

[16]   Charles Monnet, Isidore-Stanislas Helman and Antoine-Jean Duclos, *Prise de la Bastille. Le 14 Juillet 1789*, 1795–1796, engraving, eau-forte, chisel, 37.5 × 46 cm, BnF Gallica, Paris, object no. ark:/12148/btv1b8410719v, https://www.gallica.bnf.fr/ark:/12148/btv1b8410719v. © gallica.bnf.fr/BnF.

[17]   [*Prise de la Bastille*], 1789, engraving, eau-forte, 14 × 9.5 cm, BnF Gallica, Paris, object no. ark:/12148/btv1b84107156, https://www.gallica.bnf.fr/ark:/12148/btv1b84107156. © gallica.bnf.fr/BnF.

[18]   *Prise de la Bastille en 1789*, 1789, engraving, eau-forte, 21 × 26.5 cm, BnF Gallica, Paris, object no. ark:/12148/btv1b8410722b, https://gallica.bnf.fr/ark:/12148/btv1b8410722b. © gallica.bnf.fr/BnF.

[19]   Jean-François Janinet, *Prise de la Bastille par les Gardes Françaises et les Bourgeois de Paris,* le Mardi 14 Juillet 1789, 1789, engraving, wash manner, 19 × 23 cm, BnF Gallica, Paris, object no. ark:/12148/btv1b6942821h, https://www.gallica.bnf.fr/ark:/12148/btv1b6942821h. © gallica.bnf.fr/BnF.

[20]   Charles-François-Gabriel Le Vachez, *Siège de la Bastille, prise en 2 heures et demie, le 14 juillet 1789,* 1789, engraving, eau-forte, outils, col., 10.5 × 15.5 cm, BnF Gallica, Paris, object no. ark:/12148/btv1b6942798q, https://www.gallica. bnf.fr/ark:/12148/btv1b6942798q. © gallica.bnf.fr/BnF.

[21]   Charles Thévenin, Prise de la Bastille, le 14 Juillet 1789, 1790, engraving, eau-forte, 37.5 × 58.5 cm, BnF Gallica, Paris, object no. ark:/12148/btv1b6942830g, https://www.gallica.bnf.fr/ark:/12148/btv1b6942830g. © gallica.bnf.fr/BnF.

[22]   [*Prise de la Bastille*], 1789, engraving, eau-forte, pointillé, 39.5 × 57.5 cm, BnF Gallica, Paris, object no. ark:/12148/btv1b8410718f, https://www.gallica.bnf.fr/ark:/12148/btv1b8410718f. © gallica.bnf.fr/BnF.

[23]   Jacques-Louis Bance, *Prise de la Bastille par les bourgeois et les braves Gardes françaises de la bonne ville de Paris, le 14 Juillet 1789: Dédiée à la Nation*, 1789, engraving, eau-forte, monochr. bistre, 29 × 39.5 cm, BnF Gallica, Paris, object no. ark:/12148/btv1b6942822x, https://www.gallica.bnf.fr/ark:/12148/btv1b6942822x. © gallica.bnf.fr/BnF.

[24]   Charles Thévenin, *Prise de la Bastille, le 14 Juillet 1789,* 1790, engraving, eau-forte, 37.5 × 58.5 cm, BnF Gallica, Paris, object no. ark:/12148/btv1b6942830g, https://www.gallica.bnf.fr/ark:/12148/btv1b6942830g. © gallica.bnf.fr/BnF.

[25]   François Martin Testard and Le Campion, *Demolition de la Bastille,* 1789, engraving, colored aquatint, 19.5 × 28.5 cm, BnF Gallica, Paris, object no. ark:/12148/btv1b84107957, https://www.gallica.bnf.fr/ark:/12148/btv1b84107957. © gallica.bnf.fr/BnF.

[26] Janinet, Jean-François, *Événement de la nuit du 14 au 15 juillet 1789: M. de Liancourt se jette aux pieds du Roi, et lui fait le récit fidel des malheurs de la capitale,* 1789–1791, engraving, eau-forte, wash manner, 12.7 × 8.5 cm, BnF Gallica, Paris, object no. ark:/12148/btv1b84107742, https://www.gallica. bnf.fr/ark:/12148/btv1b84107742, © gallica.bnf.fr/BnF.

[27] [*Ahn Gwi-ryeong Grappling With a Gun*], videographer unknown, December 3, 2024, screenshot taken from livestream by OhmyNews, via AsiaOne, https://www.asiaone.com/asia/ south-korean-party-spokesperson-who-grappled-martial-law-soldier-insists-she-not-special.

[28] Joseph Priestley, *A Chart of Biography,* 1765, map, printed in *Cartographies of Time,* Daniel Rosenberg and Anthony Grafton, 118–119, ch. 4, fig. 19, Princeton Architectural Press, 2010, courtesy of the Library Company of Philadelphia.

Raha Golestani
Paradise Lost: Art, Caviar
and Irreconcilable Differences

[29] *Performance of Mantra by Karlheinz Stockhausen at the Saraye Moshir,* photographer unknown, September 2, 1972, photograph, Privatsammlung Stockhausen, Stockhausen Stiftung für Musik, Kürten, https://www.commons.wikimedia.org/wiki/File:Shiraz_37.jpg. © Archiv Stockhausen-Stiftung für Musik, Kürten (stockhausen.org).

[30] Abbas Hojatpanah, *Ballet by Maurice Béjart at the Shiraz Festival of Arts,* n.d., photograph. © Abbas Hojatpanah / © personal archive.

[31] Walter Bibikow, *Iran, Tehran, Niyavaran Palace Complex, Palace Of The Last Shah, Clothing Of The Royal Couple,* 2015, photograph. © Walter Bibikow/Ma.

[32] Klara Palotai, [*Photograph of Poster for the Performance of Pig, Child, Fire! at the Shiraz Festival of Arts*], 1977, photograph, poster-designer unknown. © Klara Palotai / © Squat Theatre Archives.

[33]   Abbas Hojatpanah, [*Merce Cunningham Dance Company
       Performing an Event in Persepolis*], 1972.
       © Abbas Hojatpanah/© Merce Cunningham Trust and
       the Jerome Robbins Dance Division,
       The New York Public Library.

**Merve Yıldırım
When Constantinople Was a Center
of Central Europe: (We Were Best Friends)**

[34]   *Resm-i küşaddan evvel*, n.d., photograph,
       photographer unknown, in *Servet-i Fünun* 516, January 30,
       1901, digitized periodical.
       Millî Kütüphane Süreli Yayın Koleksiyonu,
       https://www.dijital-kutuphane.mkutup.gov.tr/en/
       Periodicals/Catalog/Issue/?IssueId=6098.

[35]   [*Sultan Mehmed V. wurde vom Kaiser zum preußischen
       Feldmarschall ernannt*], n.d., photograph,
       photographer unknown, in *Die Woche* 7, 1916, 225,
       Staats- und Universitätsbibliothek Hamburg.

[36]   *Haşmetlü Almanya İmparatoru hazretleri İstanbulda
       Osmânl Müşîr oğlu forması altında*, n.d., photograph,
       photographer unknown, in *Harb Mecmuası* 2, September 30,
       1917, digitized periodical,
       Millî Kütüphane Süreli Yayın Koleksiyonu,
       https://www.dijital-kutuphane.mkutup.gov.tr/.

[37]   *Berlin, Alman Türk Dostluk Yurdu'nda satranç ve dama
       oynayan talebeler—Students Playing Chess and Checkers at
       the German Turkish Friendship Dorm in Berlin*,
       November 10, 1917, photograph, photographer unknown,
       Salt Research: Education Archive, https://www.archives.
       saltresearch.org/handle/123456789/208047.

[38]   [*Vom Besuch des Kaisers in Konstantinopel. Der Kaiser be-
       grüßt im Beisein des Sultans hohe türkische Würdenträger—
       Kaiser'in İstanbul ziyaretinden. Kaiser, padişahın huzurunda
       yüksek Türk ileri gelenlerini ağırlıyor*], October 15, 1917,
       photograph, photographer unknown, Salt Research:
       Photograph and Postcard Archive, https://www.archives.
       saltresearch.org/handle/123456789/208052.

[39]   [*Der deutsche Kaiser lässt sich auf dem Bauplatz des Hauses der Freundschaft am 16. Oktober 1917 von E. Jäckh die Vorstandsmitglieder der Türkisch-Deutschen Vereinigung vorstellen*], n.d., photograph, photographer unknown, Deutscher Werkbund und Deutsch-Türkische Vereinigung, Sammlung Werkbundarchiv, Museum der Dinge, Berlin, Bestand Deutscher Werkbund.

[40]   *Exhibition Catalogues for the Haus der Freundschaft*, n.d., Deutscher Werkbund und Deutsch-Türkische Vereinigung, Sammlung Werkbundarchiv, Museum der Dinge, Berlin, Bestand Deutscher Werkbund.

[41]   *Grundsteinlegung für das Haus der Freundschaft in Stambul am 27. April 1917 in Gegenwart der türkischen Minister und des deutschen Botschafters,* n.d., photograph, photographer unknown, Deutscher Werkbund und Deutsch-Türkische Vereinigung, in *Das Haus der Freundschaft in Konstantinopel: Ein Wettbewerb deutscher Architekten,* Theodor Heuss, F. Bruckmann, 1918.

[42]   Merve Yıldırım, *Streetsign "Dostluk Yurdu Sokağı" in Istanbul,* 2024, photograph. © Merve Yıldırım.

Dorothea Douglas
Proceeding Through Steps: The Political Aesthetics of Legal Subjectivity in the Amtsgericht Mitte, Berlin

[43]   Dorothea Douglas, [*Land- und Amtsgericht Mitte, Berlin. View from inside the Staircase between Floors One and Two*], 2020, photograph. © Dorothea Douglas.

[44]   *Ground Floor Plan of the Land- und Amtsgericht Mitte,* 1908, color lithograph on carton, 79.4 × 176.3 cm, Architecture Museum of the Technical University Berlin, object no. 29364, https://www.doi.org/10.25645/megt-jxqk. © Architekturmuseum der TU Berlin

[45]   [*Cross section of the Stairwell Pavilion at Neue Friedrichstraße (now Littenstraße)*], 1908, color lithograph on carton, 79.2 × 105.4 cm, Architecture Museum of the Technical University Berlin, object no. 29369, https://www.doi.org/10.25645/23tw-tmgx. © Architekturmuseum der TU Berlin.

[46]   Paul Thoemer, [*Ground Floor Plan of the Initial
         'Entwurfsskizze' of the Land- und Amtsgericht Mitte*], June 13,
         1896, newspaper illustration, Friedrich Raschdorff,
         "Entwurfskizzen zum Neubau eines Geschäftsgebäudes
         der Civilabtheilungen des Landgerichts I und Amtsgericht
         I in Berlin," *Centralblatt der Bauverwaltung* 16, no. 24
         (June 13, 1896): 262, https://www.digital.zlb.de/viewer/
         image/14688302_1896/279/.

[47]   Paul Thoemer, [*Façade Projection of the Initial
         'Entwurfsskizze' of the Land- und Amtsgericht Mitte*],
         June 13, 1896, newspaper illustration, in *Centralblatt der
         Bauverwaltung* 16, no. 24, Friedrich Raschdorff (ed.),
         June 13, 1896, 264, https://www.digital.zlb.de/viewer/
         image/14688302_1896/279/.

[48]   [*View of the Stairway and Tabernacle*], 1905,
         collotype on paper, in *Atlas zur Zeitschrift für Bauwesen* 55,
         46, object no. ZFB 55,046, https://www.doi.org/
         10.25645/6d7y-qsj4. © Architekturmuseum der TU Berlin.

[49]   Dorothea Douglas, [*Land- und Amtsgericht Mitte, Berlin.
         View from the Parapet onto the Stairs*], photograph, 2025.
         © Dorothea Douglas.

[50]   [*The Stairway's Landing at the Top Floor Gallery*], 1905,
         collotype on paper, in *Atlas zur Zeitschrift für Bauwesen* 55,
         47, object no. ZFB 55,047, https://www.doi.org/
         10.25645/ysak-e2wr. © Architekturmuseum der TU Berlin.

Noah Grossmann
A Moment in Time? Arendt, Moten, and the Futures
of Black Action in Little Rock

[51]   Ira Wilmer Counts Jr., *Elizabeth Eckford Outside of Little
         Rock High School,* September 4, 1957, photograph,
         https://www.img.picturealliance.sodatech.com/TTDI/
         wprev/95141168.jpg. © Picture Alliance.

[52]   Francis Miller (top) and Douglas Martin (bottom),
         [*Front Page of the New York Times: September 5, 1957,
         Showing Elizabeth Eckford Outside Little Rock Central
         High School (top) and Dorothy Counts in Charlotte (bottom)*],
         1957, photograph, in *Hannah Arendt zwischen*

den Disziplinen, Ulrich Baer and Amir Eshel (ed.), 223,
Wallstein, 2014.

Helena Crusius
Active Objects

[53]   Rembrandt Harmenszoon van Rijn, *The Entombment
         of Christ,* 1635–39, oil on canvas, 92.6 × 68.9 cm, https://
         www.sammlung.pinakothek.de/en/artwork/A9xlamzLWv.
         © Bayerische Staatsgemäldesammlungen/
         © Alte Pinakothek.

[54]   Rembrandt Harmenszoon van Rijn, *The Resurrection
         of Christ,* 1635–39, oil on canvas mounted on panel,
         91.9 × 67 cm, https://
         www.sammlung.pinakothek.de/en/artwork/apG9B2g4Zn.
         © Bayerische Staatsgemäldesammlungen/
         © Alte Pinakothek.

Susan Buck-Morss
**The 'How' of Knowledge: With a Postscript/Preview
on Planetary Perception**

[55]   Walter Benjamin, *Sketch of Layout for the Essay on
         Karl Kraus: 'Motifs of the Third Part',* 1930, sketch drawing,
         Akademie der Künste, Berlin, Walter Benjamin Archiv,
         object no. WBA 575/29 (Ms 361). © Hamburger Stiftung
         zur Förderung von Wissenschaft und Kultur.

[56]   Walter Benjamin, *Themes to "Charles Baudelaire,"* n.d.,
         sketch drawing, Akademie der Künste, Berlin,
         Walter Benjamin Archiv, object no. WBA 343/4 (Ms 1829).
         © Hamburger Stiftung zur Förderung von Wissenschaft
         und Kultur.

[57]   Boris Zemlyanitsky, *Folding Chair,* 1927–1928,
         wood and metal, photographer unknown.

[58]   Sergei Eisenstein, *October: Ten Days That Shook the World,*
         1928, film still.

[59]–[62] Dziga Vertov, *Man with a Movie Camera,* 1929, film still.

[63]   Robert Edgar, *Presenting Memory Theatre One (1985)*, 1986, film still. © Robert Edgar.

[64]   Robert Edgar, *Memory Theater One*, 1985, video game still. © Robert Edgar.

[65]   Dziga Vertov, *Man with a Movie Camera*, 1929, film still.

[66]   John Berger, [*Handwritten Correspondence in* Le Monde des livres], May 16, 1977, photograph from the personal archives of Susan Buck-Morss. © Susan Buck-Morss/ © John Berger.

[67]   [*Portrait of Ronni Moffitt*], n.d., photograph, photographer unknown. © Moffitt family/ © Institute for Policy Studies.

[68]   John Dinges and Saul Landau, *Assassination on Embassy Row,* front cover, Pantheon Books, 1980.

[69]   John Berger, [*Handwritten Correspondence*], 26 September 1976, photograph from the personal archives of Susan Buck-Morss. © Susan Buck-Morss/© John Berger.

[70]   John Berger, [*Drawing Made During Lunch,*] September 1976, photograph from the personal archives of Susan Buck-Morss. © Susan Buck-Morss/© John Berger.

[71]   Jean Mohr, *A Greek Migrant Worker in Germany,* in *A Seventh Man,* John Berger and Jean Mohr, 201, Verso Books, 2010. © Jean Mohr/© John Berger.

[72]   [*Advertisement Appearing in the New York Times: "Sunday Travel Section"*], 1982, photograph, photographer unknown, from the personal archives of Susan Buck-Morss.

[73]   Alain Nicholas, *Doves,* 2005, digital illustration, https://www.tessellations-nicolas.com. © Alain Nicolas.

[74]   Johnny Miller, *Papwa Sewgolum Golf Course in Durban,* 2022, photograph from the series *Unequal Scenes.* © Johnny Miller.

[75]   Brassaï, *Vagabond à Marseille,* 1935, photograph. © bpk | CNAC-MNAM | Estate Brassaï.

[76] Susan Buck-Morss, *The World of Things,* 1989, book scan, in *The Dialectics of Seeing: Walter Benjamin and the Arcades Project,* Susan Buck-Morss, 348–349, MIT Press, 1989. © Susan Buck-Morss.

[77] Patrick Foran, *Virtual Visual Studies Department at Cornell University,* 2005, photograph. © Patrick Foran.

[78] El Lissitzky, *Wolkenbügel,* 1924, ink and pencil on cardboard, 40 × 55.5 cm, State Tretyakov Gallery, Moscow.

[79] Susan Buck-Morss, *Constellation: The City as Dreamworld and Catastrophe,* n.d., webpage still, https://www.susanbuckmorss.info/text/the-city-as-dreamworld-and-catastrophe/, webpage conceived by studio Project Projects.

[80] Charles-Joseph Panckoucke (editor), *Gazette nationale ou le Moniteur universel,* July 20, 1789, newspaper, BnF Gallica, Paris, object no. ark:/12148/bpt6k4410970s, https://www.gallica.bnf.fr/ark:/12148/bpt6k4410970s. © gallica.bnf.fr/BnF.

[81] Jean-Paul Marat, *Journal de la République Française: L'Ami du Peuple,* September 25, 1792, journal, BnF Gallica, Paris, object no. ark:/12148/bpt6k1049090g, https://www.gallica.bnf.fr/ark:/12148/bpt6k1049090g. © gallica.bnf.fr/BnF.

[82] Emmanuel-Joseph Sieyès, *Qu'est-ce que le Tiers-État? Troisième édition,* 1789, pamphlet, BnF Gallica, Paris, object no. ark:/12148/bpt6k97743407, https://www.gallica.bnf.fr/ark:/12148/bpt6k97743407. © gallica.bnf.fr/BnF.

[83] Camille Desmoulins, *Le Vieux Cordelier,* December 15, 1793, journal, BnF Gallica, Paris, object no. ark:/12148/bpt6k1045474h, https://www.gallica.bnf.fr/ark:/12148/bpt6k1045474h. © gallica.bnf.fr/BnF.

[84] Harrison Schmitt, *The Blue Marble,* 1972, photograph, NASA, Wikimedia Commons, https://www.commons.wikimedia.org/wiki/File:The_Earth_seen_from_Apollo_17.jpg.

[85]   Ahmed Abd El-Fatah, *Tahrir Square,* July 29, 2011,
         photograph, Wikimedia Commons,
         https://www.commons.wikimedia.org/wiki/File:Tahrir_
         Square_on_July_29_2011.jpg.

[86]   Katy Connell, *Budget Bill Protest,* April 5, 2011, photograph,
         flickr, https://www.flickr.com/photos/35055840@
         N06/5591014697/. © Katy Connell.

[87]   [*Demonstrator in Cairo Shows Solidarity With Workers
         in Wisconsin*], 2011, photograph, photographer unknown,
         in Medea Benjamin, "From Cairo to Madison:
         Hope and Solidarity Are Alive," CODEPINK, February 21,
         2011, https://www.codepink.org/
         from_cairo_to_madison_hope_and_solidarity_are_alive.

Acknowledgments

We first conceived of this volume while organizing the conference "The Aesthetics of Democratic Life-Forms," which was held at Goethe University Frankfurt in September 2023. We want to thank our two co-organizers, Claudia Park-Scheld and Dominik Herold, as well as all participants in the conference. The idea for this volume was further developed in a graduate research initiative, under the same heading as the conference, in which we met regularly to read and discuss texts that would prove fundamental to this book.

There is one person in particular without whom this book would not exist. Johannes Völz supported our endeavors in all conceivable ways. It was he who encouraged us to work on the 'aesthetics of democratic life-forms' in the first place and to organize a conference. Furthermore, he was a helpful guest in our research group, offering advice on administrative issues and used some of the funds from his professorship to support the publication process.

Special thanks also go out to our copy editor and translator, Joe Paul Kroll, and to our book designer, Paula Heinrich. Without them, this book would neither look nor read the same because they were both able and willing to think through the book's contributions alongside us. Joe's linguistic intuition in both German and English was invaluable in navigating some of the difficulties of a book written mostly by non-native English speakers. He was exceptional in thinking not only about what the texts said, but about what they attempted to say. Paula's experience as a graphic designer was fundamental in helping us to think about the interplay of images, font, and text. In workshops that were conceptualized jointly, we discussed the possibilities that book design holds for academic publications in general and for this publication in particular. Her attention to detail was vital during the design process of this book.

For fruitful discussions that inspired our approach in this volume, we would like to thank Daniel Fejzo, Patchen Markell, and Sabine Müller. Mark Gorthey and Lisa Pfeifer provided critical feedback on the introduction and our contribution. For regular participation and discussion in the reading group leading up to this project, we would like to thank Jan Bunte, Jason King, Jonathan Kirn, Bianca Laliberté, Marlon Lieber, Leonie Licht, Pavan Malreddy, Malte Nielsen, Ricardo Spindola, Elif Soylu, and Friedrich Weber-Steinhaus. The reading group enjoyed a wonderful room provided by the Forschungszentrum Historische Geisteswissenschaften at Goethe-University Frankfurt, thanks to the support of Monika Beck and especially Nathan Taylor. Marietta Auer and Rita Besang of the Max-Planck-Institute for Legal History and Legal Theory were kind enough to provide us with a room in which we could write the introduction and revise our contribution.

At transcript, we always appreciated the fast-moving support from Jonas Geske and Michael Volkmer and greatly benefited from the great editorial freedom and trust they provided us. A shorter version of Susan Buck-Morss's "The 'How' of Knowledge" was previously published in the US by Inventory Press. We are grateful to Adam Michaels for the permission to reprint it here. We are also grateful to Maxime Boidy, the scientific coordinator of a volume of the French journal *Perspective*, which includes the French version of an expanded version of "The 'How' of Knowledge." For their help in navigating the German publishing landscape, we would also like to thank Tim Lanzendörfer, Morten Paul, Lukas Marstaller, Evelyn Roh, Véronique Sina, and Felix Wagner. Eyi Kim proved key in acquiring image rights from Korea, while Dennis Brzek kindly put us in touch with Hilke Wagner at the Albertinum in Dresden. In questions of image rights, the hints and recommendations of Otto Danwerth and Grischka Petri, alongside those of our in-house specialist Dorothea Douglas, helped us immensely. With the help of Andrew Davidson, the designer of the original Toblerone bear-and-mountain logo, our long quest to secure the rights to print the logo came to a successful end.

For financial support, we thank the Open Access Publication Fund at Goethe-University, GRADE and the GRADE Center Normative Orders, Adickes-Stiftung, and Bodo-Sponholz-Stiftung. Special thanks go to Ralf Nöske at Bodo-Sponholz-Stiftung, Rebecca Schmidt at Normative Orders for her swift support of the project, Sybille Küster at GRADE for her constant and now years-long support, as well as to Tatjana Thomas and Mabel Keßler, without whom we most likely would not have been able to navigate Goethe University's financial accounting system. Our final and heartfelt thanks go out to Jasmin Heuer of the Open Access Publication Fund at Goethe University, whose meticulous and cheerful assistance was truly outstanding.

Biographical Information

Susan Buck-Morss is Distinguished Professor of Political Science at CUNY Graduate Center, where she is a core member of the interdisciplinary research group 'Committee on Globalization and Social Change.' She is Jan Rock Zubrow '77 Professor Emerita of Government at Cornell University, where she was a member of the graduate fields of Comparative Literature, German Studies, History of Art and Visual Studies, Romance Studies, and the School of Art, Architecture and Planning. Her most recent books are *Year 1: A Philosophical Recounting* (MIT Press, 2021) and *Revolution Today* (Haymarket Press, 2019).

Martha Crowe is currently pursuing her Master's degree in philosophy at Humboldt University of Berlin after completing her undergraduate studies at the University of Aberdeen. With interests in political identity formation and the emotional components that underlie them, she is a research assistant for the Volkswagen Foundation funded project 'The (trans)formation of a European sense of solidarity: Visceral politics and social belonging in a comparative European context' at the Berlin School of Mind and Brain. Previously, Martha was editorial assistant at *Internet Policy Review,* published by the Humboldt Institute for Internet and Society, and was recipient of the Deutschlandstipendium 2022–2023.

Helena W. Crusius is a PhD candidate in political theory at Cornell University. Her dissertation surveys cosmographies of 5th-century Athens in Plato's *Timaeus* and *Critias,* phantasmagorias of 19th-century Paris in Walter Benjamin's *Arcades Project,* and the multiverses of the 20th century toward a critical genealogy of the utterance 'Another world is possible.' She paints birds in oils and neglects her trumpet terribly.

Dorothea Douglas studied Art and Visual History in Berlin and Basel. Currently, she is pursuing a PhD in art history as part of the DFG Research Training Group 'Organizing Architectures' based between Goethe University Frankfurt, TU Darmstadt and the University of Kassel. Coming from critical image studies, Dorothea is particularly interested in the historic and cultural contingencies of sight and perception. In addition to her work at the Research Training Group, Dorothea is a member of the 'Ästhetik und Medienkultur' working group at the Frankfurt Institute for Social Research and of the graduate research initiative 'Ästhetik demokratischer Lebensformen' at Goethe University Frankfurt. Most recently, she served as project coordinator at the 12th Berlin Biennial's curator's workshop.

Raha Golestani is a Tehran-born interdisciplinary artist, researcher, and art educator based in Frankfurt am Main. She holds a BA in Fine Arts (University of Tehran) and an MA in Aesthetics (Goethe University Frankfurt). She obtained her MA with a Goethe Goes Global scholarship and a thesis on "The Veil as a Critical Aesthetic Device in the Art of Persian Diaspora." She is currently a PhD candidate and scholarship holder at Goethe University, researching "The Entanglements of Exoticism and Self-Exoticism in the Contemporary Iranian Art Market." Raha Golestani was a fellow at the Günther Uecker Institute in 2023. Her cultural work includes stints at the Rooberoo Mansion Cultural Institute in collaboration with the Goethe Institute in Tehran, the Max Planck Institute for Empirical Aesthetics, and the Frankfurt School of Painting. She occasionally works on literary portraits for German public radio, including features on Ingmar Bergman and Hafez.

Reinhold Görling studied social sciences, social psychology, literature, and philosophy. In 1995 he qualified as Professor in Comparative Literature at the University of Hannover. From 2002 to 2018 he was Professor of Media and Cultural Studies at the University of Düsseldorf. He held visiting professorships at the University of Innsbruck, the University of California Irvine (Comparative Literature), and the University of Vienna (Film Studies). He currently holds teaching positions at the Sigmund Freud University in Berlin and at the Department of Design at the University of Applied Sciences in Düsseldorf. His research focuses on the fields of film studies, psychoanalysis, aesthetics, ethics, and media ecology.

For his Bachelor's degree in 'Allgemeine Rhetorik and Germanistik,' **Noah Grossmann** moved from Hannover all the way to Tübingen in Southwest Germany before completing his MA in Philosophy at Goethe University Frankfurt in 2022. After a six-month scholarship at the Max Weber College in Erfurt and a research position at the Leibniz Center for

Literary and Cultural Research in Berlin, he joined the Research Training Group 'Aesthetic Practices' at Hildesheim University in April 2025—less than 30 km from Hannover and thereby almost closing the circles. At Hildesheim, he is currently writing his doctoral thesis on scenes of aesthetic sociality in the texts of Paul Gilroy, Saidiya Hartman, and Fred Moten.

Sophie Loidolt is Professor of Philosophy and holds the chair in Practical Philosophy at the Technical University of Darmstadt, Germany. She is a Recurrent Visiting Professor at the Center for Subjectivity Research in Copenhagen and was the president of the German Society for Phenomenological Research from 2023 to 2025. Her work centers on issues in the fields of phenomenology, political and legal philosophy, ethics, and transcendental philosophy and philosophy of mind. Her book *Phenomenology of Plurality: Hannah Arendt on Political Intersubjectivity* (Routledge, 2017) won the Edward Goodwin Ballard Book Prize in 2018. Currently, she is preparing a book with the working title *Public Experiences: A Phenomenological Theory of the Public Realm.*

Martin Renz is a PhD candidate in American Studies at Goethe University Frankfurt, where he is finalizing his dissertation, entitled *The Prejudice Against Politics: Arendtian Explorations of the Populist Situation.* He has published on the (ir-)reality of free speech in Hannah Arendt's oeuvre (*Philosophy & Rhetoric*, 2025) and works as a freelance journalist for the German news publication *Research.Table,* where he covers science advice, research policy, and university reforms in Germany and beyond. Together with friends and colleagues, he organizes the research initiative 'Ästhetik demokratischer Lebensformen' in Frankfurt. Before embarking on his PhD, Martin studied Philosophy, Political Science, and the Humanities in Berlin, Paris, Frankfurt, and Chicago.

Julius Schwarzwälder studied philosophy and aesthetics in London, Frankfurt, Paris, and Darmstadt. He is a PhD candidate at TU Darmstadt, where he considers some aesthetic effects of the surging use of algorithmics. He has published in *Deutsche Zeitschrift für Philosophie* (on the advent of 'artistic research'), *kritische berichte* (on TikTok and 'microgenres'), and *form* (on the calculability of 'beauty'). In and beyond Frankfurt, he co-organized the graduate research initiative 'Ästhetik demokratischer Lebensformen.'

Merve Yıldırım grew up in a small town near Frankfurt before moving to Istanbul—a city she has returned to ever since. After studying architecture at the Technical University of Munich and La Sapienza in Rome (2014–2018), she worked at the Renzo Piano Building Workshop in Paris, Genoa, and Istanbul, most recently contributing to the Istanbul Modern Museum. She is currently completing her Master's degree in Aesthetics at Goethe University Frankfurt. Now based once again in Istanbul, her research and practice engage with the intersection of architecture and aesthetics, Germany and Türkiye.